Explore Your World!

Focus on case studies to understand your world.

To learn about **The United States and Canada**, you will take a close look at specific countries. In each case study, the story of that country will be told through an important world theme—such as the relationship between people and their environment or a nation's quest for independence. After studying each country, you can apply what you've learned to understand other parts of the world.

Interact with exciting online activities.

Journey to different parts of the world by using dynamic online activities on geography, history and culture. Use the web codes listed in the Go Online boxes and in the chart below to tour this region.

The United States and Canada Activities

Web Code	Activity
	History Interactive
lhp-5001	Discover a Steam Engine
lhp-5003	The Sharecropping Cycle
lhp-5009	Explore the Boston Tea Party
lhp-5010	Explore the Northwest Territory
lhp-5011	The Mexican American War
lhp-5013	Find Out How Tariffs Work
lhp-5018	The Trans-Continental Railroad
lhp-5022	Explore Capitalism
lhp-5024	Explore the Magna Carta
lhp-5025	Explore the Lessons of Battle
lhp-5026	Inside Fort Sumter
	MapMaster
lhp-5000	The Western Front
lhp-5002	The American Revolution
lhp-5004	Growth of the United States to 1853
lhp-5005	States Take Sides
lhp-5006	Land Taken from Native Americans
lhp-5007	Native American Territory
lhp-5008	Exploring the Louisiana Purchase
lhp-5012	Industrial Centers, 1865-1914
lhp-5014	Slavery After the Kansas-Nebraska Act
lhp-5015	Western Land Claims
lhp-5016	North America in 1830
lhp-5017	Early Days of War
lhp-5019	Travels to the West
lhp-5020	Final Battle of the Civil War
lhp-5021	The Texas War for Independence
lhp-5023	The Seasons

For: An activity on the Civil War
Visit:: PHSchool.com
Web Code: lhd-4202

Get hands-on with the Geographer's Apprentice Activity Pack.

Explore the geography, history and culture of the world's regions through hands-on activities. Each activity pack includes maps, data and primary sources to make learning geography fun!

PRENTICE HALL
WORLD STUDIES
the UNITED STATES and CANADA

Geography • History • Culture

In association with
DK

Discovery CHANNEL **SCHOOL**

PEARSON
Prentice
Hall

Boston, Massachusetts
Upper Saddle River, New Jersey

Program Consultants

Heidi Hayes Jacobs

Heidi Hayes Jacobs, Ed.D., has served as an education consultant to more than 1,000 schools across the nation and abroad. Dr. Jacobs serves as an adjunct professor in the Department of Curriculum on Teaching at Teachers College, Columbia University. She has written two best-selling books and numerous articles on curriculum reform. She received an M.A. from the University of Massachusetts, Amherst, and completed her doctoral work at Columbia University's Teachers College in 1981. The core of Dr. Jacobs' experience comes from her years teaching high school, middle school, and elementary school students. As an educational consultant, she works with K–12 schools and districts on curriculum reform and strategic planning.

Michal L. LeVasseur

Michal LeVasseur is the Executive Director of the National Council for Geographic Education. She is an instructor in the College of Education at Jacksonville State University and works with the Alabama Geographic Alliance. Her undergraduate and graduate work were in the fields of anthropology (B.A.), geography (M.A.), and science education (Ph.D.). Dr. LeVasseur's specialization has moved increasingly into the area of geography education. Since 1996 she has served as the Director of the National Geographic Society's Summer Geography Workshops. As an educational consultant, she has worked with the National Geographic Society as well as with schools and organizations to develop programs and curricula for geography.

Senior Reading Consultants

Kate Kinsella

Kate Kinsella, Ed.D., is a faculty member in the Department of Secondary Education at San Francisco State University. A specialist in second-language acquisition and content area literacy, she consults nationally on school-wide practices that support adolescent English learners and striving readers to make academic gains. Dr. Kinsella earned her M.A. in TESOL from San Francisco State University, and her Ed.D. in Second Language Acquisition from the University of San Francisco.

Kevin Feldman

Kevin Feldman, Ed.D., is the Director of Reading and Early Intervention with the Sonoma County Office of Education (SCOE) and an independent educational consultant. At the SCOE, he develops, organizes, and monitors programs related to K–12 literacy. Dr. Feldman has an M.A. from the University of California, Riverside in Special Education, Learning Disabilities and Instructional Design. He earned his Ed.D. in Curriculum and Instruction from the University of San Francisco.

Acknowledgments appear on page 225, which constitutes an extension of this copyright page.

PEARSON
Prentice Hall

Cartography Consultant

DK Andrew Heritage

Andrew Heritage has been publishing atlases and maps for more than 25 years. In 1991, he joined the leading illustrated nonfiction publisher Dorling Kindersley (DK) with the task of building an international atlas list from scratch. The DK atlas list now includes some 10 titles, which are constantly updated and appear in new editions either annually or every other year.

ISBN 0-13-204149-9
345678910   11 10 09 08

Academic Reviewers

Africa
Barbara B. Brown, Ph.D.
African Studies Center
Boston University
Boston, Massachusetts

Ancient World
Evelyn DeLong Mangie, Ph.D.
Department of History
University of South Florida
Tampa, Florida

**Central Asia and
the Middle East**
Pamela G. Sayre
History Department,
    Social Sciences Division
Henry Ford Community College
Dearborn, Michigan

East Asia
Huping Ling, Ph.D.
History Department
Truman State University
Kirksville, Missouri

Eastern Europe
Robert M. Jenkins, Ph.D.
Center for Slavic, Eurasian and
    East European Studies
University of North Carolina
Chapel Hill, North Carolina

Latin America
Dan La Botz
Professor, History Department
Miami University
Oxford, Ohio

Medieval Times
James M. Murray
History Department
University of Cincinnati
Cincinnati, Ohio

North Africa
Barbara E. Petzen
Center for Middle Eastern Studies
Harvard University
Cambridge, Massachusetts

Religion
Charles H. Lippy, Ph.D.
Department of Philosophy
    and Religion
University of Tennessee
    at Chattanooga
Chattanooga, Tennessee

Russia
Janet Vaillant
Davis Center for Russian
    and Eurasian Studies
Harvard University
Cambridge, Massachusetts

United States and Canada
Victoria Randlett
Geography Department
University of Nevada, Reno
Reno, Nevada

Western Europe
Ruth Mitchell-Pitts
Center for European Studies
University of North Carolina
    at Chapel Hill
Chapel Hill, North Carolina

Reviewers

Sean Brennan
Brecksville-Broadview Heights
    City School District
Broadview Heights, Ohio

Stephen Bullick
Mt. Lebanon School District
Pittsburgh, Pennsylvania

Louis P. De Angelo, Ed.D.
Archdiocese of Philadelphia
Philadelphia, Pennsylvania

Paul Francis Durietz
Social Studies
    Curriculum Coordinator
Woodland District #50
Gurnee, Illinois

Gail Dwyer
Dickerson Middle School,
    Cobb County
Marietta, Georgia

Michal Howden
Social Studies Consultant
Zionsville, Indiana

Rosemary Kalloch
Springfield Public Schools
Springfield, Massachusetts

Deborah J. Miller
Office of Social Studies,
    Detroit Public Schools
Detroit, Michigan

Steven P. Missal
Plainfield Public Schools
Plainfield, New Jersey

Catherine Fish Petersen
Social Studies Consultant
Saint James, Long Island, New York

Joe Wieczorek
Social Studies Consultant
Baltimore, Maryland

The UNITED STATES and CANADA

Develop Skills

Use these pages to develop your reading, writing, and geography skills.

Build a Regional Background

Learn about the geography, history, and culture of the region.

Focus on Countries

Create an understanding of the United States and Canada by focusing on specific regions.

MAP★MASTER™

- Learn map skills with the MapMaster Skills Handbook.
- Practice your skills with every map in this book.
- Interact with every map online and on CD-ROM.

Maps and illustrations created by DK help build your understanding of the world. The DK World Desk Reference Online keeps you up to date.

Video/DVD

The World Studies Video Program takes you on field trips to study countries around the world.

Interactive Textbook

The *World Studies* Interactive Textbook online and on CD-ROM uses interactive maps and other activities to help you learn.

Special Features

COUNTRY DATABANK

Read about the states that make up the United States.

Read about the provinces and territories that make up Canada.

REGIONAL PROFILES

Theme-based maps and charts provide a closer look at regions, provinces, and territories.

Links

See the fascinating links between social studies and other disciplines.

Literature

A selection by an American author brings social studies to life.

Skills for Life

Learn skills that you will use throughout your life.

Citizen Heroes

Meet people who have made a difference in their country.

Target Reading Skills

Chapter-by-chapter reading skills help you read and understand social studies concepts.

Eyewitness Technology

Detailed drawings show how technology shapes places and societies.

Video/DVD

Explore the geography, history, and cultures of the United States and Canada.

Maps and Charts

MAP MASTER™

MAP MASTER™ Interactive

Go online to find an interactive version of every MapMaster map in this book. Use the Web Code provided to gain direct access to these maps.

How to Use Web Codes:

1. Go to **www.PHSchool.com**.
2. Enter the Web Code.
3. Click Go!

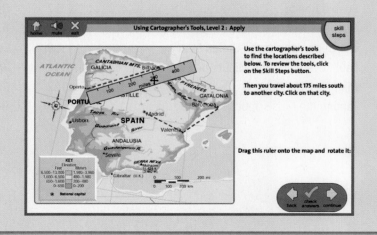

Charts, Graphs, and Tables

Building Geographic Literacy

Learning about a country often starts with finding it on a map. The MapMaster™ system in *World Studies* helps you develop map skills you will use throughout your life. These three steps can help you become a MapMaster!

The MAP★MASTER™ System

1 Learn

You need to learn geography tools and concepts before you explore the world. Get started by using the MapMaster Skills Handbook to learn the skills you need for success.

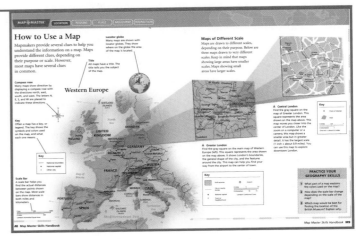

MAP★MASTER™ Skills Activity

Location The Equator runs through parts of Latin America, but it is far from other parts of the region.
Locate Find the Equator on the map. Which climates are most common in Latin America, and how far is each climate region from the Equator?
Draw Conclusions How do climates change as you move away from the Equator?

Go Online
PHSchool.com Use Web Code
lfp-1142 for step-by-step
map skills practice.

2 Practice

You need to practice and apply your geography skills frequently to be a MapMaster. The maps in *World Studies* give you the practice you need to develop geographic literacy.

3 Interact

Using maps is more than just finding places. Maps can teach you many things about a region, such as its climate, its vegetation, and the languages that the people who live there speak. Every MapMaster map is online at PHSchool.com with interactive activities to help you learn the most from every map.

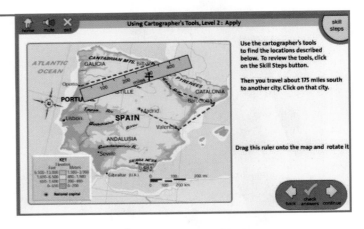

Learning With Technology

You will be making many exciting journeys across time and place in *World Studies*. Technology will help make what you learn come alive.

Go Online
PHSchool.com

For: An activity on the Civil War
Visit: PHSchool.com
Web Code: lhd-4202

For a complete list of features for this book, use Web Code lhk-1000.

Go Online at PHSchool.com

Use the Web Codes listed below and in each Go Online box to access exciting information or activities.

How to Use the Web Code:
1. Go to **www.PHSchool.com**.
2. Enter the Web Code.
3. Click Go!

The United States and Canada Activities

Web Code	Activity
History Interactive	
lhp-5001	Discover a Steam Engine
lhp-5003	The Sharecropping Cycle
lhp-5009	Explore the Boston Tea Party
lhp-5010	Explore the Northwest Territory
lhp-5011	The Mexican American War
lhp-5013	Find Out How Tariffs Work
lhp-5018	The Trans-Continental Railroad
lhp-5022	Explore Capitalism
lhp-5024	Explore the Magna Carta
lhp-5025	Explore the Lessons of Battle
lhp-5026	Inside Fort Sumter
MapMaster	
lhp-5000	The Western Front
lhp-5002	The American Revolution
lhp-5004	Growth of the United States to 1853
lhp-5005	States Take Sides
lhp-5006	Land Taken from Native Americans
lhp-5007	Native American Territory
lhp-5008	Exploring the Louisiana Purchase
lhp-5012	Industrial Centers, 1865-1914
lhp-5014	Slavery After the Kansas-Nebraska Act
lhp-5015	Western Land Claims
lhp-5016	North America in 1830
lhp-5017	Early Days of War
lhp-5019	Travels to the West
lhp-5020	Final Battle of the Civil War
lhp-5021	The Texas War for Independence
lhp-5023	The Seasons

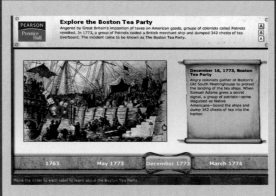

World Desk Reference Online

There are more than 190 countries in the world. To learn about them, you need the most up-to-date information and statistics. The **DK World Desk Reference Online** gives you instant access to the information you need to explore each country.

Reading Informational Texts

Reading a magazine, an Internet page, or a textbook is not the same as reading a novel. The purpose of reading nonfiction texts is to acquire new information. On page M18 you'll read about some 🔄 **Target Reading Skills** that you'll have a chance to practice as you read this textbook. Here we'll focus on a few skills that will help you read nonfiction with a more critical eye.

Analyze the Author's Purpose

Different types of materials are written with different purposes in mind. For example, a textbook is written to teach students information about a subject. The purpose of a technical manual is to teach someone how to use something, such as a computer. A newspaper editorial might be written to persuade the reader to accept a particular point of view. A writer's purpose influences how the material is presented. Sometimes an author states his or her purpose directly. More often, the purpose is only suggested, and you must use clues to identify the author's purpose.

Distinguish Between Facts and Opinions

It's important when reading informational texts to read actively and to distinguish between fact and opinion. A fact can be proven or disproven. An opinion cannot—it is someone's personal viewpoint or evaluation.

For example, the editorial pages in a newspaper offer opinions on topics that are currently in the news. You need to read newspaper editorials with an eye for bias and faulty logic. For example, the newspaper editorial at the right shows factual statements in blue and opinion statements in red. The underlined words are examples of highly charged words. They reveal bias on the part of the writer.

> More than 5,000 people voted last week in favor of building a new shopping center, but the opposition won out. The margin of victory is irrelevant. Those radical voters who opposed the center are obviously self-serving elitists who do not care about anyone but themselves.
>
> This month's unemployment figure for our area is 10 percent, which represents an increase of about 5 percent over the figure for this time last year. These figures mean unemployment is getting worse. But the people who voted against the mall probably do not care about creating new jobs.

Identify Evidence

Before you accept an author's conclusion, you need to make sure that the author has based the conclusion on enough evidence and on the right kind of evidence. An author may present a series of facts to support a claim, but the facts may not tell the whole story. For example, what evidence does the author of the newspaper editorial on the previous page provide to support his claim that the new shopping center would create more jobs? Is it possible that the shopping center might have put many small local businesses out of business, thus increasing unemployment rather than decreasing it?

Evaluate Credibility

Whenever you read informational texts, you need to assess the credibility of the author. This is especially true of sites you may visit on the Internet. All Internet sources are not equally reliable. Here are some questions to ask yourself when evaluating the credibility of a Web site.

- ❏ Is the Web site created by a respected organization, a discussion group, or an individual?
- ❏ Does the Web site creator include his or her name as well as credentials and the sources he or she used to write the material?
- ❏ Is the information on the site balanced or biased?
- ❏ Can you verify the information using two other sources?
- ❏ Is there a date telling when the Web site was created or last updated?

Writing for Social Studies

Writing is one of the most powerful communication tools you will ever use. You will use it to share your thoughts and ideas with others. Research shows that writing about what you read actually helps you learn new information and ideas. A systematic approach to writing—including prewriting, drafting, revising, and proofing—can help you write better, whether you're writing an essay or a research report.

Narrative Essays

Writing that tells a story about a personal experience

1 Select and Narrow Your Topic

A narrative is a story. In social studies, it might be a narrative essay about how an event affected you or your family.

2 Gather Details

Brainstorm a list of details you'd like to include in your narrative.

3 Write a First Draft

Start by writing a simple opening sentence that conveys the main idea of your essay. Continue by writing a colorful story that has interesting details. Write a conclusion that sums up the significance of the event or situation described in your essay.

4 Revise and Proofread

Check to make sure you have not begun too many sentences with the word *I*. Replace general words with more colorful ones.

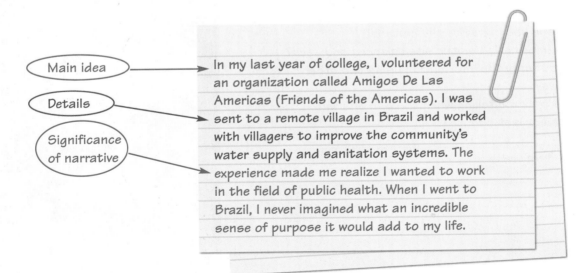

Main idea

Details

Significance of narrative

In my last year of college, I volunteered for an organization called Amigos De Las Americas (Friends of the Americas). I was sent to a remote village in Brazil and worked with villagers to improve the community's water supply and sanitation systems. The experience made me realize I wanted to work in the field of public health. When I went to Brazil, I never imagined what an incredible sense of purpose it would add to my life.

Persuasive Essays

Writing that supports an opinion or position

① Select and Narrow Your Topic

Choose a topic that provokes an argument and has at least two sides. Choose a side. Decide which argument will appeal most to your audience and persuade them to understand your point of view.

② Gather Evidence

Create a chart that states your position at the top and then lists the pros and cons for your position below, in two columns. Predict and address the strongest arguments against your stand.

③ Write a First Draft

Write a strong thesis statement that clearly states your position. Continue by presenting the strongest arguments in favor of your position and acknowledging and refuting opposing arguments.

④ Revise and Proofread

Check to make sure you have made a logical argument and that you have not oversimplified the argument.

Main Idea

Supporting (pro) argument

Opposing (con) argument

Transition words

It is vital to vote in elections. When people vote, they tell public officials how to run the government. Not every proposal is carried out; however, politicians do their best to listen to what the majority of people want. Therefore, every vote is important.

Expository Essays

Writing that explains a process, compares and contrasts, explains causes and effects, or explores solutions to a problem

1 Identify and Narrow Your Topic

Expository writing is writing that explains something in detail. It might explain the similarities and differences between two or more subjects (compare and contrast). It might explain how one event causes another (cause and effect). Or it might explain a problem and describe a solution.

2 Gather Evidence

Create a graphic organizer that identifies details to include in your essay.

Cause 1	Cause 2	Cause 3
Most people in the Mexican countryside work on farms.	The population in Mexico is growing at one of the highest rates in the world.	There is not enough farm work for so many people.

Effect

As a result, many rural families are moving from the countryside to live in Mexico City.

3 Write Your First Draft

Write a topic sentence and then organize the essay around your similarities and differences, causes and effects, or problem and solutions. Be sure to include convincing details, facts, and examples.

4 Revise and Proofread

Research Papers

Writing that presents research about a topic

1 Narrow Your Topic

Choose a topic you're interested in and make sure that it is not too broad. For example, instead of writing a report on Panama, write about the construction of the Panama Canal.

2 Acquire Information

Locate several sources of information about the topic from the library or the Internet. For each resource, create a source index card like the one at the right. Then take notes using an index card for each detail or subtopic. On the card, note which source the information was taken from. Use quotation marks when you copy the exact words from a source.

Source #1

McCullough, David. *The Path Between the Seas: The Creation of the Panama Canal, 1870-1914.* N.Y., Simon and Schuster, 1977.

3 Make an Outline

Use an outline to decide how to organize your report. Sort your index cards into the same order.

Outline
I. Introduction
II. Why the canal was built
III. How the canal was built
   A. Physical challenges
   B. Medical challenges
IV. Conclusion

> Introduction
>
> **Building the Panama Canal**
>
> Ever since Christopher Columbus first explored the Isthmus of Panama, the Spanish had been looking for a water route through it. They wanted to be able to sail west from Spain to Asia without sailing around South America. However, it was not until 1914 that the dream became a reality.

> Conclusion
>
> It took eight years and more than 70,000 workers to build the Panama Canal. It remains one of the greatest engineering feats of modern times.

4 Write a First Draft

Write an introduction, a body, and a conclusion. Leave plenty of space between lines so you can go back and add details that you may have left out.

5 Revise and Proofread

Be sure to include transition words between sentences and paragraphs. Here are some examples:

To show a contrast—*however, although, despite.*

To point out a reason—*since, because, if.*

To signal a conclusion—*therefore, consequently, so, then.*

Evaluating Your Writing

Use this table to help you evaluate your writing.

	Excellent	Good	Acceptable	Unacceptable
Purpose	Achieves purpose—to inform, persuade, or provide historical interpretation—very well	Informs, persuades, or provides historical interpretation reasonably well	Reader cannot easily tell if the purpose is to inform, persuade, or provide historical interpretation	Purpose is not clear
Organization	Develops ideas in a very clear and logical way	Presents ideas in a reasonably well-organized way	Reader has difficulty following the organization	Lacks organization
Elaboration	Explains all ideas with facts and details	Explains most ideas with facts and details	Includes some supporting facts and details	Lacks supporting details
Use of Language	Uses excellent vocabulary and sentence structure with no errors in spelling, grammar, or punctuation	Uses good vocabulary and sentence structure with very few errors in spelling, grammar, or punctuation	Includes some errors in grammar, punctuation, and spelling	Includes many errors in grammar, punctuation, and spelling

CONTENTS

Go Online
PHSchool.com Use Web Code **lap-0000** for all of the maps
in this handbook.

Five Themes of Geography

Studying the geography of the entire world is a
huge task. You can make that task easier by using the
five themes of geography: location, regions, place,
movement, and human-environment interaction. The
themes are tools you can use to organize information
and to answer the where, why, and how of geography.

▲ **Location**
This museum in England has a
line running through it. The line
marks its location at 0° longitude.

LOCATION

1 Location answers the question, "Where is it?"
You can think of the location of a continent
or a country as its address. You might give an
absolute location such as 40° N and 80° W. You
might also use a relative address, telling where
one place is by referring to another place.
Between school and the mall and
*eight miles east of Pleasant
City* are examples of
relative locations.

REGIONS

2 Regions are areas that share at least one common feature. Geographers divide the world into many types of regions. For example, countries, states, and cities are political regions. The people in any one of these places live under the same government. Other features, such as climate and culture, can be used to define regions. Therefore the same place can be found in more than one region. For example, the state of Hawaii is in the political region of the United States. Because it has a tropical climate, Hawaii is also part of a tropical climate region.

MOVEMENT

4 Movement answers the question, "How do people, goods, and ideas move from place to place?" Remember that what happens in one place often affects what happens in another. Use the theme of movement to help you trace the spread of goods, people, and ideas from one location to another.

PLACE

3 Place identifies the natural and human features that make one place different from every other place. You can identify a specific place by its landforms, climate, plants, animals, people, language, or culture. You might even think of place as a geographic signature. Use the signature to help you understand the natural and human features that make one place different from every other place.

INTERACTION

5 Human-environment interaction focuses on the relationship between people and the environment. As people live in an area, they often begin to make changes to it, usually to make their lives easier. For example, they might build a dam to control flooding during rainy seasons. Also, the environment can affect how people live, work, dress, travel, and communicate.

◄ **Interaction**
These Congolese women interact with their environment by gathering wood for cooking.

PRACTICE YOUR GEOGRAPHY SKILLS

1 Describe your town or city, using each of the five themes of geography.

2 Name at least one thing that comes into your town or city and one that goes out. How is each moved? Where does it come from? Where does it go?

Understanding Movements of Earth

The planet Earth is part of our solar system. Earth revolves around the sun in a nearly circular path called an orbit. A revolution, or one complete orbit around the sun, takes 365¼ days, or one year. As Earth orbits the sun, it also spins on its axis, an invisible line through the center of Earth from the North Pole to the South Pole. This movement is called a rotation.

▼ Spring begins
On March 20 or 21, the sun is directly overhead at the Equator. The Northern and Southern Hemispheres receive almost equal hours of sunlight and darkness.

How Night Changes Into Day

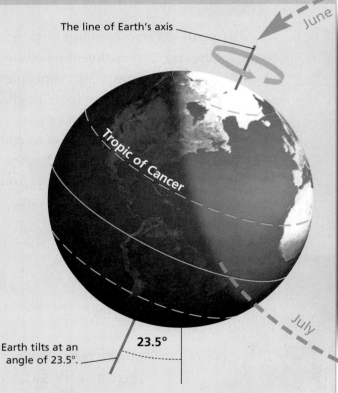

The line of Earth's axis

Tropic of Cancer

Earth tilts at an angle of 23.5°.

23.5°

May
April
June
July
August
September
Equator

Earth takes about 24 hours to make one full rotation on its axis. As Earth rotates, it is daytime on the side facing the sun. It is night on the side away from the sun.

◄ Summer begins
On June 21 or 22, the sun is directly overhead at the Tropic of Cancer. The Northern Hemisphere receives the greatest number of sunlight hours.

The Seasons

Earth's axis is tilted at an angle. Because of this tilt, sunlight strikes different parts of Earth at different times in the year, creating seasons. The illustration below shows how the seasons are created in the Northern Hemisphere. In the Southern Hemisphere, the seasons are reversed.

PRACTICE YOUR GEOGRAPHY SKILLS

1 What causes the seasons in the Northern Hemisphere to be the opposite of those in the Southern Hemisphere?

2 During which two days of the year do the Northern Hemisphere and Southern Hemisphere have equal hours of daylight and darkness?

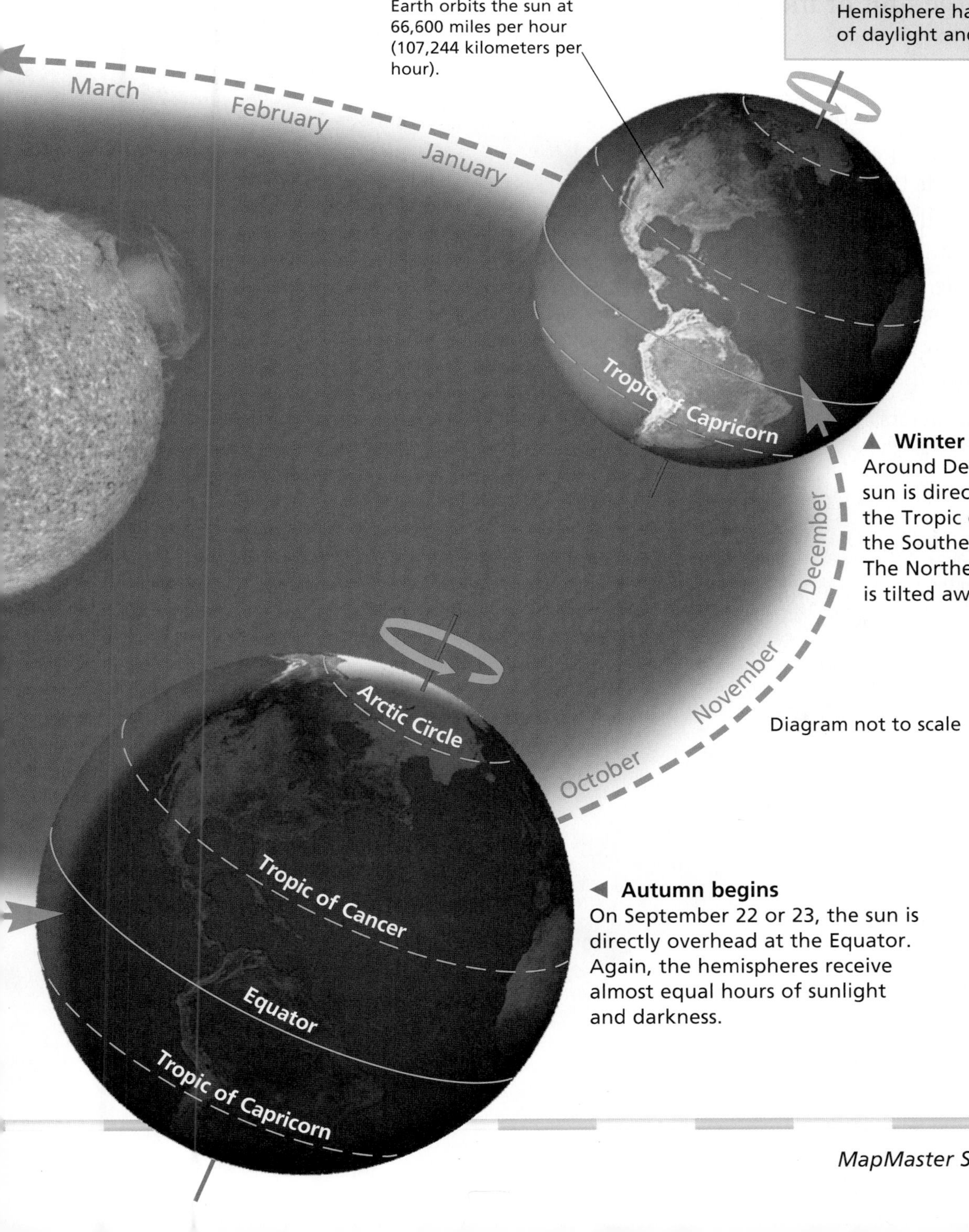

Earth orbits the sun at 66,600 miles per hour (107,244 kilometers per hour).

March
February
January

Tropic of Capricorn

December
November
October

Arctic Circle

Tropic of Cancer

Equator

Tropic of Capricorn

Diagram not to scale

▲ Winter begins
Around December 21, the sun is directly overhead at the Tropic of Capricorn in the Southern Hemisphere. The Northern Hemisphere is tilted away from the sun.

◄ Autumn begins
On September 22 or 23, the sun is directly overhead at the Equator. Again, the hemispheres receive almost equal hours of sunlight and darkness.

Understanding Globes

A globe is a scale model of Earth. It shows the actual shapes, sizes, and locations of all Earth's landmasses and bodies of water. Features on the surface of Earth are drawn to scale on a globe. This means that a small unit of measure on the globe stands for a large unit of measure on Earth.

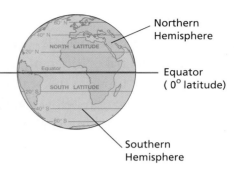

Northern Hemisphere

Equator (0° latitude)

Southern Hemisphere

Parallels of Latitude

Geographers divide the globe along imaginary horizontal lines called parallels of latitude. One of these latitude lines is the Equator, located halfway between the North and South poles. Parallels of latitude are measured in degrees (°). One degree of latitude represents a distance of about 69 miles (111 kilometers).

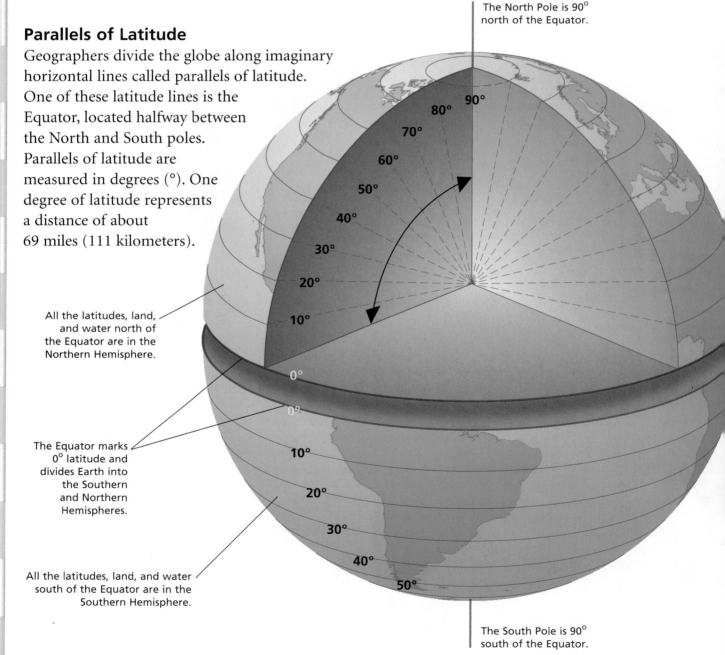

The North Pole is 90° north of the Equator.

All the latitudes, land, and water north of the Equator are in the Northern Hemisphere.

The Equator marks 0° latitude and divides Earth into the Southern and Northern Hemispheres.

All the latitudes, land, and water south of the Equator are in the Southern Hemisphere.

The South Pole is 90° south of the Equator.

Meridians of Longitude

Geographers also divide the globe along imaginary vertical lines called meridians of longitude, which are measured in degrees (°). The longitude line called the Prime Meridian runs from pole to pole through Greenwich, England. All meridians of longitude come together at the North and South Poles.

PRACTICE YOUR GEOGRAPHY SKILLS

1 Which continents lie completely in the Northern Hemisphere? In the Western Hemisphere?

2 Is there land or water at 20° S latitude and the Prime Meridian? At the Equator and 60° W longitude?

All the longitudes, land, and water west of the Prime Meridian are in the Western Hemisphere.

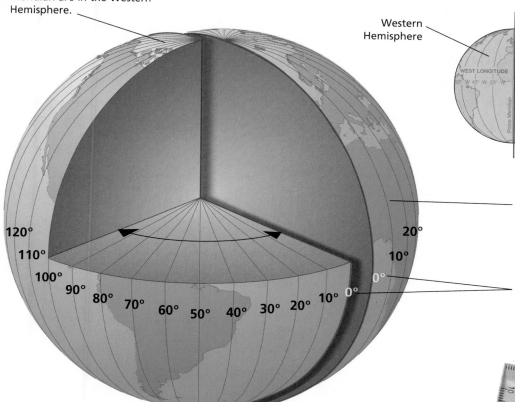

Western Hemisphere

WEST LONGITUDE   EAST LONGITUDE
60° W 40° W 20° W—0—20° E 40° E 60° E

Eastern Hemisphere

Prime Meridian (0° longitude)

All the longitudes, land, and water east of the Prime Meridian are in the Eastern Hemisphere.

120°
110°
100°
90° 80° 70° 60° 50° 40° 30° 20° 10° 0° 0°

20°
10°
0°

The Prime Meridian marks 0° longitude and divides the globe into the Eastern and Western Hemispheres.

The Global Grid

Together, the pattern of parallels of latitude and meridians of longitude is called the global grid. Using the lines of latitude and longitude, you can locate any place on Earth. For example, the location of 30° north latitude and 90° west longitude is usually written as 30° N, 90° W. Only one place on Earth has these coordinates—the city of New Orleans, in the state of Louisiana.

▲ Compass
Wherever you are on Earth, a compass can be used to show direction.

Map Projections

Maps are drawings that show regions on flat surfaces. Maps are easier to use and carry than globes, but they cannot show the correct size and shape of every feature on Earth's curved surface. They must shrink some places and stretch others. To make up for this distortion, mapmakers use different map projections. No one projection can accurately show the correct area, shape, distance, and direction for all of Earth's surface. Mapmakers use the projection that has the least distortion for the information they are presenting.

▲ **Global gores**
Flattening a globe creates a string of shapes called gores.

Same-Shape Maps

Map projections that accurately show the shapes of landmasses are called same-shape maps. However, these projections often greatly distort, or make less accurate, the size of landmasses as well as the distance between them. In the projection below, the northern and southern areas of the globe appear more stretched than the areas near the Equator.

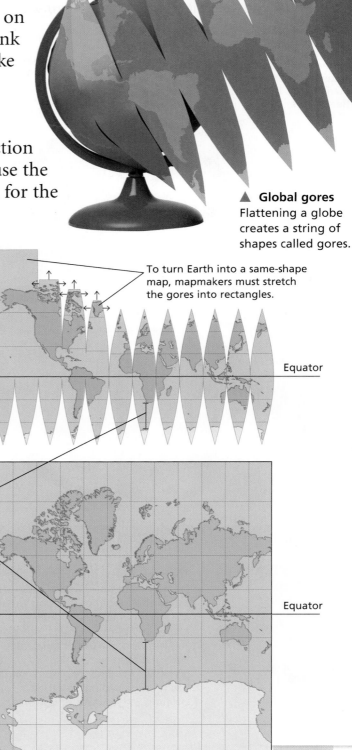

To turn Earth into a same-shape map, mapmakers must stretch the gores into rectangles.

Equator

Stretching the gores makes parts of Earth larger. This enlargement becomes greater toward the North and South Poles.

Equator

Mercator projection ▶
One of the most common same-shape maps is the Mercator projection, named for the mapmaker who invented it. The Mercator projection accurately shows shape and direction, but it distorts distance and size. Because the projection shows true directions, ships' navigators use it to chart a straight-line course between two ports.

Equal-Area Maps

Map projections that show the correct size of landmasses are called equal-area maps. In order to show the correct size of landmasses, these maps usually distort shapes. The distortion is usually greater at the edges of the map and less at the center.

PRACTICE YOUR GEOGRAPHY SKILLS

1 What feature is distorted on an equal-area map?

2 Would you use a Mercator projection to find the exact distance between two locations? Tell why or why not.

To turn Earth's surface into an equal-area map, mapmakers have to squeeze each gore into an oval.

Equator

The tips of all the gores are then joined together. The points at which they join form the North and South Poles. The line of the Equator stays the same.

North Pole

Equator

Robinson Maps

Many of the maps in this book use the Robinson projection, which is a compromise between the Mercator and equal-area projections. The Robinson projection gives a useful overall picture of the world. It keeps the size and shape relationships of most continents and oceans, but distorts the size of the polar regions.

South Pole

The entire top edge of the map is the North Pole.

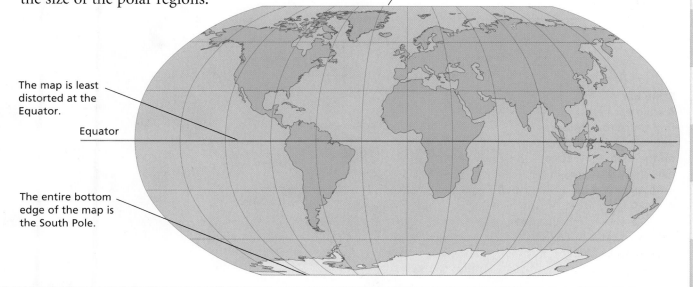

The map is least distorted at the Equator.

Equator

The entire bottom edge of the map is the South Pole.

How to Use a Map

Mapmakers provide several clues to help you understand the information on a map. Maps provide different clues, depending on their purpose or scale. However, most maps have several clues in common.

Locator globe
Many maps are shown with locator globes. They show where on the globe the area of the map is located.

Title
All maps have a title. The title tells you the subject of the map.

Compass rose
Many maps show direction by displaying a compass rose with the directions north, east, south, and west. The letters N, E, S, and W are placed to indicate these directions.

Key
Often a map has a key, or legend. The key shows the symbols and colors used on the map, and what each one means.

Scale bar
A scale bar helps you find the actual distances between points shown on the map. Most scale bars show distances in both miles and kilometers.

Western Europe

SHETLAND ISLANDS (U.K.)

North Sea

Glasgow

Copenhagen

DENMARK

UNITED KINGDOM

Dublin

IRELAND

Hamburg
Berlin

NETHERLANDS
Amsterdam

London

The Hague

GERMANY

Brussels

BELGIUM

Frankfurt

Prague

CZECH REPUBLIC

LUXEMBOURG

Luxembourg

Paris

Munich

Vienna

AUSTRIA

English Channel

FRANCE

Bern LIECHTENSTEIN

SWITZERLAND

Bay of Biscay

Lyon

Milan

SAN MARINO

Toulouse

MONACO

ITALY

Adriatic Sea

Marseille

ANDORRA

CORSICA (France)

VATICAN CITY

Rome

PORTUGAL

Madrid

Barcelona

SARDINIA (Italy)

Tyrrhenian Sea

Lisbon

SPAIN

BALEARIC ISLANDS (Spain)

Seville

Mediterranean Sea

SICILY (Italy)

60° N

10° E

60° N

20° E

0°

10° W

50° N

50° N

40° N

10° W

Key

—— National border

⊛ National capital

• Other city

0 miles   300

0 kilometers   300

Lambert Azimuthal Equal Area

Maps of Different Scales

Maps are drawn to different scales, depending on their purpose. Here are three maps drawn to very different scales. Keep in mind that maps showing large areas have smaller scales. Maps showing small areas have larger scales.

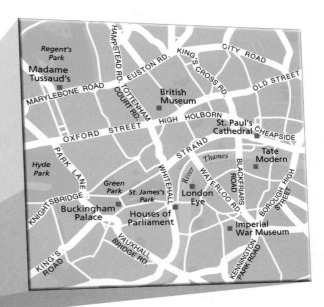

▲ **Greater London**

Find the gray square on the main map of Western Europe (left). This square represents the area shown on the map above. It shows London's boundaries, the general shape of the city, and the features around the city. This map can help you find your way from the airport to the center of town.

▲ **Central London**

Find the gray square on the map of Greater London. This square represents the area shown on the map above. This map moves you closer into the center of London. Like the zoom on a computer or a camera, this map shows a smaller area but in greater detail. It has the largest scale (1 inch represents about 0.9 mile). You can use this map to explore downtown London.

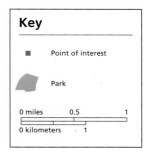

Key

■ Point of interest

⬢ Park

0 miles   0.5   1
0 kilometers   1

Key

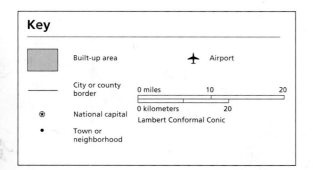

Built-up area   ✈ Airport

City or county border

0 miles   10   20
0 kilometers   20
Lambert Conformal Conic

⊛ National capital

• Town or neighborhood

PRACTICE YOUR GEOGRAPHY SKILLS

1 What part of a map explains the colors used on the map?

2 How does the scale bar change depending on the scale of the map?

3 Which map would be best for finding the location of the British Museum? Explain why.

Political Maps

Political maps show political borders: continents, countries, and divisions within countries, such as states or provinces. The colors on political maps do not have any special meaning, but they make the map easier to read. Political maps also include symbols and labels for capitals, cities, and towns.

PRACTICE YOUR GEOGRAPHY SKILLS

1 What symbols show a national border, a national capital, and a city?

2 What is Angola's capital city?

Political Africa Key

——	National border
- - -	Disputed border
⊛	National capital
•	Other city

▲ **Dakar, Senegal**
Dakar is the capital of Senegal, in West Africa. Its Presidential Palace overlooks the Atlantic Ocean.

0 miles 1,000
0 kilometers 1,000
Lambert Azimuthal Equal Area

Physical Maps

Physical maps represent what a region looks like by showing its major physical features, such as hills and plains. Physical maps also often show elevation and relief. Elevation, indicated by colors, is the height of the land above sea level. Relief, indicated by shading, shows how sharply the land rises or falls.

PRACTICE YOUR GEOGRAPHY SKILLS

1 Which areas of Africa have the highest elevation?

2 How can you use relief to plan a hiking trip?

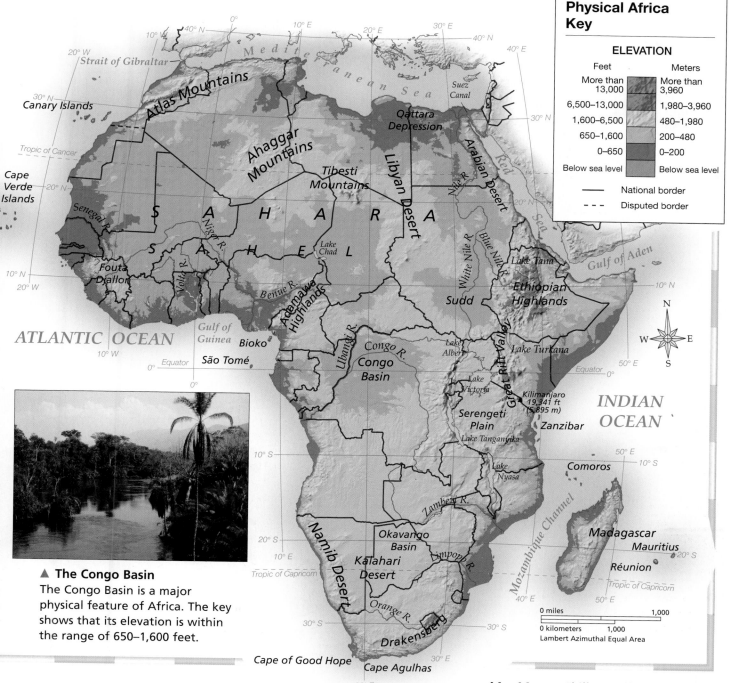

Physical Africa Key

ELEVATION

Feet	Meters
More than 13,000	More than 3,960
6,500–13,000	1,980–3,960
1,600–6,500	480–1,980
650–1,600	200–480
0–650	0–200
Below sea level	Below sea level

National border

Disputed border

Strait of Gibraltar
Atlas Mountains
Canary Islands
Tropic of Cancer
Cape Verde Islands
Senegal R.
Fouta Djallon
Volta R.
Niger R.
Mediterranean Sea
Ahaggar Mountains
Tibesti Mountains
Lake Chad
Libyan Desert
Qattara Depression
Suez Canal
Nile R.
Arabian Desert
Red Sea
S A H A R A
S A H E L
Benue R.
Adamawa Highlands
Gulf of Guinea
Bioko
São Tomé
Equator
Ubangi R.
Congo R.
Congo Basin
White Nile R.
Blue Nile R.
Lake Tana
Ethiopian Highlands
Sudd
Gulf of Aden
Lake Albert
Lake Victoria
Lake Turkana
Great Rift Valley
Kilimanjaro 19,341 ft (5,895 m)
Serengeti Plain
Zanzibar
Lake Tanganyika
Lake Nyasa
Comoros
Zambezi R.
Okavango Basin
Kalahari Desert
Limpopo R.
Namib Desert
Orange R.
Drakensberg
Cape of Good Hope
Cape Agulhas
Tropic of Capricorn
ATLANTIC OCEAN
INDIAN OCEAN
Mozambique Channel
Madagascar
Mauritius
Réunion
Tropic of Capricorn

N
W E
S

0 miles 1,000
0 kilometers 1,000
Lambert Azimuthal Equal Area

▲ **The Congo Basin**
The Congo Basin is a major physical feature of Africa. The key shows that its elevation is within the range of 650–1,600 feet.

Special-Purpose Maps: Climate

Unlike the boundary lines on a political map, the boundary lines on climate maps do not separate the land into exact divisions. For example, in this climate map of India, a tropical wet climate gradually changes to a tropical wet and dry climate.

PRACTICE YOUR GEOGRAPHY SKILLS

1. What part of a special-purpose map tells you what the colors on the map mean?

2. Where are arid regions located in India? Are there major cities in those regions?

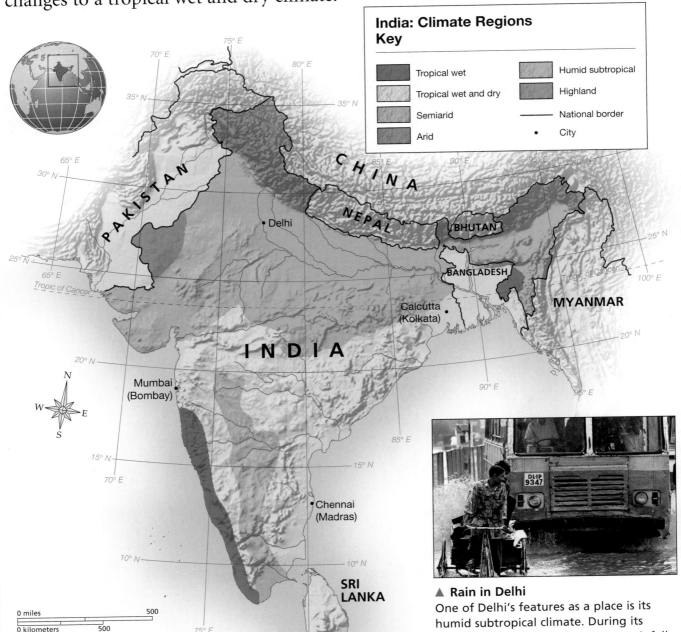

India: Climate Regions Key

- Tropical wet
- Tropical wet and dry
- Semiarid
- Arid
- Humid subtropical
- Highland
- — National border
- • City

PAKISTAN • Delhi CHINA NEPAL BHUTAN BANGLADESH MYANMAR

Calcutta (Kolkata)

INDIA

Mumbai (Bombay)

Tropic of Cancer

Chennai (Madras)

SRI LANKA

0 miles 500
0 kilometers 500
Lambert Conformal Conic

▲ **Rain in Delhi**
One of Delhi's features as a place is its humid subtropical climate. During its rainy season, Delhi receives heavy rainfall.

Special-Purpose Maps: Language

This map shows the official languages of India. An official language is the language used by the government. Even though a region has an official language, the people there may speak other languages as well. As in other special-purpose maps, the key explains how the different languages appear on the map.

PRACTICE YOUR GEOGRAPHY SKILLS

1 What color represents the Malayalam language on this map?

2 Where in India is Tamil the official language?

The Hindi language ▶
Hindi is the most widely spoken language in India. It is also the most popular language in Delhi.

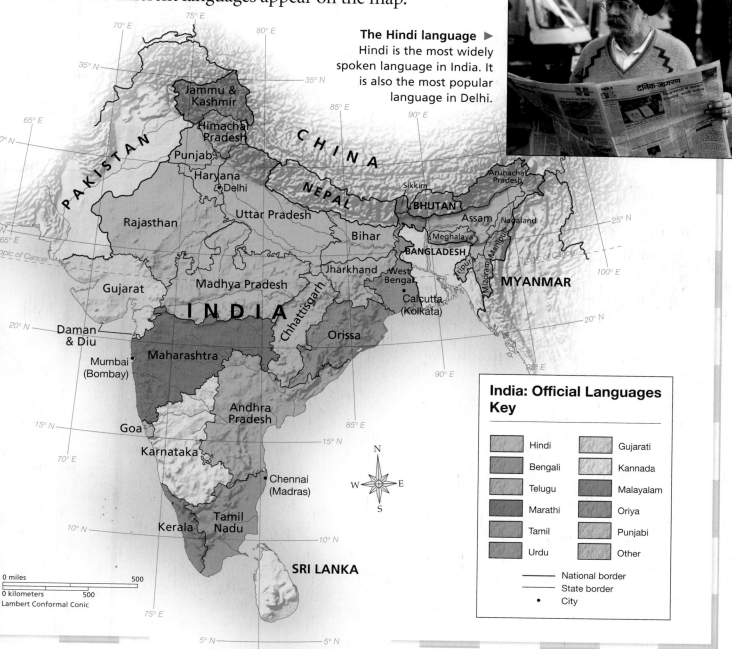

India: Official Languages Key

Hindi	Gujarati
Bengali	Kannada
Telugu	Malayalam
Marathi	Oriya
Tamil	Punjabi
Urdu	Other

—— National border
—— State border
• City

0 miles 500
0 kilometers 500
Lambert Conformal Conic

Human Migration

Migration is an important part of the study of geography. Since the beginning of history, people have been on the move. As people move, they both shape and are shaped by their environments. Wherever people go, the culture they bring with them mixes with the cultures of the place in which they have settled.

Explorers arrive ▼
In 1492, Christopher Columbus set sail from Spain for the Americas with three ships. The ships shown here are replicas of those ships.

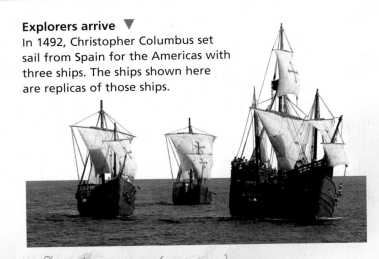

▲ **Native American pyramid**
When Europeans arrived in the Americas, the lands they found were not empty. Diverse groups of people with distinct cultures already lived there. The temple-topped pyramid shown above was built by Mayan Indians in Mexico, long before Columbus sailed.

Migration to the Americas, 1500–1800

A huge wave of migration from the Eastern Hemisphere began in the 1500s. European explorers in the Americas paved the way for hundreds of years of European settlement there. Forced migration from Africa started soon afterward, as Europeans began to import African slaves to work in the Americas. The map to the right shows these migrations.

ATLANTIC OCEAN

NEW SPAIN
(Spain)
Mexico City

Caribbean Sea

DUTCH GUIANA
(Netherlands)

Panama City

NEW GRENADA
(Spain)

FRENCH GUIANA
(France)

Amazon R.

PERU
(Spain)
Lima
Cuzco

BRAZIL
(Portugal)

Potosí
RIO DE LA PLATA
(Spain)

Concepción

Buenos Aires

0 miles   1,000
0 kilometers 1,000
Wagner VII

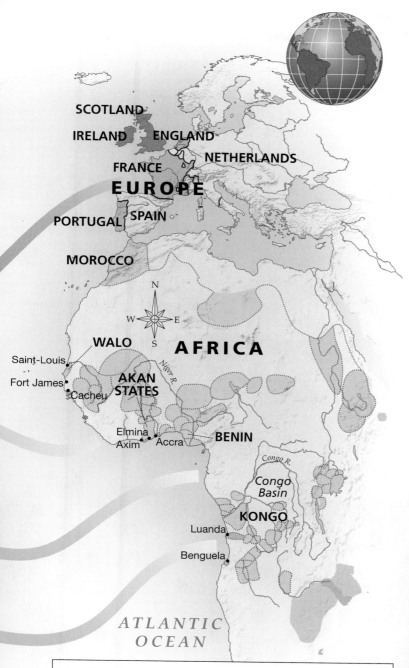

SCOTLAND
IRELAND ENGLAND
            NETHERLANDS
    FRANCE
EUROPE
PORTUGAL SPAIN

MOROCCO

N
W   E
S

WALO   AFRICA
Saint-Louis
Fort James
            AKAN   Niger R.
    Cacheu   STATES
        Elmina
        Axim   Accra   BENIN
                Congo R.
                Congo
                Basin
            KONGO
        Luanda
        Benguela

ATLANTIC
OCEAN

Migration to Latin America, 1500–1800
Key

 European migration
 African migration
——— National or colonial border
········· Traditional African border
 African State

 Spain and possessions
Portugal and possessions
Netherlands and possessions
France and possessions
England and possessions

PRACTICE YOUR GEOGRAPHY SKILLS

1 Where did the Portuguese settle in the Americas?

2 Would you describe African migration at this time as a result of both push factors and pull factors? Explain why or why not.

"Push" and "Pull" Factors

Geographers describe a people's choice to migrate in terms of "push" factors and "pull" factors. Push factors are things in people's lives that push them to leave, such as poverty and political unrest. Pull factors are things in another country that pull people to move there, including better living conditions and hopes of better jobs.

▲ **Elmina, Ghana**
Elmina, in Ghana, is one of the many ports from which slaves were transported from Africa. Because slaves and gold were traded here, stretches of the western African coast were known as the Slave Coast and the Gold Coast.

MapMaster Skills Handbook **M15**

World Land Use

People around the world have many different economic structures, or ways of making a living. Land-use maps are one way to learn about these structures. The ways that people use the land in each region tell us about the main ways that people in that region make a living.

World Land Use Key

	Nomadic herding
	Hunting and gathering
	Forestry
	Livestock raising
	Commercial farming
	Subsistence farming
	Manufacturing and trade
	Little or no activity
——	National border
- - - -	Disputed border

▲ **Wheat farming in the United States**
Developed countries practice commercial farming rather than subsistence farming. Commercial farming is the production of food mainly for sale, either within the country or for export to other countries. Commercial farmers like these in Oregon often use heavy equipment to farm.

Levels of Development

Notice on the map key the term *subsistence farming*. This term means the production of food mainly for use by the farmer's own family. In less-developed countries, subsistence farming is often one of the main economic activities. In contrast, in developed countries there is little subsistence farming.

▲ **Growing barley in Ecuador**
These farmers in Ecuador use hand tools to harvest barley. They will use most of the crop they grow to feed themselves or their farm animals.

NORTH
AMERICA

SOUTH
AMERICA

0 miles
0 kilometers   2,000
Robinson

▲ Growing rice in Vietnam
Women in Vietnam plant rice in wet rice paddies, using the same planting methods their ancestors did.

PRACTICE YOUR GEOGRAPHY SKILLS

1 In what parts of the world is subsistence farming the main land use?

2 Locate where manufacturing and trade are the main land use. Are they found more often near areas of subsistence farming or areas of commercial farming? Why might this be so?

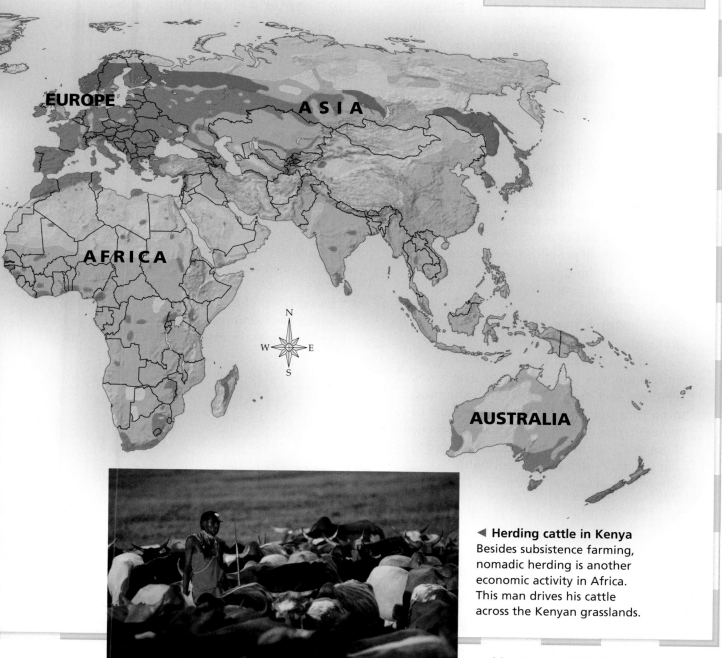

EUROPE

ASIA

AFRICA

AUSTRALIA

◄ Herding cattle in Kenya
Besides subsistence farming, nomadic herding is another economic activity in Africa. This man drives his cattle across the Kenyan grasslands.

How to Read Social Studies

Target Reading Skills

The Target Reading Skills introduced on this page will help you understand the words and ideas in this book and in other social studies reading you do. Each chapter focuses on one of these reading skills. Good readers develop a bank of reading strategies, or skills. Then they draw on the particular strategies that will help them understand the text they are reading.

Chapter 1 Target Reading Skills

Reading Process Previewing can help you understand and remember what you read. In this chapter you will practice using these previewing skills: setting a purpose for reading, predicting what the text will be about, and asking questions before you read.

Chapter 2 Target Reading Skills

Clarifying Meaning If you do not understand something you are reading right away, you can use several skills to clarify the meaning of the word or idea. In this chapter you will practice these strategies for clarifying meaning: rereading, reading ahead, paraphrasing, and summarizing.

Chapter 3 Target Reading Skills

Main Idea Since you cannot remember every detail of what you read, it is important to identify the main ideas. The main idea of a section or paragraph is the most important point and the one you want to remember. In this chapter you will practice these skills: identifying both stated and implied main ideas and identifying supporting details.

Chapter 4 Target Reading Skills

Comparison and Contrast You can use comparison and contrast to sort out and analyze information you are reading. Comparing means examining the similarities between things. Contrasting is looking at differences. In this chapter you will practice these skills: comparing and contrasting, using signal words, identifying contrasts, and making comparisons.

Chapter 5 Target Reading Skills

Using Context Using the context of an unfamiliar word can help you understand its meaning. Context includes the words, phrases, and sentences surrounding a word. In this chapter you will practice using these context clues: definitions, interpreting nonliteral meanings, your own general knowledge, and cause and effect.

The UNITED STATES and CANADA

Spreading "from sea to shining sea," the United States and Canada take up nearly seven eighths of North America. In this book, you'll see how the United States and Canada are working to create a good life for every citizen in these vast countries.

Guiding Questions

The text, photographs, maps, and charts in this book will help you discover answers to these Guiding Questions.

1. **Geography** How has physical geography affected the cultures of the United States and Canada?

2. **History** How have historical events affected the cultures of the United States and Canada?

3. **Culture** How has the variety of people in the United States and Canada benefited and challenged the two nations?

4. **Government** How do the governments of the United States and Canada differ? How are they alike?

5. **Economics** How did the United States and Canada become two of the wealthiest nations in the world?

Project Preview

You can also discover answers to the Guiding Questions by working on projects. Several project possibilities are listed on page 188 of this book.

Investigate the United States and Canada

Stretching from the Pacific Ocean to the Atlantic Ocean, the United States is the world's fourth largest country. Canada is slightly larger and stretches across five time zones. Though roughly the same size, the United States has far more people—nearly 10 times the population of Canada.

▲ **The Northern Territories, Canada**
Snowmobiles and dogsleds make travel possible in the far north.

LOCATION

1 Locate the United States and Canada

How would you describe Canada's location? One way would be to compare its location to that of the United States. Which country extends farther north? Which country is closer to Russia? Which country has more of its land touching the Arctic Ocean? Based on the relative locations of these two countries, estimate which has a colder climate.

REGIONS

2 Estimate the Length of the United States and Canada

How does Canada's length from north to south compare to the length of the continental United States? With a ruler, measure the United States from its southernmost border to its border with Canada. Now measure the length of Canada. Which is longer? Now measure both countries from east to west. Which is wider?

Political United States and Canada

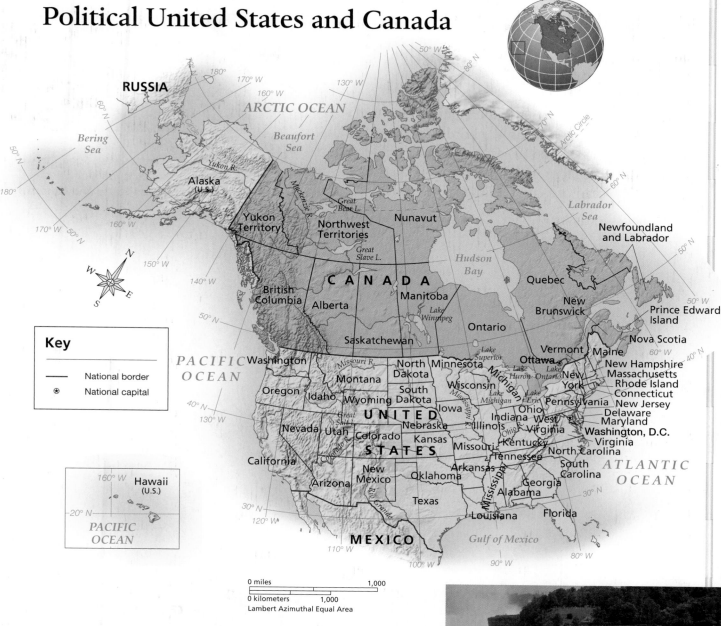

Key

— National border

⊛ National capital

0 miles ———— 1,000
0 kilometers ———— 1,000
Lambert Azimuthal Equal Area

PLACE

3 Find States, Provinces, and Territories

Which two of the 50 United States do not share a border with any other state? Which Canadian territory reaches the farthest north? Which states border Canada? Which provinces border the United States? Name the cities that are the national capitals of the United States and Canada. Notice that the United States and Canada together make up most of the continent of North America. What other country is on the same continent?

▲ **Niagara Falls**
The Niagara Falls lie on the border between Canada and the United States.

Physical United States and Canada

INTERACTION

4 Find Important Bodies of Water

What three oceans surround the United States and Canada? What bodies of water lie on the border between the United States and Canada? The largest bay in the world is located in Canada. What is its name? Would you enter the bay from the Pacific Ocean or from the Atlantic Ocean?

▲ **Lake Superior**
One of the five Great Lakes, Superior is the farthest north. It lies along the border of the United States and Canada.

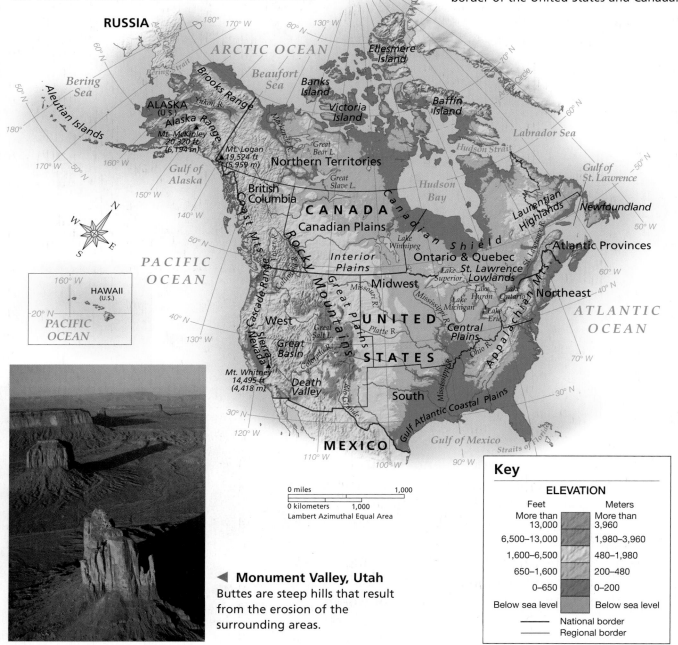

0 miles 1,000
0 kilometers 1,000
Lambert Azimuthal Equal Area

Key

ELEVATION	
Feet	Meters
More than 13,000	More than 3,960
6,500–13,000	1,980–3,960
1,600–6,500	480–1,980
650–1,600	200–480
0–650	0–200
Below sea level	Below sea level
——— National border	
——— Regional border	

◀ **Monument Valley, Utah**
Buttes are steep hills that result from the erosion of the surrounding areas.

Climates of the United States and Canada

The climates of the United States and Canada range widely. Average annual temperatures vary from 71° F in Florida to 27° F in Alaska. Because of its greater distance from the Equator, Canada has much cooler temperatures than the United States. In both countries it is hotter in the interior in the summer and colder and windier in the winter.

Key

——	National border
▮	Tropical wet
▯	Tropical wet and dry
▮	Semiarid
▮	Arid
▮	Mediterranean
▮	Humid continental
▮	Marine west coast
▮	Humid subtropical
▯	Subarctic
▯	Tundra
▮	Highland

REGIONS

5 Explore Influences on Climate

Compare the physical map of the United States and Canada on the previous page with the climate map above. How might landforms affect weather and rainfall? Notice that from Miami, Florida to Yellowknife, Canada the climate changes from tropical wet and dry to subarctic. Give reasons for this great shift in climates.

PRACTICE YOUR GEOGRAPHY SKILLS

1 On your hike in the western mountains you camped at the foot of Mount Rainier. Then you crossed an international border. What country are you in now?

2 You just flew over the mouth of the Mackenzie River and are headed for Victoria Island in Canada. Are you north or south of the Arctic Circle?

3 You are traveling through the Gulf of St. Lawrence toward the Great Lakes. What river will you take?

▲ **Mount Rainier National Park, Washington**

Focus on Regions of the United States and Canada

Now that you've investigated the geography of the United States and Canada, take a closer look at some of the regions that make up these two countries.

Go Online
PHSchool.com
Use Web Code lhp-4000 for the interactive maps on these pages.

RUSSIA

ARCTIC OCEAN

Bering Sea

Beaufort Sea

Yukon R.

ALASKA (U.S.)

Mackenzie R.

Great Bear

Northern

British Columbia

Prair

PACIFIC OCEAN

West

HAWAII (U.S.)

PACIFIC OCEAN

▲ British Columbia
British Columbia has important ties to the Pacific Rim nations across the ocean. Its largest city, Vancouver, is one of North America's great cities. Almost all trade between Canada and the Pacific Rim passes through its harbor, which never freezes.

◄ The West
The West has an abundance of natural and human resources. Although the West produces 85 percent of America's gold, water is one of the most precious natural resources in the region.

The South ▶
The South is a warm region with a climate perfect for growing crops. Its booming industries have drawn many people from within the country and overseas. The Mardi Gras festival is one example of the region's cultural diversity.

Atlantic Provinces ▶

The four Canadian provinces that make up the Atlantic Provinces all border the Atlantic Ocean. Fishing and other maritime industries have always supported the economy and way of life of this region.

▲ Ontario and Quebec

These two provinces are Canada's most populous provinces. Ontario contains Ottawa, the national capital, shown above. French speakers make up a majority of the population of Quebec.

◀ The Midwest

Though the Midwest is still "America's Breadbasket," most family farms there have given way to larger corporate farms. The region is also an important transportation center.

Key

——	National border
——	Regional border
⊛	Capital city

0 miles · 1,000
0 kilometers · 1,000
Lambert Azimuthal Equal Area

The U.S. and Canada: Physical Geography

Chapter Preview

This chapter will introduce you to the geography of the United States and Canada and show how geography affects the people who live in the region.

Section 1
Land and Water

Section 2
Climate and Vegetation

Section 3
Resources and Land Use

 **Target Reading Skill**

Reading Process In this chapter you will use previewing to help you understand and remember what you read.

▶ Talbot Lake, Canada

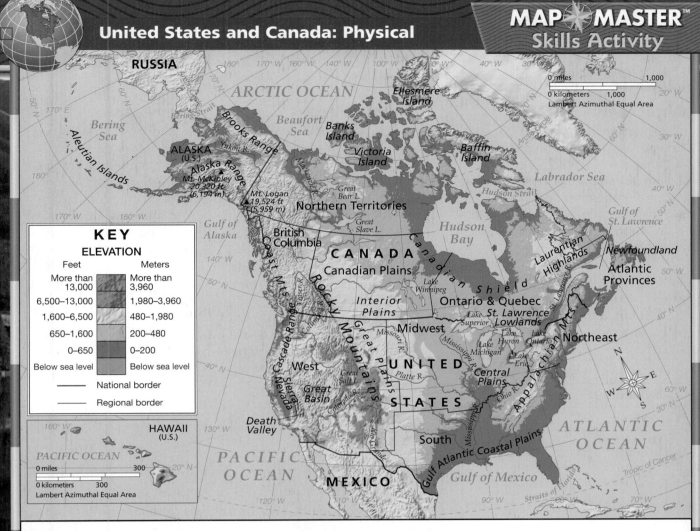

United States and Canada: Physical

KEY

ELEVATION

Feet		Meters
More than 13,000		More than 3,960
6,500–13,000		1,980–3,960
1,600–6,500		480–1,980
650–1,600		200–480
0–650		0–200
Below sea level		Below sea level
———	National border	
———	Regional border	

RUSSIA

ARCTIC OCEAN

Ellesmere Island

Bering Strait

Bering Sea

Brooks Range

Aleutian Islands

ALASKA (U.S.)

Yukon R.

Alaska Range

Mt. McKinley 20,320 ft (6,194 m)

Mt. Logan ▲19,524 ft (5,959 m)

Beaufort Sea

Banks Island

Victoria Island

Baffin Island

Labrador Sea

Hudson Strait

Gulf of St. Lawrence

Arctic Circle

Gulf of Alaska

British Columbia

Coast Mts.

Great Bear L.

Mackenzie R.

Northern Territories

Great Slave L.

CANADA

Canadian Plains

Canadian Shield

Hudson Bay

Laurentian Highlands

Newfoundland

Atlantic Provinces

Lake Winnipeg

Interior Plains

Rocky Mountains

Great Plains

Columbia R.

Snake R.

Missouri R.

Ontario & Quebec

St. Lawrence Lowlands

Lake Superior

St. Lawrence R.

Midwest

Lake Michigan

Lake Huron

Lake Ontario

Lake Erie

Appalachian Mts.

Northeast

Cascade Range

Sierra Nevada

West

Great Basin

Great Salt L.

Platte R.

Mississippi R.

Central Plains

Ohio R.

UNITED STATES

Death Valley

Colorado R.

Rio Grande

South

Gulf Atlantic Coastal Plains

Mississippi R.

ATLANTIC OCEAN

MEXICO

Gulf of Mexico

Tropic of Cancer

Straits of Florida

PACIFIC OCEAN

0 miles 1,000
0 kilometers 1,000
Lambert Azimuthal Equal Area

HAWAII (U.S.)

PACIFIC OCEAN

0 miles 300
0 kilometers 300
Lambert Azimuthal Equal Area

Place Notice that the United States and Canada share many physical features. **Locate** Which areas of the United States and Canada have the highest elevation? **Predict** How might people use the land in these mountainous regions?

Go Online
PHSchool.com Use Web Code **lhp-4110** for step-by-step **map skills practice**.

Prepare to Read

Objectives

In this section you will
1. Learn where the United States and Canada are located.
2. Find out about the major landforms of the United States and Canada.
3. Explore major bodies of water that are important to the United States and Canada.

Taking Notes

As you read the section, look for the main ideas about land and water. Copy the table below and record your findings in it.

Country	Landforms	Bodies of Water
United States		
Canada		

Target Reading Skill

Set a Purpose for Reading Before you read this section, look at the headings, maps, and photographs to see what the section is about. Then set a purpose for reading this section. For example, your purpose might be to find out about the geography of the United States and Canada. Use the Taking Notes table to help you meet your purpose.

Key Terms

- **Rocky Mountains** (RAHK ee MOWN tunz) *n.* the major mountain range in western North America
- **glacier** (GLAY shur) *n.* a huge, slow-moving mass of snow and ice
- **Great Lakes** (grayt layks) *n.* the world's largest group of freshwater lakes
- **tributary** (TRIB yoo tehr ee) *n.* a river or stream that flows into a larger river

Alaska's Mount McKinley is the highest mountain in North America. In 1992, Ruth Kocour joined a team of climbers to scale the 20,320-foot (6,194-meter) peak. After the team had set up camp at 9,500 feet (2,896 meters), the first storm arrived. The team quickly built walls of packed snow to shield their tents from the wind. They dug a snow cave to house their kitchen and waited for the storm to end. Kocour recalls, "Someone on another team went outside for a few minutes, came back, and had a hot drink. His teeth cracked."

Maybe camping in the mountains is not for you. Perhaps you would prefer the sunny beaches of Florida, the giant forests of the Northwest, or the rugged coastline of Nova Scotia. Maybe you would like to see the Arizona desert or the plains of central Canada. The landscape of the United States and Canada varies greatly.

Climbers on Mount McKinley

A Scenic Landscape
This view of the Pioneer Valley along the Connecticut River in Massachusetts was taken from Mount Sugarloaf. **Draw Conclusions** *What can you conclude about the northeastern region of the United States from this photo?*

A Global Perspective

The United States and Canada are located in North America. To the east is the Atlantic Ocean, and to the west is the Pacific Ocean. To the north, Canada borders the Arctic Ocean, while to the south, the United States borders Mexico and the Gulf of Mexico. The United States also includes Alaska, a huge state bordering northwest Canada, and Hawaii, a group of Pacific islands more than 2,000 miles (3,220 kilometers) west of California.

✓ Reading Check **Which bodies of water border the United States and Canada?**

Landforms

From outer space, the United States and Canada appear as one landmass, with mountain ranges or systems, and vast plains running from north to south. Locate these mountains and plains on the United States and Canada: Physical map on page 9.

Extending about 3,000 miles (4,830 kilometers) along the western section of the continent, the **Rocky Mountains** are the largest mountain system in North America. In the east, the Appalachian (ap uh LAY chun) Mountains are the United States' second-largest mountain system. They stretch about 1,500 miles (2,415 kilometers). In Canada, the Appalachian Mountains meet the Laurentian (law REN shun) Highlands.

Between the Rockies and the Appalachians lies a huge plains area. In Canada, these lowlands are called the Interior Plains. In the United States, they are called the Great Plains and the Central Plains. Much of this region has rich soil. In the wetter, eastern area, farmers grow crops like corn and soybeans. In the drier, western area, farmers grow wheat and ranchers raise livestock.

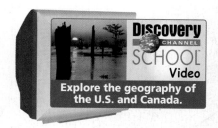

DISCOVERY CHANNEL
SCHOOL Video
Explore the geography of the U.S. and Canada.

Links to Science

The Next Hawaiian Island
Volcanic eruptions in the Pacific Ocean, like the one shown above in Volcano National Park, created the islands of Hawaii. Loihi (loh EE hee), off the southern tip of Hawaii, is the world's most active volcano. But no one has seen it erupt. Its peak is 3,000 feet (914 meters) below the ocean's surface. Years of continuous eruption have produced layer after layer of molten lava. Scientists predict that in 100,000 years or less, Loihi will rise above the surface of the ocean and become the next Hawaiian island.

Special Features of the United States   The United States has several unique features. The Gulf-Atlantic Coastal Plain runs along its eastern and southern coasts. In the Northeast, this plain is narrow; it broadens as it spreads south and west. Flat, fertile land and access to the sea attracted many settlers to this area.

A region of plateaus and basins lies west of the Rockies. Perhaps the most notable feature of this area is the Great Basin. In the northeast section of this bowl-shaped region is the Great Salt Lake. Death Valley is in the southwest section. Much of Death Valley lies below sea level. It is also the hottest place in North America. Summer temperatures there exceed 125°F (52°C).

Volcanoes   To the west of this region lie three more mountain ranges. They are the Coast Ranges along the Pacific, the Sierra Nevada in California, and the Cascades in Washington and Oregon. Volcanoes produced the Cascades. Volcanoes form when magma, or molten rock, breaks through Earth's crust. Once it comes up to the surface, the molten rock is called lava. One of the volcanoes in the Cascades—Mount St. Helens— erupted in 1980. The eruption was so powerful that people as far away as Montana had to sweep volcanic ash off of their cars.

Glaciers   Far to the north, snow and ice cover Alaska's many mountains. **Glaciers,** huge, slow-moving sheets of ice, fill many of the valleys among these mountains. Glaciers form over many years when layers of snow press together, thaw a little, and then turn to ice. Valley glaciers are found in high mountain valleys where the climate is too cold for the ice to melt. In North America, these valley glaciers move through the Rocky and Cascade mountains, the Sierra Nevada, and the Alaskan ranges.

Special Features of Canada   Canada, too, has a number of unique features. East of Alaska lies the Yukon (YOO kahn) Territory. Mount Logan, Canada's highest peak, is located there in a range called the Coast Mountains. The Coast Mountains, which stretch south along the Pacific Ocean, are located only in Canada. They are not part of the United States Coast Ranges.

Farther east, beyond the Interior Plains, lies the Canadian Shield. This huge region of ancient rock covers about half of Canada. The land on the shield is rugged, so few people live there.

Southeast of the shield along the St. Lawrence River are the St. Lawrence Lowlands. These lowlands are Canada's smallest land region. However, they are home to more than half of the country's population. The region is also Canada's manufacturing center. And because the lowlands have fertile soil, farmers in this region produce about one third of the country's crops.

✓ **Reading Check**   **Describe two physical features of the United States and Canada.**

Set a Purpose for Reading
If your purpose is to learn about the geography of Canada, how do the three paragraphs at the left help you meet your goal?

Major Bodies of Water

Both the United States and Canada have important lakes and rivers. People use these bodies of water for transportation, recreation, and industry. Many American and Canadian cities developed near these bodies of water. Find these waterways on the United States and Canada: Physical map on page 9.

A satellite image of the Great Lakes, which create a natural border between the United States and Canada

The Great Lakes   Lakes Superior, Michigan, Huron, Erie, and Ontario make up the **Great Lakes,** the world's largest group of freshwater lakes. Lake Superior is the deepest lake, with a mean depth of 487 feet (148 meters). Lake Erie is the shallowest lake at only 62 feet (19 meters) deep. Only Lake Michigan lies entirely in the United States. The other four lie on the border between the United States and Canada.

Glaciers formed the Great Lakes during an ice age long ago. As the glaciers moved, they dug deep trenches in the land. Water from the melting glaciers filled these trenches to produce the Great Lakes. Today, the Great Lakes are important waterways in both the United States and Canada. Shipping on the Great Lakes has helped to develop the industries of both countries.

The Continental Divide
The Rocky Mountains form the continental divide and are the site of several national parks, including Grand Teton National Park in Wyoming (large photo).
White-water rafters paddle along Flathead River in Montana, west of the Rockies (small photo).
Explain *In what direction does the Flathead River flow?*

Major Rivers of the United States The largest river in the United States is the Mississippi River. Its source, or starting point, is in Minnesota. From there, the river flows through the Central Plains to the Gulf of Mexico. Two other major rivers, the Ohio and the Missouri, are tributaries of the Mississippi. A **tributary** (TRIB yoo tehr ee) is a stream or river that flows into a larger river. The Mississippi River system includes hundreds of tributaries and branches. Together they form about 12,000 miles (19,000 kilometers) of navigable water.

The Mighty Mississippi Water levels tend to rise in the spring when heavy rain combines with melting snow from the mountains. If the soil cannot soak up the excess water, flooding can occur. In 1993, the Upper Mississippi Valley experienced a disastrous flood. It caused nearly 50 deaths and damages totaling more than 15 billion dollars.

People have used the Mississippi River as an important transportation route for hundreds of years. Today, it is one of the busiest waterways in the world. Cargo ships transport many products, including iron, steel, chemicals, and even space rockets.

Look at the United States and Canada: Physical map on page 9 and find the Rocky Mountains. Notice that the Fraser, Columbia, and Colorado rivers form in the Rockies and flow west. Now find the Platte and Missouri rivers. They flow east from the Rockies. This is because the Rockies form the Continental Divide, the boundary that separates rivers flowing to the Pacific Ocean from those flowing to the Atlantic Ocean.

Major Rivers of Canada The Mackenzie River, Canada's longest, forms in the Rocky Mountains and flows north to the Arctic Ocean. It runs for more than 2,600 miles (4,197 kilometers). Although for most of its course the Mackenzie winds through sparsely populated, dense forest area, it is an important transportation route.

In the 1880s, steamboats on the Mackenzie took supplies to local trading posts. Today, ships carry energy and mineral resources from the oil and natural gas fields in the region.

Canada's second major river is the St. Lawrence River. It is one of North America's most important transportation routes, flowing from the Great Lakes to the Atlantic Ocean. A system of locks and canals enables large ships to navigate it. From the St. Lawrence, ships can reach the Great Lakes ports that serve the farmland and industries of the region. Thus, the St. Lawrence is an important trade route between the United States and Canada. Millions of tons of cargo move along the St. Lawrence River each year.

✓ **Reading Check** **Name the five Great Lakes.**

Section 1 Assessment

Key Terms
Review the key terms at the beginning of this section. Use each term in a sentence that explains its meaning.

 Target Reading Skill
How did having a purpose for reading help you to understand important ideas in this section?

Comprehension and Critical Thinking
1. (a) Recall Describe the borders of the United States and Canada.
(b) Predict How do you think the climates of Hawaii and Alaska differ?

2. (a) Describe What is the largest mountain system in North America?
(b) Identify Effects How have the physical features of the United States and Canada affected the lives of the people there?
3. (a) Locate Which bodies of water lie on the border between the United States and Canada?
(b) Explain Why are these bodies of water important?
(c) Draw Conclusions Why did many people coming to the United States and Canada hundreds of years ago settle along coastal plains and rivers?

Writing Activity
Suppose that you are on vacation in the United States or Canada. Write a postcard to a friend describing the physical features that you have seen. Before you begin, review the information you recorded in your Taking Notes table.

For: An activity on Mt. McKinley
Visit: PHSchool.com
Web Code: lhd-4101

"It's a freak storm," Ian e-mailed excitedly to his friends. "Four inches of snow already, and we might get six inches total. It's awful!"

"Awful?" Janet replied. "It's just a few inches. What's the big deal?"

"JUST a few inches?" Ian typed. "This city is paralyzed. Cars are stuck everywhere. Our camping trip this weekend is cancelled. It's a disaster."

Luann responded to both of her friends. "Of course it's a disaster to Ian. He lives in Georgia. No way is the South prepared to deal with a snowstorm in April."

"Well, up here in Quebec, we're not afraid of a little snow!" Janet wrote back.

"Okay, calm down," wrote Luann. "Your opinion depends on what you're used to."

In other words, your opinion depends on your frame of reference.

Learn the Skill

Follow the steps below to understand frame of reference.

1. **Identify the topic being discussed.** Look for evidence that an opinion is being expressed. When people state their opinions, they often reveal information about their frame of reference.

2. **Identify the author's opinion on the issue.** An opinion is what someone believes. It is not a fact, which is something that can be proved.

3. **Identify what you know about the author's background.** Some background factors are age, personality, family, culture, nationality, concerns, and historical era.

4. **Ask how the author's background might have influenced his or her beliefs.** Think about whether the person's opinions would be different if he or she came from a different place, culture, family, or time in history.

Practice the Skill

The text in the box on the right comes from Inuit students in Nunavut. The Inuit, a Native American culture group, persuaded the Canadian government to create the territory of Nunavut in 1999. Read what the students wrote just before the creation of their new homeland.

1 This text has no title, but you can give it a title that reflects the main topic. What title would you give it?

2 The students give both description and opinion. Which parts of the text are description, and which are opinion?

3 You already know some facts about the students' background: They are Canadian, and they are Inuit. What else can you discover about the students' background?

4 The students' opinions are shaped by their frame of reference. Explain how your own frame of reference might make you feel differently about Nunavut.

"There are not very many people, but all of us are friends. We share the same culture and language, Inuktitut. You can learn from elders. We help each other. . . .

"[W]e go to school, church, cadets, the hall, and the gym. We play [games], watch T.V., listen to music, play and watch sports (especially hockey), . . . dance, and sleep. We also stay home, visit with our parents, clean, look after children, and try to finish our homework. . . . We eat seal meat, caribou, arctic char, walrus, . . . and also we eat various types of birds. . . .

"Nunavut is independence. The creation of Nunavut means that we, the Inuit, are going to have our own land. . . . It means a lot to us, the Inuit youth. It means making choices for ourselves. We are proud of Nunavut."
—*Grade 10 students at Ataguttaaluk High in Igloolik, a town in central Nunavut, above the Arctic Circle*

Inuit sculptor

Apply the Skill

Think of an issue that you feel strongly about. Describe your own frame of reference, and show how it has influenced your opinion.

Prepare to Read

Objectives

In this section you will
1. Learn what climate zones the United States and Canada have.
2. Identify the natural vegetation zones of the United States and Canada.

Taking Notes

As you read the section, look for details about climate and vegetation. Copy the chart below and write each detail under the correct heading.

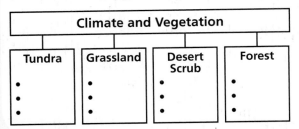

Climate and Vegetation

Tundra	Grassland	Desert Scrub	Forest
•	•	•	•
•	•	•	•
•	•	•	•

Target Reading Skill

Predict Making predictions about your text helps you set a purpose for reading and remember what you read. Before you begin, preview the section by looking at the headings, photographs, and maps. Then predict what the text might discuss about climate and vegetation. As you read the section, connect what you read to your prediction. If what you learn doesn't support your prediction, change it.

Key Terms

- **tundra** (TUN druh) *n.* a cold, dry region covered with snow for more than half the year
- **permafrost** (PUR muh frawst) *n.* a permanently frozen layer of ground below the top layer of soil
- **prairie** (PREHR ee) *n.* a region of flat or rolling land covered with grasses
- **province** (PRAH vins) *n.* a political division of land in Canada

On a hot and sunny February morning, a reporter left his home in Miami Beach, Florida, and headed for the airport. Wearing lightweight pants and a short-sleeved shirt, he boarded a plane to snowy Toronto. Was he forgetting something? Surely he knew that the temperature would be below freezing in Canada.

He did, indeed, know all about the bitter cold that would greet him when he got off the plane. But he was going to research an article on Toronto's tunnels and underground malls. He wanted to find out whether people could really visit hotels, restaurants, and shops without having to go outside and brave the harsh Canadian winter.

A climate-controlled shopping center in Toronto, Ontario

Climate Zones

Climate is weather patterns that an area experiences over a long period of time. Climate zones in the United States and Canada range from a desert climate to a polar climate. Factors such as latitude, or a location's distance north or south of the Equator, mountains, and oceans all affect the climates found in different regions.

Climates of Canada   Generally, the farther a location is from the Equator, the colder its climate. Look at the climate regions map on page 5 of the Regional Overview. Notice that much of Canada lies well north of the 40° N line of latitude, a long way from the Equator. Therefore, much of Canada is very cold!

Ocean Effects The ocean affects Canada's climates, too. Water heats up and cools down more slowly than land. Winds blowing across water on to land tend to warm the land in winter and cool the land in summer. Therefore, areas that are near an ocean generally have milder climates. Also, winds blowing across the ocean pick up moisture. When these winds blow over land, they drop the moisture in the form of rain or snow.

Being a great distance from the ocean also affects climate. Inland areas often have climate extremes. Find Winnipeg, in Canada's Interior Plains, on the climate map. Winter temperatures here are very cold, averaging around 0°F (−18°C). Yet summer temperatures run between 70°F and 90°F (20°C and 32°C).

Mountain Effects Mountains are another factor that influence climate. Winds blowing from the Pacific Ocean rise as they meet mountain ranges in the west. As they rise, the winds cool and drop their moisture. The air is dry by the time it reaches the other side of the mountains, and it warms up as it returns to lower altitudes. This is called the Chinook effect. The area on the side of the mountains away from the wind is in a rain shadow. A rain shadow is an area on the dry, sheltered side of a mountain, which receives little rainfall.

Graph Skills

Located in different climate regions, Miami, Florida, and Toronto, Canada, experience very different average temperatures. **Identify** In which month does Miami experience the coolest temperatures? Which month is the coolest in Toronto?
Compare Which month has the least difference between the average temperature in Miami and Toronto?

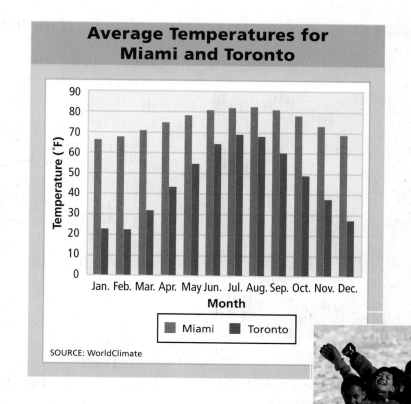

Average Temperatures for Miami and Toronto

SOURCE: WorldClimate

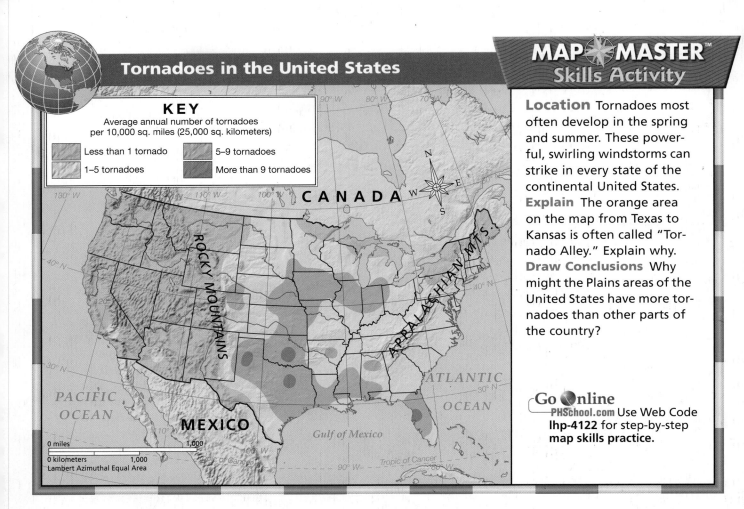

KEY

Average annual number of tornadoes
per 10,000 sq. miles (25,000 sq. kilometers)

Less than 1 tornado

1–5 tornadoes

5–9 tornadoes

More than 9 tornadoes

CANADA

ROCKY MOUNTAINS

APPALACHIAN MTS.

PACIFIC OCEAN

MEXICO

Gulf of Mexico

ATLANTIC OCEAN

Tropic of Cancer

0 miles 1,000
0 kilometers 1,000
Lambert Azimuthal Equal Area

Location Tornadoes most often develop in the spring and summer. These powerful, swirling windstorms can strike in every state of the continental United States. **Explain** The orange area on the map from Texas to Kansas is often called "Tornado Alley." Explain why. **Draw Conclusions** Why might the Plains areas of the United States have more tornadoes than other parts of the country?

Go Online
PHSchool.com Use Web Code **lhp-4122** for step-by-step map skills practice.

A tornado produces high winds and flying debris that can cause heavy damage to structures in its path.

Climates of the United States Location also influences climate. On the climate map on page 5, notice that Alaska lies north of the 60° N line of latitude. Far from the Equator, Alaska is cold for much of the year. Now find Hawaii and the southern tip of Florida. They lie near or within the tropics, the area between the 23½° N and 23½° S lines of latitude. There, it is almost always warm.

The Pacific Ocean and mountains affect climate in the western United States. Wet winds from the ocean drop their moisture before they cross the mountains. As a result, the eastern sections of California and Arizona are semiarid or desert. Death Valley, which is located there, has the lowest average rainfall in the country—about 2 inches (5 centimeters) a year.

East of the Great Plains, the country has continental climates. In the north, summers are warm and winters are cold and snowy. In the south, summers tend to be long and hot, while winters are mild. The coastal regions of these areas sometimes experience violent weather. In summer and fall, hurricanes and tropical storms develop in the Atlantic Ocean.

✓ **Reading Check** What factors affect climate?

Natural Vegetation Zones

Climate in the United States and Canada helps produce four major kinds of natural vegetation, or plant life. As you can see on the United States and Canada: Vegetation map on page 22, these are tundra, grassland, desert scrub, and forest.

Northern Tundras   The **tundra,** found in the far north, is a cold, dry region that is covered with snow for more than half the year. The Arctic tundra contains **permafrost,** a layer of permanently frozen soil. During the short, cool summer, the soil above the permafrost thaws. Mosses, grasses, and bright wildflowers grow there. Life is hard in the tundra. However, some Inuits (IN oo its), a native people of Canada and Alaska, once called Eskimos, live there. They make a living by fishing and hunting.

Grasslands   Grasslands are regions of flat or rolling land covered with grasses. They are located in areas where there is enough rain to support grasses but not enough to support forests. In North America, grasslands are called **prairies.** The world's largest prairie lies in the Central and Great Plains of North America. It stretches from the American central states into the Canadian provinces of Alberta, Saskatchewan (sas KACH uh wahn), and Manitoba. These three provinces are sometimes called the Prairie Provinces. **A province** is a political division of Canada, much like one of our states. Look at the temperate grasslands region of the United States and Canada: Vegetation map on page 22 to locate the prairies, or plains areas, of the United States and Canada.

Predict
Based on what you've read so far, is your prediction on target? If not, revise or change your prediction now.

Two Vegetation Zones
The natural vegetation of the northern tundra (large photo) differs greatly from the natural vegetation of the grasslands (smaller photo).
Draw Conclusions *How does climate affect the vegetation that grows in the tundra and grasslands?*

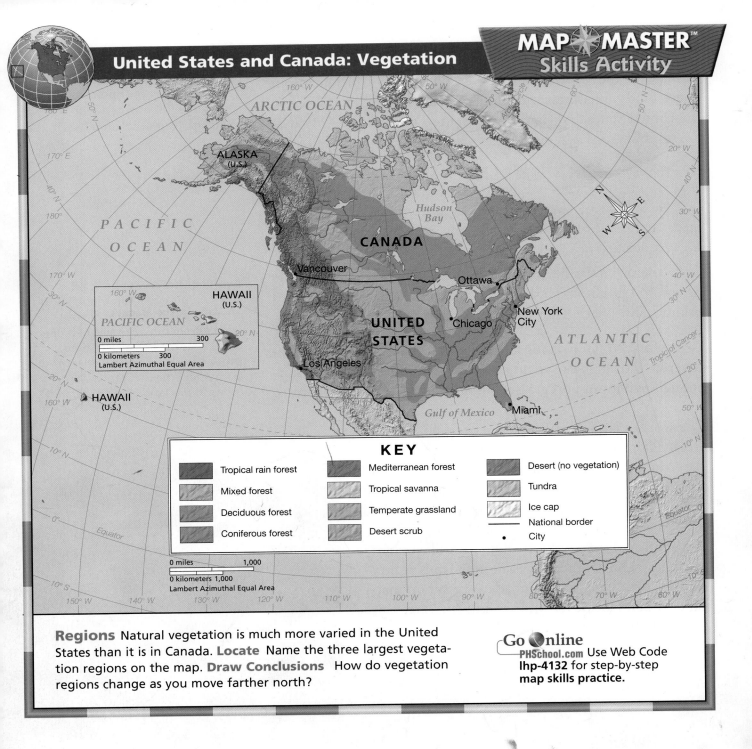

ARCTIC OCEAN

ALASKA
(U.S.)

PACIFIC
OCEAN

Hudson
Bay

CANADA

Vancouver

Ottawa

HAWAII
(U.S.)

PACIFIC OCEAN

New York
City

0 miles   300

UNITED
STATES

Chicago

0 kilometers   300
Lambert Azimuthal Equal Area

ATLANTIC

Los Angeles

OCEAN

HAWAII
(U.S.)

Gulf of Mexico

Miami

KEY

Tropical rain forest	Mediterranean forest	Desert (no vegetation)
Mixed forest	Tropical savanna	Tundra
Deciduous forest	Temperate grassland	Ice cap
Coniferous forest	Desert scrub	——— National border
		• City

0 miles   1,000
0 kilometers 1,000
Lambert Azimuthal Equal Area

Regions Natural vegetation is much more varied in the United States than it is in Canada. **Locate** Name the three largest vegetation regions on the map. **Draw Conclusions** How do vegetation regions change as you move farther north?

Go Online
PHSchool.com Use Web Code
lhp-4132 for step-by-step
map skills practice.

When pioneers first encountered the prairies in what is now the Midwest, they described it as "a sea of grass." Today, farmers grow fields of corn and soybeans there. Farther west, the Great Plains receive less rainfall. Therefore, only short grasses will grow. These grasses are ideal for grazing cattle. The land is also suitable for growing wheat. The Prairie Provinces, too, have many wheat farms and cattle ranches.

Desert Scrub With little rainfall, desert and semiarid regions have limited vegetation. What plants there are have adapted to drought conditions or survive through their deep root systems. The Great Basin, a large, dry region between the Rocky Mountains and the Sierra Nevada in the United States, is one example of a desert region. It covers about 190,000 square miles (492,000 square kilometers) of the West and includes Death Valley. The majority of Nevada and western Utah lie within the Great Basin.

The Sierras block the Great Basin from moisture-bearing winds that come off the Pacific Ocean. Thus, the entire region is in a rain shadow. With annual rainfall of only six to twelve inches (15 to 30 centimeters), the basin cannot support large numbers of people. But, many sheep graze on the area's shrubs.

For many years, the Great Basin was an obstacle that delayed the development of the West, because conditions made it difficult for explorers to cross it. Many people sought alternate routes around the Great Basin as they headed west during the California Gold Rush in 1849.

Life in the Desert
Despite little rain and scorching heat, hundreds of plants and animals, such as the scorpion below, live in the desert. **Draw Conclusions** *How might these plants and animals have adapted to the harsh desert environment?*

An autumn landscape in the Charlevoix region of Quebec, Canada

Forests Forests cover nearly one third of the United States and almost one half of Canada. The mild climate of the northern Pacific coast encourages great forests of coniferous (koh NIF ur us) trees, such as pine, fir, and spruce. Coniferous trees have cones that carry and protect their seeds. The Rockies are blanketed with coniferous forests. From the Great Lakes across southeastern Canada and New England, and down to the southeastern United States, you will find mixed forests. These are forests of coniferous trees mixed with deciduous (dee SIJ oo us) trees. Deciduous trees shed their leaves in the fall.

One of Canada's best-known symbols is the deciduous sugar maple tree. The sugar maple leaf appears on Canada's flag. In addition, sugar maples produce a sweet sap that can be made into maple syrup and maple sugar—two Canadian specialties.

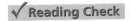 **Reading Check** **Name the four major kinds of natural vegetation in the United States and Canada.**

 ## Section 2 Assessment

Key Terms
Review the key terms at the beginning of this section. Use each term in a sentence that explains its meaning.

Target Reading Skill
What did you predict about this section? How did your prediction guide your reading?

Comprehension and Critical Thinking
1. (a) Recall Describe the major climate zones of the United States and Canada.

(b) Summarize How do oceans influence climate?
(c) Generalize What geographic features might lead someone to settle in Vancouver rather than in Winnipeg?
2. (a) Locate Where is the largest prairie in the world?
(b) Infer Why do more people live in the prairies than in the tundra?
(c) Identify Effects How does the vegetation of the prairies affect economic activity there?

Writing Activity
Describe the climate zones you would pass through if you traveled from northwestern Canada to the southeastern United States.

For: An activity on Florida's Everglades
Visit: PHSchool.com
Web Code: lhd-4102

Resources and Land Use

Prepare to Read

Objectives

In this section you will
1. Learn about the major resources of the United States.
2. Find out about the major resources of Canada.

Taking Notes

As you read the section, look for details about the resources of the United States and Canada. Copy the table below and write each detail under the correct subject heading.

Resource	United States	Canada
Farmland		
Water		
Energy and minerals		
Forests		

Target Reading Skill

Preview and Ask Questions Before you read this section, preview the headings and photographs to see what the section is about. Write one or two questions that will help you understand or remember something important in the section. Then read to answer your questions.

Key Terms

- **alluvial soil** (uh LOO vee ul soyl) *n.* fertile topsoil left by a river, especially after a flood
- **agribusiness** (AG ruh biz niz) *n.* a large company that runs huge farms
- **hydroelectricity** (hy droh ee lek TRIH suh tee) *n.* electric power produced by moving water
- **fossil fuel** (FAHS ul FYOO ul) *n.* a fuel formed over millions of years from animal and plant remains

Surrounded by majestic redwood forests, Carlotta, California, has little more than a gas station and a general store. Yet on one day in September 1996, police arrested more than 1,000 people there. Was Carlotta filled with outlaws like some old Wild West town? No, but it was the scene of a showdown. A logging company wanted to cut down some of the oldest redwood trees in the world. Protesters wanted to preserve the forest and the animals that live there. Both sides believed in the importance of natural resources. But they disagreed strongly about how to use them. As in Carlotta, people all over North America use their natural resources for recreation, industry, and energy.

Redwood National Park, California

Resources of the United States

Native Americans, pioneers, and explorers in North America knew centuries ago that it was a land of plenty. Abundant resources helped to build two of the world's leading economies.

Farmland   Both the Midwest and the South have rich, dark soils that are suitable for farming. Along the Mississippi and other river valleys are **alluvial** (uh LOO vee ul) **soils**, the fertile topsoil left by a river after a flood. Until the 1900s, most American farms were owned by families. Since then, large companies have bought many family farms. Southern California's Imperial Valley has vast vegetable fields operated by agribusinesses. An **agribusiness** is a large company that runs huge farms.

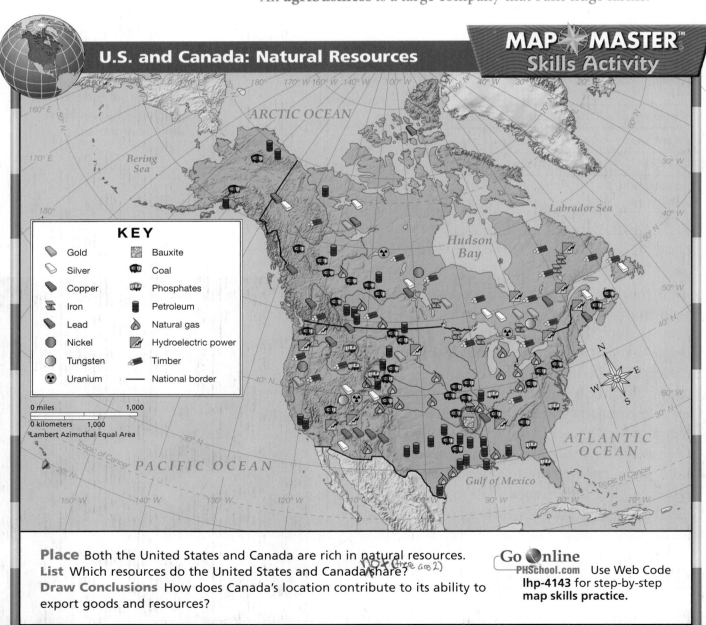

U.S. and Canada: Natural Resources

MAP MASTER™
Skills Activity

KEY

Gold		Bauxite	
Silver		Coal	
Copper		Phosphates	
Iron		Petroleum	
Lead		Natural gas	
Nickel		Hydroelectric power	
Tungsten		Timber	
Uranium		National border	

0 miles 1,000
0 kilometers 1,000
Lambert Azimuthal Equal Area

Place Both the United States and Canada are rich in natural resources.
List Which resources do the United States and Canada share?
Draw Conclusions How does Canada's location contribute to its ability to export goods and resources?

Go Online
PHSchool.com   Use Web Code
lhp-4143 for step-by-step
map skills practice.

Water Water is a vital resource. People need water to drink and to grow crops. Factories rely on water for many industrial processes, including cooling machinery. Both industry and farmers use rivers to transport goods. The Mississippi, Ohio, and Missouri rivers are important shipping routes.

Water is used for other purposes, too. Dams along many rivers produce **hydroelectricity** (hy droh ee lek TRIH suh tee), or electric power generated by moving water. The Grand Coulee (KOO lee) Dam on the Columbia River in the state of Washington produces more hydroelectricity than any other dam in the United States.

An irrigation system watering several fields on a California farm

Forests People have claimed that before Europeans arrived, a squirrel could leap from one tree to another all the way from the Atlantic Coast to the Mississippi River. That is no longer true, but America's forests are still an important resource. Large forests extend across the Pacific Northwest, the South, the Appalachians, and areas around the Great Lakes. They produce lumber, wood pulp for paper, and fine wood for furniture.

Energy and Mineral Resources The United States produces and consumes more fossil fuels than any other country. **Fossil fuels** are sources of energy that formed from animal and plant remains. Petroleum, natural gas, and coal are all fossil fuels. Although the United States imports most of its oil from other countries, the biggest oil reserves in North America are along the northern coast of Alaska. A pipeline carries oil from the wells in Prudhoe Bay to the port of Valdez in the south. From here, giant tankers carry the oil away to be refined.

The Trans-Alaska Pipeline Workers prepare a section of the 800-mile (1,280-kilometer) pipeline for welding. **Identify Effects** *How did the construction of the Trans-Alaska Pipeline produce growth for both the population and the economy of Alaska?*

Natural Gas Natural gas is a mixture of gases found beneath Earth's surface. To be usable, natural gas must be processed after it is removed from the ground. Its major use is as a fuel. Natural gas heats many homes in the United States. Large gas fields can be found in the Texas Panhandle, Louisiana, and Alaska. Natural gas can be transported by pipeline or in specially designed tanker ships.

Coal Coal is another important fossil fuel. Many power plants burn coal to produce electricity. It is also used to produce steel, as well as to heat and power industrial facilities. The United States has about 2,500 coal mines, totaling nearly 25 percent of the world's coal reserves. Over the past 30 years, modern mining equipment has nearly tripled the productivity of these mines. Wyoming, Kentucky, West Virginia, and Pennsylvania are the main coal-producing states in the country.

Mining In addition, the United States has valuable deposits of copper, gold, iron ore, and lead. Mining accounts for a small percentage of the country's economy and employs less than one percent of its workers. But these minerals are very important to other industries and have fueled industrial expansion.

✓ Reading Check **Why is water an important natural resource?**

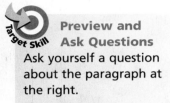

Preview and Ask Questions
Ask yourself a question about the paragraph at the right.

Mining Machinery
A coal miner uses a mining machine to dig into the face of a coal deposit. **Analyze** *Why is coal such an important resource in the United States?*

Resources of Canada

Canada's first European settlers earned their living as fur trappers, loggers, fishers, and farmers. Today, the economic picture has changed. Less than five percent of Canada's workers earn their living in these ways.

Farmland Less than 10 percent of Canada's land is suitable for farming. Most is located in the Prairie Provinces. This region produces most of Canada's wheat and beef. The St. Lawrence Lowlands are another major agricultural region. This area produces grains, milk, vegetables, and fruits.

Water Canada has more lakes than any other country in the world. About nine percent of the world's fresh water is in Canada. Before the first railroads were built in the 1800s, the only way to reach some parts of the country was by water. Today, the St. Lawrence and Mackenzie rivers serve as important shipping routes.

Minerals and Energy Resources The Canadian Shield contains much of Canada's mineral wealth. Most of the nation's iron ore comes from mines near the Quebec-Newfoundland border. The region also has large deposits of gold, silver, zinc, copper, and uranium. The Prairie Provinces, particularly Alberta, have large oil and natural gas deposits.

Canada harnesses the rivers of Quebec Province to make hydroelectricity. These rivers generate enough hydroelectric power that some of it can be sold to the northeastern United States.

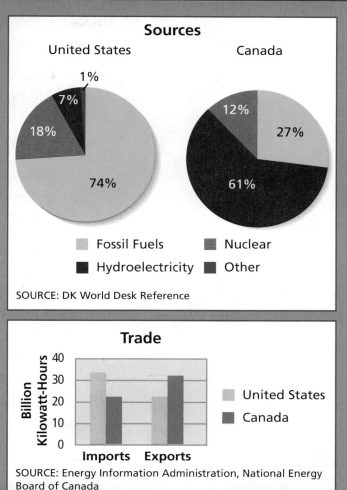

Electric Power

Sources

United States

Canada

Fossil Fuels
Nuclear
Hydroelectricity
Other

SOURCE: DK World Desk Reference

Trade

Billion Kilowatt-Hours

United States
Canada

Imports Exports

SOURCE: Energy Information Administration, National Energy Board of Canada

■ Chart Skills

Both the United States and Canada use fossil fuels to produce electricity. Fossil fuels are nonrenewable resources, meaning that once used they are not easily replaced. The United States and Canada also make use of renewable resources such as the hydroelectricity produced by the dam above. **Name** What energy source produces the largest percentage of Canada's electricity? **Analyze** Which nation is more dependent on the other for its energy? Explain.

Tugboats tow huge booms, or lines of connected floating logs, harvested from Canada's forests.

Forests   With almost half its land covered in forests, Canada is a leading producer and exporter of timber products. These products include lumber, paper, plywood, and wood pulp. The climate in British Columbia produces Canada's densest tall-timber forests. Large amounts of rain and a long growing season contribute to the growth of large evergreens with hard wood ideal for construction lumber. The provinces of Ontario and Quebec also produce large amounts of timber.

✓ **Reading Check**   **What resources are found in the Canadian Shield?**

Section 3 Assessment

Key Terms
Review the key terms at the beginning of this section. Use each term in a sentence that explains its meaning.

Target Reading Skill
What questions did you ask that helped you to learn and remember something from this section?

Comprehension and Critical Thinking
1. (a) List Describe the major natural resources of the United States.

(b) Explain How have energy resources shaped the economy and the standard of living of the United States?
(c) Infer What economic challenges might a country with few natural resources face?
2. (a) Note How much of Canada's land can be used for farming?
(b) Summarize How is water used as a resource in Canada?
(c) Compare Based on what you know about the physical geography of the two countries, in what ways do you think the resources are similar?

Writing Activity
What do you think is the most important resource in the United States and Canada? Write a paragraph explaining your choice.

> **Writing Tip** Be sure to include examples, details, facts, and reasons that support the main idea of your paragraph.

Review and Assessment

◆ Chapter Summary

Section 1: Land and Water
- Both the United States and Canada are located in North America.
- The United States and Canada have many mountain ranges and plains areas.
- Bodies of water such as the Great Lakes provide transportation and support industry.

Section 2: Climate and Vegetation
- Climate zones in the United States and Canada range from a desert climate to a polar climate.
- Varied climates in the United States and Canada help to produce varied vegetation.

Section 3: Resources and Land Use
- Farmland, forests, water, and minerals are all important resources for the United States and Canada.
- Natural resources affect the economies of the United States and Canada.

Montana

Scorpion in a desert in California

◆ Key Terms

Use each key term below in a sentence that shows the meaning of the term.

1. agribusiness
2. alluvial soil
3. glacier
4. Great Lakes
5. hydroelectricity
6. Rocky Mountains
7. tributary
8. tundra
9. permafrost
10. prairie
11. province
12. fossil fuel

◆ Comprehension and Critical Thinking

13. (a) Identify What landform lies between the Rocky and Appalachian mountains?
(b) Draw Conclusions How does climate affect the crops grown there?

14. (a) Define What is the Canadian Shield?
(b) Compare and Contrast Why do more people live in the St. Lawrence Lowlands than on the Canadian Shield?

15. (a) Explain How does the Pacific Ocean help to keep Canada's west coast climate mild?
(b) Contrast How does the west coast climate differ from the climate that Canada's Interior Plains experiences? Explain.

16. (a) Explain How does latitude affect climate?
(b) Apply Information How might geography and climate affect the way people live in the Canadian territory of Nunavut?

17. (a) Recall Tundra, grassland, desert scrub, and forests are major types of what?
(b) Identify Cause and Effect How do the climate and vegetation of the tundra affect how Inuits live?

18. (a) Identify Until the 1900s, who owned and ran most American farms?
(b) Explore the Main Idea How are most American farms run today?
(c) Draw Conclusions How has this change in ownership affected American farmers?

◆ Skills Practice

Identifying Frame of Reference Review the steps you followed in the Skills for Life activity in this chapter. Then reread the first two paragraphs of Section 3. First, identify the topic being discussed. Then, list some reasons why the logging company and the protesters might have different opinions on how to use natural resources. Finally, identify the frames of reference for people on both sides of the issue.

◆ Writing Activity: Science

Suppose that you are a meteorologist, or a scientist who studies Earth's weather patterns. Create two possible weather maps for the United States and Canada. One map should show a typical winter day and the other a typical summer day. The weather maps should show changes in the weather across the two countries.

MAP MASTER™
Skills Activity

Place Location Write the letter from the map that shows its location.
1. Canadian Shield
2. Great Basin
3. Great Plains ✓
4. Rocky Mountains ✓
5. Appalachian Mountains ✓
6. Pacific Ocean ✓
7. Atlantic Ocean ✓
8. Great Lakes ✓

Go Online
PHSchool.com Use Web Code **lhp-4153** for an **interactive map.**

The United States and Canada

Standardized Test Prep

Test-Taking Tips

Some questions on standardized tests ask you to make mental maps. Read the paragraph below. Then follow the tips to answer the sample question about Canada.

> Jessie is working on a crossword puzzle. She studies the following clue and knows the correct answer: Which large Canadian city is located on one of the Great Lakes?
>
> What is her answer?

TIP Try to picture a map of the United States and Canada. Then try to place each of the cities on this mental map—from east to west.

Make a mental map of the United States and Canada. Then pick the letter that best answers the question.

A Ottawa
B Toronto
C ~~Chicago~~
D ~~Vancouver~~

TIP Rule out choices that do not make sense. Then choose the best answer from the remaining choices.

Think It Through You can rule out Vancouver because it is on the west coast of Canada. Chicago is on Lake Michigan, but it is in the United States. That leaves Ottawa and Toronto. Ottawa is farther north than Toronto. It is on a waterway, the Ottawa River, but not on one of the Great Lakes. The answer is B, Toronto, which is on Lake Ontario.

Practice Questions

Use the tips above and other tips in this book to help you answer the following questions.

1. Because of its location near the Pacific Ocean and the Coast Mountains, Canada's northwestern coast is
   A hot and dry.
   B bitterly cold.
   C wet and snowy.
   D wet and mild.

2. Which vegetation region shared by the United States and Canada is the largest in the world of its kind?
   A prairie
   B tundra
   C desert
   D savanna

3. The United States is the world's second-largest producer of
   A coal, petroleum, and natural gas.
   B iron ore.
   C hydroelectricity.
   D wood and wood products.

Make a mental map of Canada. Then answer the question below.

4. This region of Canada lies east of the Interior Plains. It covers about half of Canada. Few people live in this region.
   A the St. Lawrence Lowlands
   B the Canadian Shield
   C the Laurentian Highlands
   D the St. Lawrence Seaway

Use Web Code **lha-4103** for a **Chapter 1 self-test.**

Chapter Preview

This chapter presents the history of the United States and Canada and shows how that history affects the region to this day.

Target Reading Skill

Clarifying Meaning In this chapter you will focus on skills you can use to clarify meaning as you read.

▶ The Washington Monument as seen from the Lincoln Memorial in Washington, D.C.

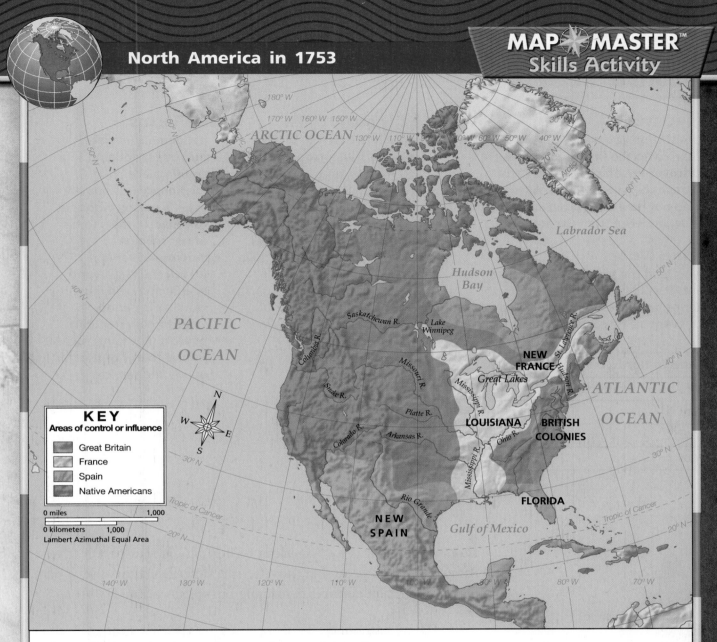

North America in 1753

MAP MASTER™
Skills Activity

ARCTIC OCEAN

Labrador Sea

Hudson Bay

PACIFIC OCEAN

Saskatchewan R.

Lake Winnipeg

St. Lawrence R.

NEW FRANCE

Columbia R.

Missouri R.

Great Lakes

Hudson R.

ATLANTIC OCEAN

Snake R.

Mississippi R.

LOUISIANA

BRITISH COLONIES

Platte R.

Ohio R.

Colorado R.

Arkansas R.

Mississippi R.

Rio Grande

FLORIDA

NEW SPAIN

Gulf of Mexico

KEY
Areas of control or influence

- Great Britain
- France
- Spain
- Native Americans

0 miles 1,000
0 kilometers 1,000
Lambert Azimuthal Equal Area

Location Notice that Native Americans and three European countries controlled North America in 1753. **Identify** Find the area of the country in which you live. Who had influence over that area in 1753? **Analyze** Which country controlled the area that includes access to the mouth of the Mississippi River?

Go Online
PHSchool.com Use Web Code
lhp-4211 for step-by-step
map skills practice.

Chapter 2 **35**

The Arrival of the Europeans

Prepare to Read

Objectives

In this section you will
1. Learn who the first Americans were.
2. Discover the effects the arrival of Europeans had on Native Americans.
3. Find out how the United States won its independence from Great Britain.

Taking Notes

As you read the section, look for important events that have taken place in North America. Copy the table below and write each event in the correct time period.

Events in North American History	
1400s	
1500s	
1600s	
1700s	

Target Reading Skill

Reread Rereading is a strategy that can help you understand words and ideas in the text. If you do not understand a certain passage, reread it to look for connections among the words and sentences.

Key Terms

- **indigenous** (in DIJ uh nus) *adj.* belonging to a certain place
- **missionary** (MISH un ehr ee) *n.* a person who tries to convert others to his or her religion
- **indentured servant** (in DEN churd SUR vunt) *n.* a person who must work for a period of years to gain freedom
- **boycott** (BOY kaht) *n.* a refusal to buy or use goods and services

Native American artifacts

Louise Erdrich is an American writer. She is also part Native American. In one of her novels, she describes the variety of Native American cultures before the Europeans arrived:

> **"[They] had hundreds of societies . . . whose experience had told them that the world was a pretty diverse place. Walk for a day in any direction and what do you find: A tribe with a whole new set of gods, a language as distinct from your own as Tibetan is from Dutch. . . . "**
>
> —*Louise Erdrich,* The Crown of Columbus

The First Americans

Many scientists think that Native Americans migrated from Asia. Perhaps as early as 30,000 years ago, they theorize, small groups of hunters and gatherers reached North America from Asia.

This migration from Asia to North America took place during the last ice age. At that time, so much water froze into thick ice sheets that the sea level dropped. As a result, a land bridge was exposed between Siberia and Alaska. Hunters followed herds of bison and mammoths across this land bridge. Other migrating people may have paddled small boats and fished along the coasts.

Over time, the first Americans spread throughout North and South America. They developed different ways of life to suit the environment of the places where they settled.

Many Native Americans disagree with this theory, believing they have always lived in the Americas. In any case, all people consider Native Americans **indigenous** (in DIJ uh nus) people, meaning they belong to and are native to this place.

✓ Reading Check   **How did migrating people reach North America?**

The Europeans Arrive

Life for the millions of indigenous people in the Americas began to change after 1492. That year, Christopher Columbus, a sea captain sailing from Spain, explored islands in the Caribbean Sea. His voyage opened the way for European colonization.

Spanish Claims to the Americas   The Spanish settlers who followed Columbus spread out across the Americas. Some went to the present-day southwestern United States and Mexico. Others went to Florida, the Caribbean islands, and South America. Spain gained great wealth from its American colonies.

Learn about early Native American houses.

Taos, New Mexico
Although Native Americans had inhabited the area for centuries, Spanish explorers arrived in present-day Taos (TAH ohs), New Mexico in 1540. They built the church below in 1617. **Predict** *How might life have changed for Native Americans after Spanish explorers arrived?*

Pueblo Village

When the Pueblo Indians of the Southwest learned how to grow corn and other crops, they no longer had to move about to hunt and gather food. As they became more settled and grew larger harvests, they built stone corn cribs. Over time, these storerooms became larger, and the Pueblos began to build their houses and villages around them.

Acoma Pueblo, New Mexico
The Acoma Pueblo sits high on a 357-foot (109-meter) sandstone rock. It is also known as "Sky City."

The village walls were made of adobe bricks, cemented together with mud. A coating of mud plaster, lime plaster, or stucco covered the bricks and protected the wall.

The Pueblos planted and tended crops of squash, beans, and corn close to the village.

After mud and straw were mixed together, people poured the mixture into molds where they dried into bricks.

Light reached the inside of the pueblo through doors and windows, allowing people inside to weave and cook.

Making adobe bricks
A present-day craftsman in Rancho de Taos, New Mexico, uses ancient methods to create bricks out of mud.

ANALYZING IMAGES
Why were the tops of the village rooms flat, instead of roofed?

The colonists often enslaved Native Americans. They forced Native Americans to work in mines or on farms. Working conditions were so harsh that thousands died. Spanish missionaries tried to make Native Americans more like Europeans, often by force. **Missionaries** (MISH un ehr ees) are religious people who want to convert others to their religion.

French Claims to the Americas Seeing Spain's success, other countries also wanted colonies in the Americas. French explorers claimed land along the St. Lawrence and Mississippi rivers. Unlike the Spanish, who were interested in gold, the French were interested in fur. French traders and missionaries often lived among the Native Americans and learned their ways. However, both the French and the Spanish brought disease along with them. Millions of Native Americans died from diseases that they had never been exposed to before, such as smallpox and measles.

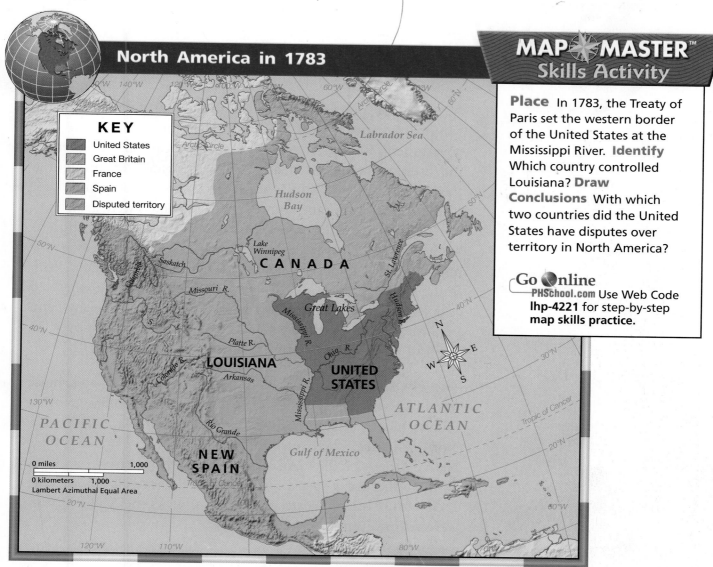

North America in 1783

KEY
- United States
- Great Britain
- France
- Spain
- Disputed territory

MAP MASTER™ Skills Activity

Place In 1783, the Treaty of Paris set the western border of the United States at the Mississippi River. **Identify** Which country controlled Louisiana? **Draw Conclusions** With which two countries did the United States have disputes over territory in North America?

Go Online
PHSchool.com Use Web Code **lhp-4221** for step-by-step map skills practice.

THE LANDING OF THE PILGRIMS,
ON PLYMOUTH ROCK, DEC. 11TH 1620.

In 1620, a group of about 100 Pilgrims sailed to New England on the *Mayflower* (right). In 1682, William Penn (left) arrived in the colony of Pennsylvania, which means "Penn's woods."

The English Colonists English settlers also arrived, establishing a strip of colonies along the Atlantic Coast. These settlers came to start a new life. Some wanted to be free from debt. Others wanted to own land or practice their religions freely. Some came as **indentured servants,** or people who had to work for a period of years to gain freedom.

The first permanent English settlement was Jamestown, Virginia, founded in 1607. By 1619, it had the beginnings of self-government. In the same year, the first Africans arrived there as indentured servants. Later, about 1640, Africans were brought to the colonies as slaves. Many were forced to work on plantations, or the large farms in the South where cash crops were grown.

In 1620, the Pilgrims arrived in Plymouth, Massachusetts from England. They wanted to worship God in their own way and to govern themselves. About 60 years later, William Penn founded the Pennsylvania Colony. He wanted a place where all people, regardless of race or religion, were treated fairly. Penn paid Native Americans for their land. Later, settlers took over the land, and then fought Native Americans to control it.

The French and Indian War In the 1700s, Britain and France fought several wars. When they fought, their colonists often fought, too. In 1754, Britain and France went to war over land in North America. The British fought against the French and their Native American allies. An ally is a country or person that joins with another for a special purpose. Americans call this war the French and Indian War. With the colonists' help, the British were victorious in 1763.

Target Skill **Reread** Reread to see why the French and Indian War was fought.

✓ Reading Check Why did English settlers establish the colonies?

The Break With Britain

Despite their victory, the British wanted an army in North America to protect the colonists. The British thought the colonists should help pay for the war and for their defense. They put taxes on many British goods the colonists bought. Because no one represented the colonists in the British Parliament, they could not protest these taxes. Many of them began to demand "no taxation without representation." They also **boycotted**, or refused to buy, British goods.

Resentment grew against British rule, causing the Revolutionary War to break out in 1775. Thomas Jefferson summarized the colonists' views in the Declaration of Independence. His words inspired many colonists to fight. In 1781, George Washington led the American forces to victory. The Treaty of Paris, signed in 1783, made American independence official.

Before they won independence, the 13 colonies worked on a plan of government called the Articles of Confederation. But Congress was not given the power to tax. After the war, the 13 new states agreed to form a stronger central government. They wrote the Constitution, which set up the framework for our federal government. Approved in 1788, it is still the highest law of the United States.

 Reading Check What was the problem with the Articles of Confederation?

This statue commemorates the Minutemen of the American Revolution who stood their ground against British troops on April 19, 1775.

Section 1 Assessment

Key Terms
Review the key terms at the beginning of this section. Use each term in a sentence that explains its meaning.

Target Reading Skill
What word or idea were you able to clarify by rereading?

Comprehension and Critical Thinking
1. (a) Recall Where do many scientists think the first Americans came from?

(b) Identify Point of View Why might Native Americans today disagree with the theory of migration?

2. (a) Explain Describe how different European groups settled in the Americas.

(b) Summarize How did Europeans affect Native American life?

3. (a) Name What document is the framework for the United States government?

(b) Identify Cause and Effect Why did the colonists object to the taxes placed on them by the British?

Writing Activity
Write a paragraph discussing how life in the Americas might have been different if Columbus's voyage had not taken place.

Writing Tip Begin your paragraph with a topic sentence that states your main idea. Give at least two examples of how life might have been different.

Growth and Conflict in the United States

Prepare to Read

Objectives

In this section you will
1. Explore the effects of westward expansion in the United States.
2. Discover the causes and effects of the Civil War.

Taking Notes

As you read the section, look for details about the causes and effects of westward expansion and the Civil War. Copy the flow-chart below and write each detail under the correct heading.

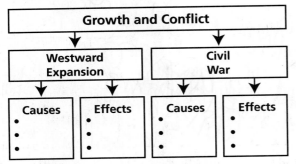

Growth and Conflict

Westward Expansion		Civil War	
Causes	Effects	Causes	Effects
•	•	•	•
•	•	•	•
•	•	•	•

Target Reading Skill

Read Ahead Reading ahead is a strategy that can help you understand words and ideas in the text. If you do not understand a certain passage, it might help to read ahead. A word or an idea may be clarified further on.

Key Terms

- **Louisiana Purchase** (loo ee zee AN uh PUR chus) *n.* the sale of land in North America in 1803 by France to the United States

- **immigrant** (IM uh grunt) *n.* a person who moves to a new country in order to settle there
- **Industrial Revolution** (in DUS tree ul rev uh LOO shun) *n.* the change from making goods by hand to making them by machine
- **abolitionist** (ab uh LISH un ist) *n.* a person who believed that enslaving people was wrong and who wanted to end the practice
- **segregate** (SEG ruh gayt) *v.* to set apart, typically because of race or religion

Meriwether Lewis and William Clark with their Native American translator Sacajawea

In 1804, President Thomas Jefferson sent Meriwether Lewis and William Clark with a company of men to explore the land west of the Mississippi River. They would eventually travel all the way to the Pacific Coast and back—about 8,000 miles (13,000 kilometers).

As they journeyed up the Missouri River, Lewis and Clark found plants and animals completely new to them. They also created accurate, highly valuable maps of the region. As they traveled with their Native American translator, a Shoshone (shoh SHOH nee) woman named Sacajawea, Lewis and Clark met many Native American groups. Sacajawea helped Lewis and Clark communicate with the various groups. During these meetings, the two men tried to learn about the region and set up trading alliances. Few of the Native Americans they met had any idea how the visit would change their way of life.

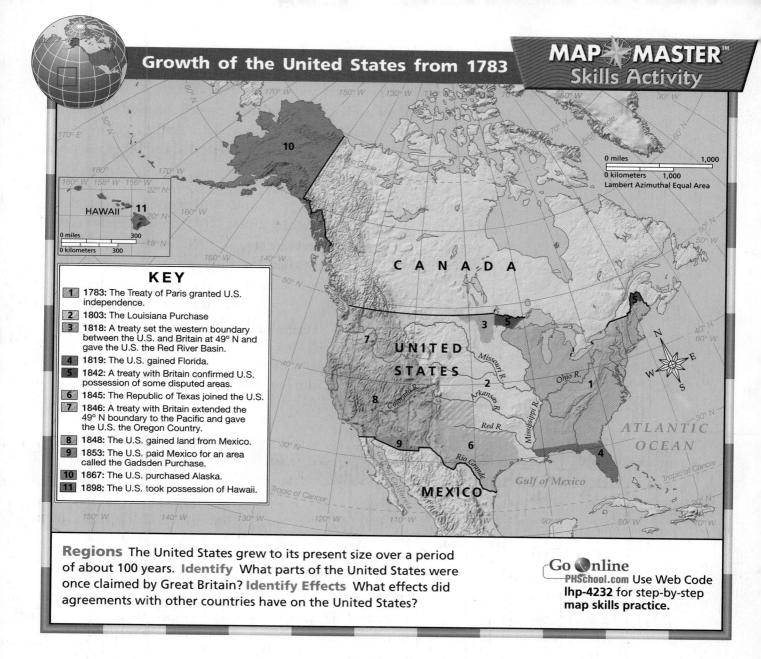

Growth of the United States from 1783

MAP MASTER™ Skills Activity

KEY

1 **1783:** The Treaty of Paris granted U.S. independence.
2 **1803:** The Louisiana Purchase
3 **1818:** A treaty set the western boundary between the U.S. and Britain at 49° N and gave the U.S. the Red River Basin.
4 **1819:** The U.S. gained Florida.
5 **1842:** A treaty with Britain confirmed U.S. possession of some disputed areas.
6 **1845:** The Republic of Texas joined the U.S.
7 **1846:** A treaty with Britain extended the 49° N boundary to the Pacific and gave the U.S. the Oregon Country.
8 **1848:** The U.S. gained land from Mexico.
9 **1853:** The U.S. paid Mexico for an area called the Gadsden Purchase.
10 **1867:** The U.S. purchased Alaska.
11 **1898:** The U.S. took possession of Hawaii.

0 miles 1,000
0 kilometers 1,000
Lambert Azimuthal Equal Area

HAWAII

0 miles 300
0 kilometers 300

CANADA
UNITED STATES
MEXICO
ATLANTIC OCEAN
Gulf of Mexico
Gulf of California
Rio Grande
Red R.
Colorado R.
Arkansas R.
Missouri R.
Mississippi R.
Ohio R.
Tropic of Cancer
Arctic Circle

Regions The United States grew to its present size over a period of about 100 years. **Identify** What parts of the United States were once claimed by Great Britain? **Identify Effects** What effects did agreements with other countries have on the United States?

Go Online
PHSchool.com Use Web Code **lhp-4232** for step-by-step map skills practice.

A Nation Grows

The United States had not always owned the land that Lewis and Clark explored, called the Louisiana Territory. But, the purchase of this land set the country on a new course of westward expansion.

The Louisiana Purchase   First France, and then Spain, owned the Louisiana Territory. In 1800, war in Europe forced Spain to give it back to France. In 1803, France offered to sell all the land between the Mississippi River and the eastern slopes of the Rocky Mountains to the United States—for only $15 million. This sale of land, called the **Louisiana Purchase,** doubled the size of the United States. The land would later be split into more than a dozen states.

As the country grew, so did the meaning of democracy. In the 13 original states, only white males who owned property could vote. New states passed laws giving the vote to all white men 21 years old or older, whether they owned property or not. Eventually, all states gave every adult white male the right to vote. Women, African Americans, Native Americans, and other minorities, however, could not vote.

The Indian Removal Act Native Americans had struggled to keep their land since colonial times. Their struggle grew more difficult in 1828, when voters elected Andrew Jackson President. President Jackson looked after the interests of poor farmers, laborers, and settlers who wanted Native American lands in the Southeast. In 1830, he persuaded Congress to pass the Indian Removal Act. It required the Cherokees and other Native Americans in the area to leave their homelands. They were sent to live on new land in present-day Oklahoma. So many Cherokees died on the journey that the route they followed is known as the Trail of Tears.

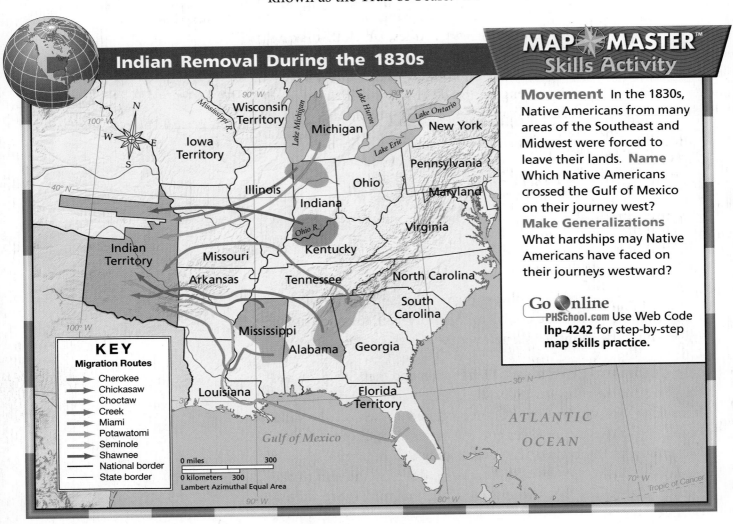

Indian Removal During the 1830s

MAP MASTER™ Skills Activity

Movement In the 1830s, Native Americans from many areas of the Southeast and Midwest were forced to leave their lands. **Name** Which Native Americans crossed the Gulf of Mexico on their journey west? **Make Generalizations** What hardships may Native Americans have faced on their journeys westward?

Go Online
PHSchool.com Use Web Code lhp-4242 for step-by-step map skills practice.

KEY
Migration Routes
→ Cherokee
→ Chickasaw
→ Choctaw
→ Creek
→ Miami
→ Potawatomi
→ Seminole
→ Shawnee
— National border
— State border

0 miles 300
0 kilometers 300
Lambert Azimuthal Equal Area

Manifest Destiny Many Americans believed that the United States had a right to own all the land from the Atlantic to the Pacific. This belief, called Manifest Destiny, was used to justify further westward expansion. In the 1840s, American wagon trains began to cross the continent heading for the West.

The United States also looked to the Southwest. In 1836, American settlers in the Mexican territory of Texas had rebelled against Mexican rule. The Texans had then set up the Lone Star Republic. In 1845, Texas became part of the United States. Only a year later, the United States went to war with Mexico. The United States won the war and gained from Mexico much of what is now the Southwest region.

The Industrial Revolution At the same time, thousands of people were pouring into cities in the Northeast. Some had left farms to work in factories. Others were **immigrants**, or people who move to one country from another. These people came from Europe in search of jobs in the United States. They were spurred by the **Industrial Revolution**, or the change from making goods by hand to making them by machine.

The first industry to change was textiles, or cloth-making. New spinning machines and power looms enabled people to make cloth more quickly than they could by hand. Other inventions, such as the steam engine, made travel easier and faster. Steamboats and steam locomotives moved people and goods rapidly. By 1860, railroads linked most major northeastern and southeastern cities.

✓ **Reading Check** **What did the Indian Removal Act do?**

The Clermont, 1807
Robert Fulton demonstrates his steam-powered paddle-wheel boat, the *Clermont*, which used a steam engine improved by James Watt.
Draw Conclusions *How did the inventions of the Industrial Revolution change people's lives?*

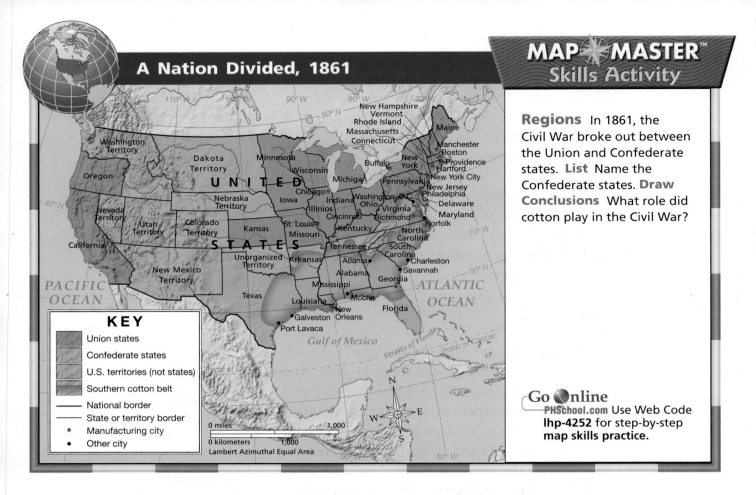

Regions In 1861, the Civil War broke out between the Union and Confederate states. **List** Name the Confederate states. **Draw Conclusions** What role did cotton play in the Civil War?

KEY

Union states
Confederate states
U.S. territories (not states)
Southern cotton belt
National border
State or territory border
● Manufacturing city
• Other city

0 miles 1,000
0 kilometers 1,000
Lambert Azimuthal Equal Area

Go Online
PHSchool.com Use Web Code
lhp-4252 for step-by-step map skills practice.

Read Ahead
Keep reading to see how harvesting cotton affected the nation's history.

The Civil War and Reconstruction

With the textile industry growing as a result of the Industrial Revolution, the demand for cotton grew as well. Cotton required many laborers for planting and harvesting. This is one reason why slaves were an important part of plantation life.

In 1793, Eli Whitney invented the cotton gin, which quickly removed seeds from cotton. The cotton gin made cotton easier to process after it was picked. Cotton farming boomed. However, growing cotton quickly wore out the soil. To keep up production, farmers wanted to expand into western lands. But that meant that slavery would spread into the new territories. Some people did not want this. The debate began. Should the states or the federal government decide about the issue of slavery in the new territories?

Causes of Conflict Before California asked to be admitted to the union as a free state in 1850, there were equal numbers of slave and free states. After a heated debate, Congress granted California's request. The Southern states were not pleased. To gain their support, Congress also passed the Fugitive Slave Act. It required that runaway slaves must be returned to their owners. This action only intensified the argument over slavery.

The South Breaks Away In 1852, Harriet Beecher Stowe published *Uncle Tom's Cabin,* a novel about the evils of slavery. After reading this book, thousands of Northerners became abolitionists (ab uh LISH un ists). **Abolitionists** were people who believed that slavery was wrong and wanted to end, or abolish, its practice. Many helped enslaved people escape to Canada. There, slavery was illegal. Most Southerners, however, felt that abolitionists were robbing them of their property.

The debate over slavery raged. When Abraham Lincoln, a Northerner, was elected President in 1860, many Southerners feared they would have little say in the government. As a result, some Southern states seceded, or withdrew, from the United States. They founded a new country—the Confederate States of America, or the Confederacy.

The Civil War In 1861, the Civil War between the Northern states and the Confederacy erupted. It lasted four years. The North, known as the Union, had more industry, wealth, and soldiers. The Confederacy had experienced military officers. It also had cotton. Many foreign countries bought southern cotton. Southerners hoped that these countries would help support the Confederacy in its struggle.

Despite the North's advantages, the war dragged on. In 1863, Lincoln issued the Emancipation Proclamation. This declared that enslaved people in areas loyal to the Confederacy were free, and it gave the North a new battle cry—freedom! Thousands of African Americans joined the fight against the South.

Fighting for Their Cause
These African American soldiers are outside of their barracks at Fort Lincoln, Washington, D.C. Twenty-three African Americans received the Congressional Medal of Honor (below right), the country's highest military honor. **Draw Conclusions** *Why do you think African Americans were willing to fight for the Union?*

Clara Barton

When the Civil War began, Clara Barton learned that many soldiers were suffering because of the lack of supplies on the front lines. She decided to help by setting up an organization to deliver supplies to men wounded in battle. She also worked as a nurse in hospitals located near battlefields. Because of her gentle and helpful ways, Barton earned the name Angel of the Battlefield. Years later, she founded the American branch of the Red Cross.

Reconstruction The Civil War ended in 1865 when the Confederates surrendered. Lincoln wanted the Southern states to return willingly to the Union. This was the first step in his plan for the Reconstruction, or rebuilding, of the nation. Less than a week after the end of the war, Lincoln was assassinated, or murdered. Vice President Andrew Johnson tried to carry out Lincoln's plan. But Congress resisted his efforts. Finally, Congress took complete control of Reconstruction. The Union Army governed the South until new state officials were elected.

In 1877, the Union Army withdrew. But Southern lawmakers soon voted to **segregate**, or separate, black people from white people. Segregation affected all aspects of life. Southern states passed laws, called Jim Crow laws, that separated blacks and whites in schools, restaurants, theaters, trains, streetcars, playgrounds, hospitals, and even cemeteries. Some African Americans brought lawsuits to challenge segregation. The laws passed during Reconstruction would become the basis of the civil rights movement in later years. The difficult struggle to preserve the United States had succeeded. But the long struggle to guarantee equality to all Americans still lay ahead.

 **Reading Check** **Why did some Southern states secede from the United States?**

 Section 2 Assessment

Key Terms
Review the key terms at the beginning of this section. Use each term in a sentence that explains its meaning.

Target Reading Skill
What word or idea were you able to clarify by reading ahead?

Comprehension and Critical Thinking
1. (a) List In what ways did the United States increase the area of its land?

(b) Identify Effects How did the growing nation affect Native Americans?
(c) Identify Causes What factors led to a population boom in northeastern cities?
2. (a) Identify Why did the Southern states withdraw from the Union?
(b) Explore the Main Idea How did the issue of slavery become a cause of the Civil War?
(c) Analyze How did segregation affect African Americans?

Writing Activity
Write an entry on a plan for Reconstruction that President Lincoln might have made in his diary.

For: An activity on the Civil War
Visit: PHSchool.com
Web Code: lhd-4202

Prepare to Read

Objectives

In this section you will

1. Explore what happened in the United States from 1865 to 1914.
2. Find out what happened during the World Wars.
3. Explore the challenges the United States faces at home and abroad.

Taking Notes

As you read the section, look for details about the United States becoming a world power. Copy the outline below and fill in each main idea and detail.

I. The United States from 1865 to 1914
   A. Moving to the Midwest
      1.
      2.
   B.
II.

Target Reading Skill

Paraphrase Paraphrasing can help you understand what you read. When you paraphrase, you restate in your own words what you have read. As you read this section, paraphrase, or "say back," the information following each red or blue heading.

Key Terms

- **labor force** (LAY bur fawrs) *n.* the supply of workers
- **Holocaust** (HAHL uh kawst) *n.* the murder of six million Jews during World War II
- **Cold War** (kohld wawr) *n.* a period of great tension between the United States and the Soviet Union
- **civil rights** (SIV ul ryts) *n.* the basic rights due to all citizens
- **terrorist** (TEHR ur ist) *n.* a person who uses violence and fear to achieve goals

Jacob Riis was an angry man. In one of his books, he introduced his readers to slum life in the late 1800s. He wanted other people to be angry, too—angry enough to change things.

> **Come over here. Step carefully over this baby—it is a baby, in spite of its rags and dirt—under these iron bridges called fire escapes, but loaded down . . . with broken household goods, with washtubs and barrels, over which no man could climb from a fire. . . . That baby's parents live in the rear tenement [apartment] here. . . . There are plenty of houses with half a hundred such in [them].**
>
> —*Jacob Riis,* How the Other Half Lives

An 1886 photo of a slum by Jacob Riis

Settling the Plains
A wagon train travels in the Oklahoma Territory around 1900 (above). Railroads such as the Hannibal and St. Joseph recruited farmers to buy and settle land, as advertised in the poster above. **Draw Conclusions** *How did the Homestead Act and the railroads help to speed up settlement of the Midwest?*

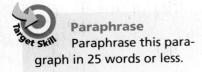

Paraphrase
Paraphrase this paragraph in 25 words or less.

From 1865 to 1914

By the late 1800s, a handful of rich people had made millions of dollars in industry. The Industrial Revolution had also made life easier for the middle class—the group of people that included skilled workers and successful farmers. But life did not improve for the poor. City slums were crowded with immigrants. These newcomers were a huge **labor force**, or supply of workers. Many couldn't speak English. Employers paid them little. Even small children worked so that families could make ends meet.

Reformers like Jacob Riis began to protest such poverty. In Chicago, Jane Addams set up a settlement house, or community center, for poor immigrants. Mary Harris Jones helped miners organize for better wages. Because of her work to end child labor, people called her Mother Jones.

Moving to the Midwest To leave poverty behind, many people moved to the open plains and prairies of the Midwest. The United States government attracted settlers to this region with the Homestead Act of 1862. This act gave free land to settlers. Settlers faced a difficult life on the plains. Still, thousands came west, helped by the development of railroads that connected the East Coast with the West.

New Territories The United States also expanded beyond its continental borders. In 1867, the United States bought the territory of Alaska from Russia. In 1898, the United States took control of Hawaii. In that same year, the United States fought and won the Spanish-American War. The victory gave the United States control of the Spanish lands of Puerto Rico, Guam, and the Philippines. By the 1900s, America had a strong economy, military might, and overseas territory.

✓ **Reading Check** **How did the United States get Alaska?**

The World at War

Now the United States had a major role in world affairs. As a result, the country was drawn into international conflicts. In 1914, World War I broke out in Europe. President Woodrow Wilson did not want America to take part, but when Germany began sinking American ships, Wilson had no choice. He declared war. The United States joined the Allied Powers of Great Britain and France. In 1917, thousands of American soldiers sailed to Europe. They fought against the Central Powers, which included Germany, Austria-Hungary, and Turkey. With this added strength, the Allies won the war in 1918. The terms of peace in the Treaty of Versailles punished Germany severely. Its harshness led to another worldwide conflict 20 years later.

The Economy Collapses Following World War I, the United States' economy boomed. Women enjoyed new freedoms and the hard-won right to vote. More and more people bought cars, refrigerators, radios, and other modern conveniences.

In 1929, however, the world was overcome by an economic disaster called the Great Depression. In America, factories closed, people lost their jobs, and farmers lost their farms. Many banks closed, and people lost their life's savings. In 1933, President Franklin D. Roosevelt took office. He created a plan called the New Deal. This was a series of government programs to help people get jobs and to restore the economy. Some of these programs, like Social Security, are still in place today. Social Security provides income to people who are retired or disabled.

Americans at War
Nurses place a wounded soldier on a stretcher during World War I (below). Recruitment posters such as the one below called on Americans to join the military. **Draw Inferences** *Why do you think this poster was effective in getting Americans to volunteer for military duty?*

This Rosie the Riveter poster from World War II encouraged women to join the workforce.

We Can Do It!

A Second World War The Great Depression affected people around the world. In Germany, Adolf Hitler rose to power, promising to restore Germany's wealth and power. He began World War II. In 1941, Germany's ally, Japan, attacked the United States naval base at Pearl Harbor, Hawaii. The United States declared war on Japan. Germany then declared war on the United States.

The United States sent armed forces to fight in Europe and in the Pacific. President Roosevelt, who led the nation in war, did not live to see peace. He died in April 1945, and Vice President Harry S Truman became President.

In May of 1945, the Allies defeated the Germans. During the summer of 1945, President Truman decided to drop two atomic bombs on Japan. That convinced Japan to surrender. Finally, World War II was over.

By the end of the war in 1945, Europe was in ruins. People around the world learned that Hitler had forced Jews, Gypsies, Slavs, and others into brutal prison camps. Millions of people, including some six million Jews, were murdered. This horrible mass murder is called the **Holocaust** (HAHL uh kawst).

✓ **Reading Check** What led the United States to take part in World War II?

Timeline Skills

The United States has been involved in both domestic and international conflicts since the Civil War ended. **Identify** Which of the wars shown did not involve open warfare? **Compare** How long was this war, compared to the others shown on the timeline?

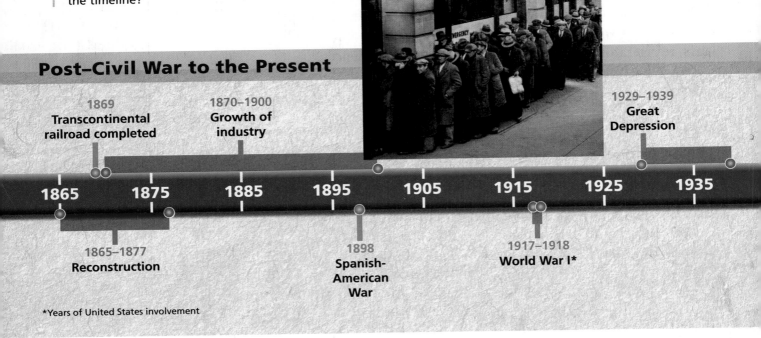

Post–Civil War to the Present

1869 Transcontinental railroad completed

1870–1900 Growth of industry

1929–1939 Great Depression

1865   1875   1885   1895   1905   1915   1925   1935

1865–1877 Reconstruction

1898 Spanish-American War

1917–1918 World War I*

*Years of United States involvement

The U.S. at Home and Abroad

Following World War II, the United States was a world superpower. It faced new challenges and responsibilities both at home and abroad.

Tension with the Soviets In 1922, the Soviet Union had been created. It adopted a form of government called communism. Under this system, the state owns all property, such as farms and factories, on behalf of its citizens.

After World War II, the Soviet Union took control of many Eastern European countries. The United States feared the Soviets were trying to spread communism throughout the world. As a result, the United States and the Soviet Union entered the **Cold War,** a period of great tension. The Cold War lasted about four decades. Although the two countries never faced each other in an actual war, two wars grew out of this tension—the Korean War and the Vietnam War.

The Fight for Civil Rights The economy boomed in the post-war years, but not all citizens shared in the benefits. In the South, racial segregation was a way of life. Many African Americans began to unite to win their **civil rights,** or the rights belonging to all citizens. The movement had many leaders, including Martin Luther King, Jr. He led peaceful marches and organized boycotts against companies that practiced discrimination, or unfair treatment of a group or person. The movement's success inspired others who felt they were treated unfairly, including women and Mexican Americans.

Links Across Time

Living Underground During the Cold War, many Americans became concerned about the possibility of a nuclear war with the Soviet Union. The United States government encouraged families to build fallout, or bomb, shelters as shown below. A fallout shelter is a concrete and steel structure designed to protect people from nuclear radiation. Many of these shelters were underground. A typical bomb shelter would have canned food, bottled water, first-aid supplies, and other necessities.

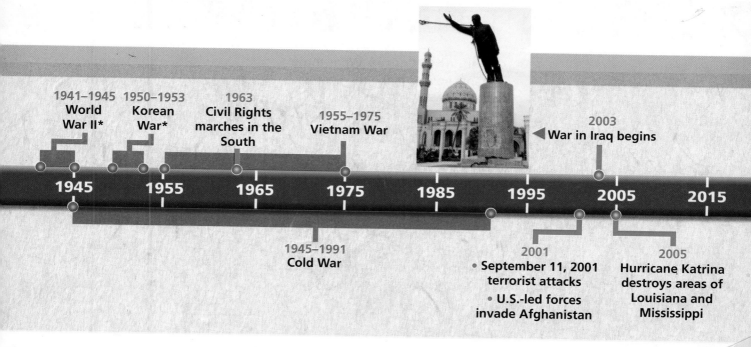

- **1941–1945** World War II*
- **1950–1953** Korean War*
- **1963** Civil Rights marches in the South
- **1955–1975** Vietnam War
- **2003** War in Iraq begins

1945 · 1955 · 1965 · 1975 · 1985 · 1995 · 2005 · 2015

- **1945–1991** Cold War
- **2001** September 11, 2001 terrorist attacks • U.S.-led forces invade Afghanistan
- **2005** Hurricane Katrina destroys areas of Louisiana and Mississippi

Firefighters walk away from the rubble of the World Trade Center towers in New York City.

America in the World Today At the beginning of the twenty-first century, Americans continued to look for solutions to long-term problems, such as homelessness, low wages, and pollution.

The economy reached new heights in the 1990s, powered by the Internet business revolution. The Internet is a network of interconnected computers that allows users to access computerized information. After a downturn in the early 2000s, the economy continued to grow. At the same time, it faced challenges such as high oil prices and rising federal debt.

The United States also faced a new challenge at home and abroad—on September 11, 2001, terrorists attacked the World Trade Center in New York City and the Pentagon in Washington, D.C. **Terrorists** use violence to frighten people or governments or to express their views. In response to these and possible future attacks, the United States took military action in both Afghanistan and Iraq. Saddam Hussein (sah DAHM hoo SAYN), Iraq's brutal dictator, was captured by coalition troops in December 2003. However, the United States continues to maintain a military presence in Iraq. The United States works with its allies around the world, especially Great Britain, to fight terrorism.

✓ **Reading Check** **What countries were involved in the Cold War?**

Section **3** Assessment

Key Terms
Review the key terms at the beginning of this section. Use each term in a sentence that explains its meaning.

Target Reading Skill
Paraphrase the paragraph on page 51 under the red heading The World at War.

Comprehension and Critical Thinking
1. (a) Recall How did the Industrial Revolution affect poor immigrants in the late 1800s?

(b) Identify Causes What three events helped make the United States a world power?
2. (a) List What countries made up the Central Powers in World War I?
(b) Sequence Describe the events that led to World War II.
3. (a) Explain What gains in equality did African Americans make after World War II?
(b) Identify Cause and Effect How might African American gains in civil rights affect other groups?

Writing Activity
Write a paragraph about what it means for a country to be a world power. What challenges would a world power face? What special responsibilities might it have?

For: An activity on the Homestead Act
Visit: PHSchool.com
Web Code: lhp-4203

The History of Canada

Prepare to Read

Objectives

In this section you will

1. Learn about why France and Britain were rivals in Canada.
2. Discover how Canada became an independent nation.
3. Explore how Canada became a world power in the 1900s.

Taking Notes

As you read the section, look for events that happened before and after the British North America Act in 1867. Copy the table below and write each event in the correct column.

British North America Act (1867)	
Before	**After**
•	•
•	•
•	•

Target Reading Skill

Summarize When you summarize, you review and state, in the correct order, the main points you have read. Summarizing what you read is a good technique to help you comprehend and study. As you read, pause occasionally to summarize what you have read.

Key Terms

- **dominion** (duh MIN yun) *n.* a self-governing area subject to Great Britain
- **bilingual** (by LIN gwul) *adj.* able to speak two languages

Haida portrait mask

The Haida people of British Columbia tell this tale. As in many Native American tales, nature plays an important role.

> **While he was crying and singing his dirge [sad song], a figure emerged from the lake. It was a strange animal, in its mouth a stick that it was gnawing. On each side of the animal were two smaller ones also gnawing sticks. Then the largest figure . . . spoke, 'Don't be so sad! It is I, your wife, and your two children. We have returned to our home in the water. . . . Call me the Beaver woman.'**
>
> —*Haida tale*

To the Haida and other native peoples in Canada, beavers were especially important. Imagine how they felt when European trappers killed almost all of the beavers to make fur hats.

The Battle of Quebec, 1759
The Battle of Quebec was a turning point in the Seven Years' War. This painting illustrates how British troops found a passage through the cliffs that protected Quebec. **Analyze Images** *Do you think that Quebec would have fallen to the British if troops had not found a passage in? Explain why or why not.*

The French and the British

The profitable fur trade in Canada was a source of conflict for France and Great Britain. They had fought wars all over the world, but had signed a peace treaty in 1713. The treaty gave Great Britain the Hudson Bay region, Newfoundland, and part of Acadia, which later became the southeastern corner of Canada.

The peace was uneasy. Against their will, French Catholics in Acadia came under the rule of British Protestants. The French controlled the lowlands south of Hudson Bay and lands around the St. Lawrence River. Both countries wanted to control the Ohio River valley, farther to the south. The French wanted the beavers for furs. The British wanted the land for settlement.

Great Britain Gains Control   The contest for this region erupted into the Seven Years' War in 1756. The British won the decisive Battle of Quebec in 1759. The Treaty of Paris, signed in 1763, gave Great Britain complete control over Canada. Some French settlers returned to France. Those who stayed resisted English culture. The first two British governors of Canada were sympathetic to the French and passed the Quebec Act. It gave the French people in Quebec the right to speak their own language, practice their own religion, and follow their own customs.

Two Colonies Emerge   During the American Revolution, some Americans did not want independence from Britain. They were called Loyalists. After the war, many Loyalists moved to Canada. But most did not want to live in a French culture. To avoid problems, Great Britain divided the land into two colonies, Upper Canada and Lower Canada. Most Loyalists moved into Upper Canada, which is now called Ontario. French Canadians remained in Lower Canada, which is now Quebec.

✓ Reading Check   **Why was Canada divided into two colonies?**

Canada Seeks Independence

The people of Upper and Lower Canada worked together during the War of 1812. They fought to protect Canada from invasion by the United States. Once the War of 1812 ended, however, Canadians with different backgrounds stopped cooperating with one another. Both French Canadians and British Canadians hated British rule. Many felt Britain was too far away to understand their needs. But the two groups did not join in rebellion. In 1837, a French Canadian named Louis Papineau (LOO ee pah pea NOH) organized a revolt in Lower Canada. His goal was to establish the region as a separate country. The British easily defeated the rebels. The same thing happened in Upper Canada. William Mackenzie led the people against British rule. Again, the British put down the separatist rebellion.

A Peaceful Revolution Still, British leaders were afraid more trouble was coming. They sent the Earl of Durham to learn what was wrong. When Durham returned, he had many suggestions. First, he suggested that the Canadians be given more control of their government. He also thought all of the colonies should be united. But the British government united only Upper and Lower Canada to form the Province of Canada. Nova Scotia, Newfoundland, Prince Edward Island, and New Brunswick were not included in this union. If Canada were completely united, the British feared the Canadians might make a successful rebellion.

Citizen Heroes

Louis Riel

A Voice of Protest
In 1869, the Canadian government wanted to finish the cross-country railroad across the flat plains region. Louis Riel, leader of the Métis (may TEEZ)—mixed European and Native American people—objected to the plan. The Métis said that the railroad would bring new settlers, who would take away their land. The government refused to stop, so Riel led an armed revolt. It failed, and Riel was later executed for treason, but the government did set aside land for the Métis. Today, the Métis consider Riel a hero.

The Canadian Pacific Railway
On November 7, 1885, Canada's far-flung provinces were tied together as the last spike was driven in, completing the Canadian Pacific Railway. **Draw Conclusions** *Why was a railroad connecting all of Canada important to Canadians?*

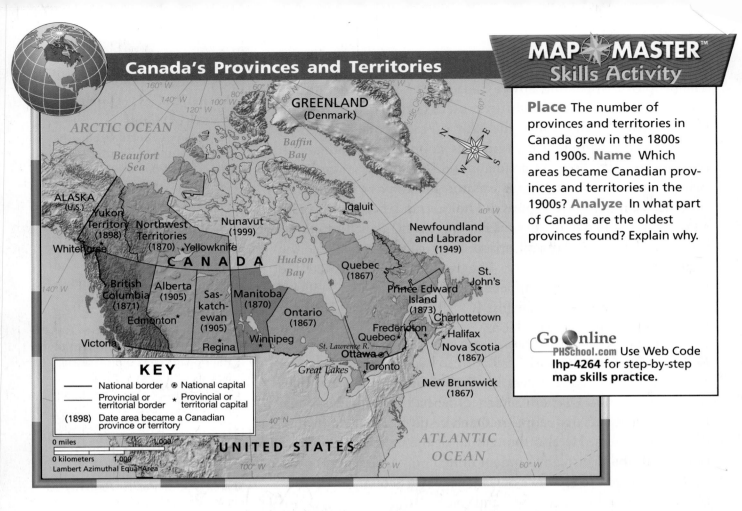

Canada's Provinces and Territories

Place The number of provinces and territories in Canada grew in the 1800s and 1900s. **Name** Which areas became Canadian provinces and territories in the 1900s? **Analyze** In what part of Canada are the oldest provinces found? Explain why.

Go Online
PHSchool.com Use Web Code **lhp-4264** for step-by-step map skills practice.

KEY

—— National border	⊛ National capital
—— Provincial or territorial border	★ Provincial or territorial capital
(1898) Date area became a Canadian province or territory	

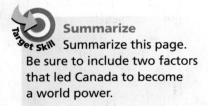

Summarize
Summarize this page. Be sure to include two factors that led Canada to become a world power.

Canadians believed that all provinces should be represented in their government. In 1864, leaders met to work out a plan to form a union. On July 1, 1867, the British Parliament accepted the British North America Act. This made Canada "one Dominion under the name of Canada." A **dominion** is a self-governing area. Canada was not completely independent from Great Britain, but now a central government would run the country. Canadians would elect their own leaders. Without a war, Canadians had won the right to control their own government.

After its "peaceful revolution," Canada saw years of growth and change. Skilled European farmers settled in Canada's western plains. Gold and other valuable minerals were discovered in the Yukon Territory in the 1890s. That brought miners to the far northwest. Canada was becoming rich and important.

Canada Becomes a World Power When Britain entered World War I, Canadians were still British subjects. Canada, therefore, entered the war, too. Canada willingly sent soldiers and resources overseas. Canada contributed so much to the Allied victory that the young country became a world power.

✓ **Reading Check** Why didn't the British want Canada to be united?

Canada: Postwar to the Present

During World War II, Canadians built factories. They made war supplies and goods such as clothes and shoes. Because of the war, people could not get such products from Europe. After the war, Canadian goods found a ready market in the United States and Europe.

Also, during the postwar years, immigrants poured into Canada. They came from Asia, Europe, Africa, and the Caribbean. The newcomers filled jobs in factories and businesses. Soon, Canada became one of the world's most important industrial nations.

The Growth of Industry   Industrialization strengthened the economy but brought back old arguments. British Canadians built new factories in Quebec. That alarmed French Canadians. In 1969, the government passed new laws that made Canada a **bilingual** country. That is, Canada had two official languages— English and French. However, by 1976 some French Canadians did not want to be part of Canada. Quebec, they argued, should be independent. Many people in Quebec still feel that way today.

Canadian Industry
Canadians, such as this factory worker tending to spools of nylon (above), made important supplies during World War II. One year after the war, plans for the first Canadian-designed and built jet fighter (left) began. Nearly 700 planes were built to defend North America in case of a future attack and to participate in overseas operations. **Draw Conclusions** *What were the effects of WWII on Canadian industries?*

A New Constitution

Although the British North America Act in 1867 gave Canadians the right to control their own government, it was still necessary for Great Britain to approve amendments to the Canadian constitution. That changed in 1982 when the Canadians adopted a new constitution. It gave Canadians the power to change their constitution without Great Britain's permission. Canada was now completely independent.

A Parliamentary System

Canada's government is modeled on the British parliamentary system. Canada has a constitutional monarchy. A set of laws states what the monarch—the king or queen—can or cannot do. Because the monarch lives in Great Britain, he or she must appoint someone in Canada to act as a representative. This position is called the governor-general. Since World War II, the governor-general has been a Canadian citizen. Although the monarch is the head of state, he or she does not make any political decisions. That is the job of the prime minister, who is the head of government.

Canada is also called a parliamentary democracy. The group of representatives that makes its laws is modeled on the British parliament. Canada's Parliament, like Great Britain's, has two chambers: the House of Commons and the Senate. The House of Commons is made up of elected representatives. The governor-general appoints the members of the Senate. Senators are allowed to hold office until they are 75 years old.

Canada's Parliament Buildings
The Parliament Buildings are an example of the Gothic style of architecture, which is from medieval times. This type of architecture developed in Western Europe between the 1100s and 1500s.
Draw Conclusions *How do the Parliament Buildings reflect Canada's heritage?*

The Commonwealth of Nations Another tie between Canada and Great Britain is its membership in the Commonwealth of Nations. It is a voluntary organization, whose member countries are former British colonies. The purpose of the Commonwealth of Nations is to consult and cooperate with one another, particularly in matters of trade and economics. In addition, Great Britain gives members financial aid and advice. At one time, the Commonwealth of Nations was the only worldwide political organization besides the United Nations.

Although Great Britain's Queen Elizabeth II is the head of the Commonwealth of Nations, her role is symbolic. In 2002, for the celebration of her fiftieth year as monarch, she traveled from one end of the Commonwealth to the other, from Nunavut to Australia.

Supporters greet Queen Elizabeth in Iqaluit, Nunavut, at the start of her twelve-day tour of Canada.

Canada in the World Today Today, Canada works both on its own and closely with international agencies to carry out foreign policy. It provides humanitarian aid to nations struck by natural disasters, such as Indonesia after a 2006 earthquake. Canada is involved in diplomatic and humanitarian missions to troubled countries from Haiti to Sudan. It has contributed to rebuilding both Afghanistan and Iraq. In addition, Canada maintains close trade and diplomatic ties with the United States.

✓ **Reading Check** **Why did Canadians write a new constitution?**

 Section 4 Assessment

Key Terms

Review the key terms at the beginning of this section. Use each term in a sentence that explains its meaning.

Target Reading Skill

Write a summary of the paragraph on page 58 called Canada Becomes a World Power.

Comprehension and Critical Thinking

1. (a) List What two countries came into conflict in Canada in the 1700s?

(b) Sequence How did the fur trade lead to war in Canada?

2. (a) Explain Why did Canadians object to British rule?

(b) Summarize How did Canadians win control of their government without going to war?

3. (a) Recall How did Canada become an industrial power after World War II?

(b) Link Past and Present How is Canada still tied to Britain today?

Writing Activity

Compare and contrast the ways in which Canada and the United States became independent nations.

> **Writing Tip** One way to organize your comparison is subject by subject, or by first explaining how the United States became independent and then how Canada did.

Suppose that your pen pal in Canada wants to know what your school looks like. Which should you do: write her a letter describing your school or send her a photograph?

A photo would show her in an instant what your school looks like. But a letter could describe details a photograph might not show. Perhaps you would send both.

There is another way to show what something looks like *and* describe it in words: You could draw a diagram. A diagram is a picture that shows how something works or is made. It usually includes labels that tell about certain parts of the picture. It is a combination of the letter and the photograph you would send to your pen pal.

A diagram is like a game of show-and-tell—the picture shows and the labels tell.

Learn the Skill

To understand how to interpret information in a diagram, follow the steps below.

1 **Study the picture.** Notice the various parts of the picture. Get visual information from it.

2 **Read the labels.** Sometimes the labels will be numbered or will appear in a certain order to explain a step-by-step process.

3 **Summarize the information in the diagram.** From the information you gather by studying the picture and the labels, write a summary describing what the diagram shows you.

Practice the Skill

Look at How a Locomotive Works, below, as you practice interpreting a diagram.

1 From the title, you can tell what the diagram shows. As you look at the picture, what information can you learn—even before you read the labels?

2 The labels in this diagram are meant to be read in a particular order. Do you know why? Notice that this diagram has both labels and arrows. What do the arrows show?

3 Write a paragraph describing how a locomotive works. Write as if the reader did not have the picture to look at. Don't simply repeat the text in the labels, but summarize the information in the labels and picture.

How a Locomotive Works

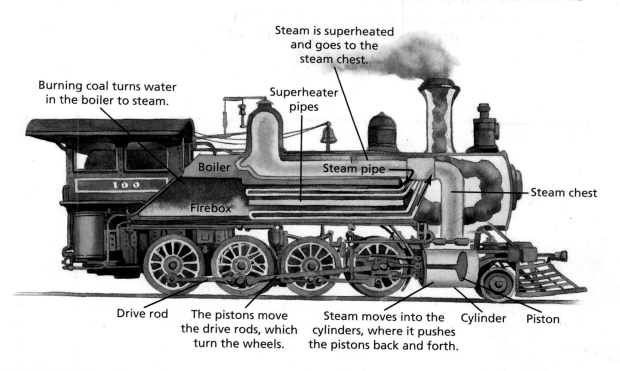

Steam is superheated and goes to the steam chest.

Burning coal turns water in the boiler to steam.

Superheater pipes

Boiler

Steam pipe

Firebox

Steam chest

Drive rod

The pistons move the drive rods, which turn the wheels.

Steam moves into the cylinders, where it pushes the pistons back and forth.

Cylinder

Piston

Apply the Skill

Find a photograph of a bicycle in a catalog or a magazine. Then, write a paragraph describing what the bicycle looks like, what parts it has, and how the parts work.

Now draw a diagram of a bicycle. Make labels showing how it works.

Compare the picture, the paragraph, and the diagram. Which one does the best job of showing and explaining how a bicycle works?

Section 5

The United States and Canada Today

Prepare to Read

Objectives

In this section you will
1. Identify the environmental concerns the United States and Canada share today.
2. Find out about the economic ties the United States and Canada have to each other and to the world.

Taking Notes

As you read the section, look for details about the environmental concerns and economic ties that the United States and Canada share. Copy the concept web below and fill in the details.

Target Reading Skill

Reread or Read Ahead Rereading and reading ahead are strategies that can help you understand words and ideas in the text. If you do not understand a certain passage, reread it to look for connections among the words and sentences. It might also help to read ahead, because a word or an idea may be clarified further on.

Key Terms

- **acid rain** (as id rayn) n. rain containing acids that are harmful to plants and trees
- **tariff** (tar if) n. a fee charged on imported goods
- **free trade** (free trayd) n. trade without taxes on imported goods

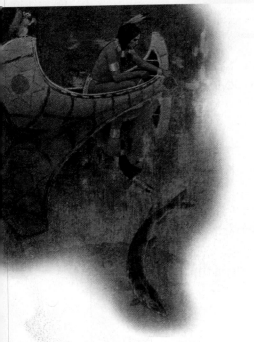

A painting of an Iroquois fishing from a canoe

The birch-bark canoes paddled into the village of Sault Sainte Marie, on the border of the present-day United States and Canada. The canoes carried fishing nets made from strands of willow bark and baskets full of lake trout. The Native American fishermen unloaded their baskets at the shore. Any fish they did not eat that day would be dried on racks and saved for later or ground up and used as fertilizer for crops.

For centuries, the lake trout of the Great Lakes provided food for both Native Americans and European settlers. By the mid-1950s, lake trout were the most valuable fish in the Upper Great Lakes. Lake trout were soon overharvested. In some of the Great Lakes, the lake trout almost disappeared.

In 1955, Canada and the United States joined to create the Great Lakes Fishery Commission. Members of the commission worked together to find ways of protecting lake trout and many other species of fish in the Great Lakes. This is just one of the ways the United States and Canada have become cooperative neighbors.

Environmental Issues

The United States and Canada share many geographic features—the coasts of the Atlantic and Pacific oceans, the Great Lakes, and the Rocky Mountains, for example. Both countries use natural resources in similar ways. And both have used technology to meet their needs. But technology has left its mark on their water, air, forests, and futures.

Solving Water Problems   Can you picture a river on fire? Impossible, you say? In 1969, a fire started on the Cuyahoga River (ky uh HOH guh RIV er). That river flows past Cleveland, Ohio, and then empties into Lake Erie. For many years, Cleveland had poured waste, garbage, and oil into the river. The layer of pollutants was so thick that it caught on fire.

The Cuyahoga was typical of the rivers that empty into Lake Erie. So much pollution had been dumped into the lake that most of the fish had died. Swimming in the river was unthinkable. The fire on the Cuyahoga was a wake-up call. The United States and Canada signed an agreement promising to cooperate in cleaning up the lake. Agreements such as this have greatly reduced freshwater pollution in the United States. Today, people again enjoy fishing and boating on the Cuyahoga.

The Cuyahoga River
In June 1969, firefighters hosed down flames from the Cuyahoga River fire (below). **Analyze Images** *Looking at the river today (inset), what positive effects came out of the cleanup effort?*

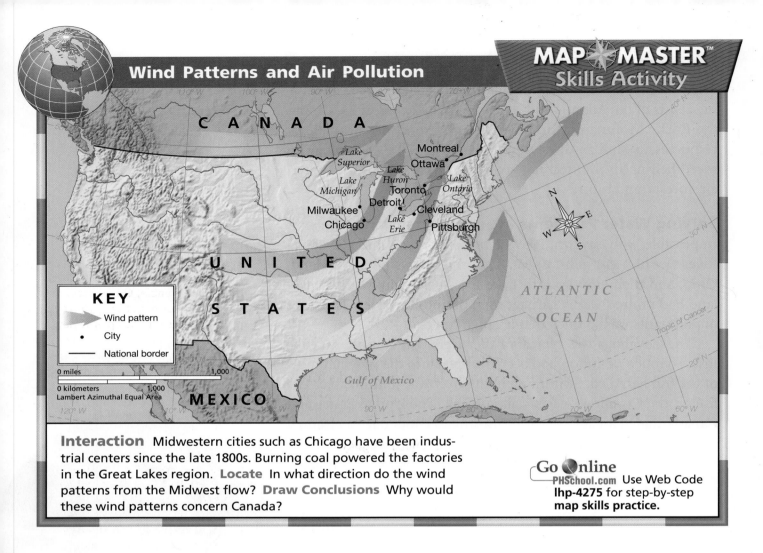

CANADA

Lake Superior

Lake Huron

Lake Michigan

Montreal
Ottawa
Toronto
Detroit
Lake Ontario
Milwaukee
Chicago
Cleveland
Lake Erie
Pittsburgh

UNITED STATES

ATLANTIC OCEAN

MEXICO

Gulf of Mexico

Tropic of Cancer

KEY

- Wind pattern
- City
- National border

0 miles 1,000
0 kilometers 1,000
Lambert Azimuthal Equal Area

Interaction Midwestern cities such as Chicago have been industrial centers since the late 1800s. Burning coal powered the factories in the Great Lakes region. **Locate** In what direction do the wind patterns from the Midwest flow? **Draw Conclusions** Why would these wind patterns concern Canada?

Go Online
PHSchool.com Use Web Code
lhp-4275 for step-by-step map skills practice.

Improving Air Quality On many days, you can look around most big cities and see that the air is filled with a brown haze. This pollution is caused by cars and factories burning fossil fuels. Not only is this air unhealthy to breathe, but it can also create other serious problems hundreds of miles away. Pollutants in the air combine with moisture to form acid. **Acid rain** is rain that dissolves these acids and carries them to Earth. This acid kills plants, trees, and fish. Coal-burning power plants in the West and Midwest United States create acid rain problems in the Northeast and in the Great Lakes area. Winds carry these acids long distances.

Acid rain caused by United States power plants has affected forests and lakes in Canada. The two countries signed agreements to control air quality in the 1980s. A 2002 government progress report showed that rain acidity was reduced in Canada by 45 percent and in the United States by 35 percent.

Aerial view of Toronto's hazy skyline and harbor, Ontario, Canada

Renewing Forests "I'm like a tree—you'll have to cut me down," cried Kim McElroy in 1993. The other demonstrators with her agreed. They were blocking the path of logging trucks trying to enter the forest of Clayoquot Sound on Vancouver Island, British Columbia. The protesters believed that cutting down the trees would damage the environment. In similar forests throughout the United States and Canada, logging companies practiced clear-cutting, or cutting down all the trees in an area. Without trees, soil washes away, other plants die, and animals lose their homes.

On the other hand, people need lumber for building. Paper companies need wood pulp to make their products. People who work for logging companies need their jobs.

The Canadian and American governments want to maintain both the forests and the timber industry. They are working to develop ways of doing that. For example, British Columbia passed a law that sets aside parts of the Clayoquot Sound's forests for logging. The law also imposes new rules on loggers to prevent damage in the areas where cutting is allowed.

✓ **Reading Check** **Why is there disagreement about logging in some forests?**

The Old and the New
A hill in the Queen Charlotte Islands of British Columbia, Canada (below), shows clear-cut forest growth. The man in the inset photo plants new trees. **Draw Conclusions** *How does planting new trees help to keep soil from washing away? Why is that important?*

Target Skill

Reread
Reread or keep reading to see the economic links between the United States and Canada.

"Economics Has Made Us Partners"

Not all next-door neighbors get along as well as the United States and Canada. President John F. Kennedy once described the relationship this way: "Geography has made us neighbors. History has made us friends. Economics has made us partners." With 5,527 miles (8,895 kilometers) of border between the two countries, economic cooperation has benefited both. Part of this cooperation has been in transportation between the countries, particularly around the Great Lakes.

The St. Lawrence Seaway Have you ever heard of someone going over Niagara Falls in a barrel? The barrel would drop about 190 feet (58 meters)—a crazy stunt! Suppose you have a cargo of manufactured goods in Cleveland to send to Montreal. You would like to ship by water, because it is the cheapest and most direct means of transportation. But Niagara Falls lies between Cleveland and Montreal. And after passing the falls, your cargo would have to travel down another 250 feet (76 meters) in the St. Lawrence River before it reached Montreal. What do you do?

The Great Lakes and the St. Lawrence Seaway

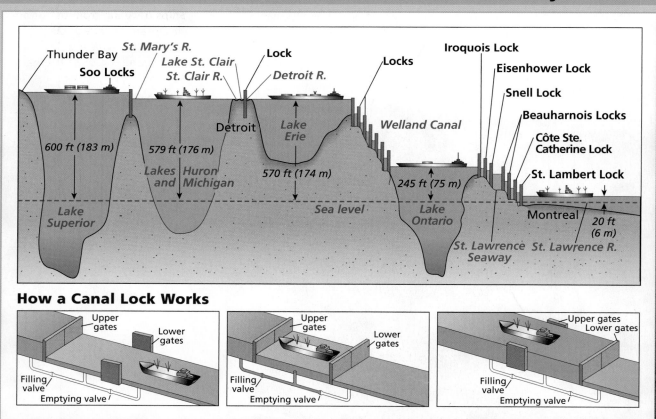

How a Canal Lock Works

To solve this problem, the United States and Canada built the St. Lawrence Seaway. Completed in 1959, it is a system of locks, canals, and dams that allows ships to move from one water level to another. A lock is an enclosed area on a canal that raises or lowers ships from one water level to another. Now, ships can travel from Duluth, Minnesota, on Lake Superior, all the way to the Atlantic Ocean. The St. Lawrence Seaway makes it much easier for the United States and Canada to trade with each other and with Europe. The St. Lawrence Seaway has been called Canada's highway to the sea because of the volume of goods that travels its length.

Trade   What country is the biggest trading partner of the United States? It is Canada. And, the United States is Canada's largest trading partner, too. About three fourths of all of Canada's foreign trade—both exports and imports—is with the United States. Our economies are interdependent. That means that in order to be successful, each country needs to do business with the other.

Diagram Skills

Ships traveling from the Atlantic Ocean to Lake Superior must go through a series of locks along the St. Lawrence Seaway. **Describe** How do the locks allow ships to make the great change in elevation between the Atlantic and the Great Lakes? **Identify Effects** How did building the St. Lawrence Seaway affect the economies of the United States and Canada?

The emblem of the Organization of American States shows the furled flags of its member nations.

Since 1988, the United States and Canada have signed two important trade agreements. The Free Trade Agreement (FTA) put an end to **tariffs**, or fees charged on imported goods. Tariffs raise the cost of goods, so the amount of trade can be limited. By eliminating tariffs, Canada and the United States agreed to have **free trade**, trade without taxes on imported goods. In 1994, this agreement was expanded to include Mexico. The goal of the North American Free Trade Agreement (NAFTA) is to encourage trade and economic growth in all three countries. The agreement affects many major industries, including agriculture, trucking, and manufacturing. Since these agreements were made, trade among the three countries has increased. Although some jobs in the United States have been created because of increased imports, other jobs have been lost because American companies have moved to Mexico.

Interdependent Countries The United States and Canada are interdependent politically as well as economically. Both Canada and the United States belong to the Organization of American States, or OAS. This international organization was formed to promote cooperation among countries in the Western Hemisphere. The member countries work with one another to promote political, economic, military, and cultural cooperation. The main goals of OAS are to maintain peace in the Western Hemisphere and to prevent other countries from interfering within the region.

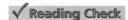 **Reading Check** What are the main goals of the member countries in the Organization of American States?

 ## Section 5 Assessment

Key Terms
Review the key terms at the beginning of this section. Use each term in a sentence that explains its meaning.

Target Reading Skill
What word or idea were you able to clarify by rereading or reading ahead?

Comprehension and Critical Thinking
1. (a) Explain What are some environmental problems the United States and Canada share?

(b) Summarize How have these two countries worked together to solve these problems?

(c) Identify Effects How can one nation's problems affect another?

2. (a) Note What country is the largest trading partner of the United States?

(b) Make Generalizations How has the St. Lawrence Seaway made trade easier for the United States and Canada?

(c) Identify the Main Idea What is the goal of NAFTA?

Writing Activity
Write a paragraph that explains the main reasons that Canada and the United States are important to each other.

> **Writing Tip** Begin your paragraph with a topic sentence that states your main idea. Be sure to include examples, details, and facts that support your main idea.

Review and Assessment

◆ Chapter Summary

Native American artifact

Section 1: The Arrival of the Europeans
- The first Americans are called Native Americans.
- The lives of Native Americans changed after Europeans arrived.
- The 13 colonies won independence after the Revolutionary War.

Section 2: Growth and Conflict in the United States
- The United States doubled its size in 1803 with the Louisiana Purchase.
- The Industrial Revolution changed the way people in America lived.
- The Civil War pitted the North against the South.

Section 3: The United States on the Brink of Change
- The Industrial Revolution helped the rich but not the poor.
- The United States fought two world wars and became a superpower.
- After years of fighting various wars, Americans faced new terrorist threats.

Section 4: The History of Canada
- Britain fought France to gain control of Canada.
- Canadians won the right to control their own government.
- Today, Canada is completely independent of Great Britain.

Section 5: The United States and Canada Today
- The United States and Canada work together to solve environmental issues.
- The United States and Canada are each other's largest trading partners.

Civil War soldiers

◆ Key Terms

Each of the statements below contains a key term from the chapter. If the statement is true, write *true*. If it is false, rewrite the statement to make it correct.

1. A **missionary** is a person who must work for a period of years to gain freedom.

2. A **tariff** is a fee charged on imported goods.

3. **Acid rain** forms over millions of years from plant and animal remains.

4. The **Industrial Revolution** was a period of great tension between the United States and the Soviet Union.

5. A **dominion** is a self-governing area that is subject to the United States.

6. Canada is a **bilingual** country, meaning that it has two official languages.

7. A **boycott** is a refusal to buy or use goods and services.

8. An **abolitionist** is a person who moves to a new country in order to settle there.

Review and Assessment (continued)

◆ Comprehension and Critical Thinking

9. (a) Compare Why were Spanish and French explorers interested in the Americas?
(b) Identify Cause and Effect How did the treatment of Native Americans reflect the different interests of the Spanish and the French explorers?

10. (a) Explain How did the Industrial Revolution change the textile industry?
(b) Draw Conclusions How might this change have affected workers?

11. (a) Identify What was the Homestead Act?
(b) Draw Inferences How did railroads help settle the American West more quickly?

12. (a) Name Where did some Loyalists move after the American Revolution?
(b) Identify Frame of Reference Why would Loyalists have opposed independence from Britain?

13. (a) Define What kind of government does Canada have?
(b) Name What system is the Canadian government modeled on?
(c) Draw Conclusions What duties might a monarch have, since he or she is not the head of the government?

14. (a) Describe How has geography contributed to the trade partnership between Canada and the United States?
(b) Draw Inferences What other factors might explain this strong trade relationship?

◆ Skills Practice

Interpreting Diagrams In the Skills for Life activity in this chapter, you learned how to interpret information in a diagram. You also learned that labels on a diagram often should be read in a certain order.

Review the steps you followed to learn this skill. Then reread the part of Section 5 called Improving Air Quality. Create a diagram showing the cycle of acid rain. Remember to label your diagram clearly.

◆ Writing Activity: Language Arts

Compare and contrast the histories of the United States and of Canada. Write a paragraph describing the ways in which the growth, settlement, and independence of the United States and Canada were similar and ways in which they were different.

MAP MASTER™
Skills Activity

Place Location For each place listed below, write the letter from the map that shows its location.

1. Ontario
2. Quebec
3. Yukon
4. Lake Erie
5. St. Lawrence Seaway

Go Online
PHSchool.com Use Web Code **lhp-4285** for an **interactive map.**

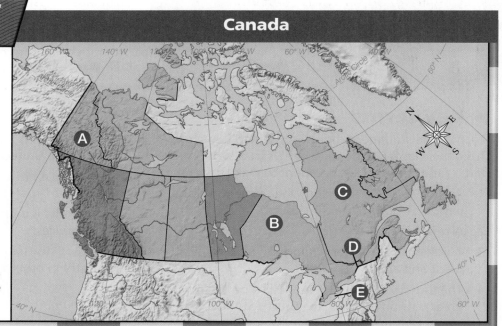

Canada

Standardized Test Prep

Test-Taking Tips

Some questions on standardized tests ask you to analyze primary sources. Read the excerpt below from a famous United States document. Then follow the tips to answer the sample question.

> "All legislative Powers herein granted shall be vested in a Congress of the United States, which shall consist of a Senate and House of Representatives. . . . The House of Representatives shall be composed of Members chosen every second Year by the People of the several states. . . . The Senate of the United States shall be composed of two Senators from each State for six Years; and each Senator shall have one Vote."

TIP Try to identify the main idea, or most important point, of the passage.

Pick the letter that best answers the question.

Which document does this extract come from?

A ~~Declaration of Independence~~

B United States Constitution

C Federalist Papers

D ~~Pledge of Allegiance~~

TIP Use what you already know about United States history and government to help you find the *best* answer.

Think It Through Start with the main idea of the extract: *The Congress is supposed to make laws.* Which document explains the powers of each branch of government? You can rule out A and D. The Pledge is a statement of loyalty. The Declaration of Independence explains why colonists cut their ties to England. That leaves B and C. Maybe you aren't sure about the Federalist Papers, but you probably know that the Constitution is the plan for our government—including Congress. The correct answer is B.

Practice Questions

Use the tips above and other tips in this book to help you answer the following questions.

1. Which event encouraged immigrants and farmworkers to look for jobs in cities?
   A the Civil War
   B the Industrial Revolution
   C the Louisiana Purchase
   D the Indian Removal Act

2. What was the result of the Seven Years' War?
   A Canada became independent.
   B France lost, but kept control over Quebec.
   C Great Britain gained control over all of Canada.
   D Canada became a dominion of Great Britain.

Read the excerpt on Article 102, and then answer the question that follows.

> **Article 102: Objectives**
> a) eliminate barriers to trade in, and facilitate the cross-border movement of, goods and services between the territories of the Parties;
> b) promote conditions of fair competition in the free-trade area.

3. Which document does this excerpt most likely come from?
   A the British North America Act
   B the Treaty of Paris
   C NAFTA
   D the Quebec Act

Use Web Code **lha-4205** for a **Chapter 2 self-test.**

Chapter

3

Cultures of the United States and Canada

Chapter Preview

This chapter will introduce you to the cultures of the United States and Canada.

Section 1
A Heritage of Diversity and Exchange

Section 2
The United States: A Nation of Immigrants

Section 3
The Canadian Mosaic

Target Reading Skill

Main Idea In this chapter you will focus on skills you can use to identify the main ideas as you read.

▶ Young people enjoy an amusement park ride in Orlando, Florida.

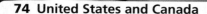
74 United States and Canada

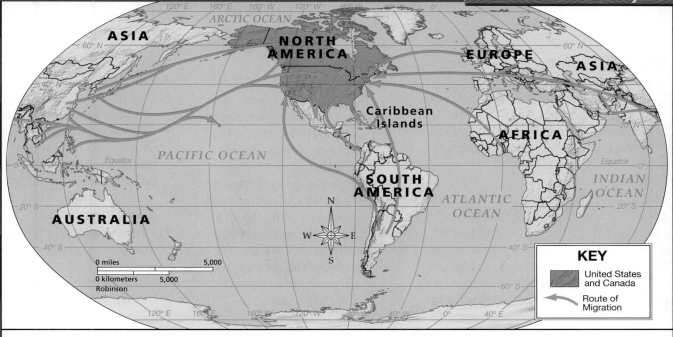

KEY

United States and Canada

Route of Migration

Movement Both the United States and Canada have long histories of welcoming immigrants from around the world. **Locate** Where are most of the arrows pointing to on the map? **Predict** What factors in people's lives might cause them to immigrate to the United States or Canada?

Go Online
PHSchool.com Use Web Code **lhp-4311** for step-by-step map skills practice.

A Heritage of Diversity and Exchange

Prepare to Read

Objectives

In this section you will

1. Explain how cultural patterns developed in the United States and Canada.
2. Discuss the cultural patterns that exist today in the United States and Canada.

Taking Notes

As you read this section, add facts and details to the outline. Use Roman numerals to indicate the major headings of the section, capital letters for the subheadings, and numbers for the supporting details.

> **A Heritage of Diversity and Exchange**
> I. Patterns of culture develop
>   A.
>   B.
> II.

Target Reading Skill

Identify Main Ideas   It is not possible to remember every detail that you read. Good readers therefore identify the main idea in every paragraph or section. The main idea is the most important or the biggest point—the one that includes all the other points in the section. As you read, write the main idea that is stated in each section.

Key Terms

- **cultural diversity** (KUL chur ul duh VUR suh tee) *n.* a variety of cultures
- **cultural exchange** (KUL chur ul eks CHAYNJ) *n.* the process by which different cultures share ideas and ways of doing things
- **ethnic group** (ETH nik groop) *n.* a group of people who share a common language, history, and culture

Fur traders at Fort Garry, present-day Winnipeg, in Manitoba, Canada

By 1763, Canada and the eastern half of the present-day United States were one land, governed by Great Britain. When the Revolutionary War ended in 1783, new political boundaries were created. A new country, the United States, was born.

New political borders, however, did not divide cultural regions that already existed. The same patterns of **cultural diversity,** or a wide variety of cultures, continued.

> **❝By 1810, many . . . merchants were . . . immigrants, as were almost all the millers, mechanics, store-keepers, . . . and the majority of the farmers. . . . [They] had been lured by economic opportunities. . . . ❞**
>
> —*D. W. Meinig,* The Shaping of America

This passage describes American immigrants to Canada. At that time, Americans in the northeastern United States were more comfortable with the culture of southern Canada than with some of the cultures within their own country.

Patterns of Culture Develop

The United States and Canada have always been culturally diverse. Both countries are geographically diverse, too—that is, they have a variety of landforms, climates, and vegetation. The cultures of the first Americans reflected their environments. Native Americans near the ocean ate a great deal of fish and told stories about the sea. Native Americans in forests learned how to trap and hunt forest animals. They also traded with each other. When groups trade, they receive more than just goods. They also get involved in **cultural exchange,** or the process by which different cultures share ideas and ways of doing things.

Cultural Exchange When Europeans arrived in North America, they changed Native American life. Some changes came from things that Europeans brought with them. For example, there were no horses in the Americas before the Spanish explorers arrived. Once horses were introduced, they became an important part of Native American culture.

Native American in the Badlands of South Dakota

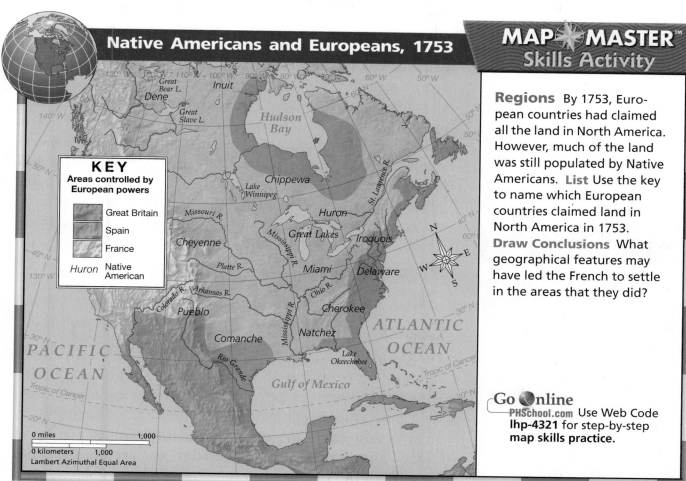

Native Americans and Europeans, 1753

KEY
Areas controlled by European powers

- Great Britain
- Spain
- France
- *Huron* Native American

Map labels: Inuit, Dene, Great Bear L., Great Slave L., Hudson Bay, Chippewa, Lake Winnipeg, Missouri R., Huron, Great Lakes, St. Lawrence R., Iroquois, Cheyenne, Mississippi R., Platte R., Miami, Delaware, Colorado R., Arkansas R., Pueblo, Cherokee, Comanche, Ohio R., Natchez, ATLANTIC OCEAN, Rio Grande, Lake Okeechobee, PACIFIC OCEAN, Tropic of Cancer, Gulf of Mexico

0 miles 1,000
0 kilometers 1,000
Lambert Azimuthal Equal Area

MAP★MASTER™ Skills Activity

Regions By 1753, European countries had claimed all the land in North America. However, much of the land was still populated by Native Americans. **List** Use the key to name which European countries claimed land in North America in 1753.

Draw Conclusions What geographical features may have led the French to settle in the areas that they did?

Go Online
PHSchool.com Use Web Code **lhp-4321** for step-by-step map skills practice.

Harvesting Wheat
These farmers in Manitoba, Canada, are harvesting wheat with a horse-drawn reaper, which cuts grain.
Identify Causes *Why did farming attract many immigrants to the United States and Canada?*

Using Your Fingers and Toes Native American groups developed number systems to help when conducting trade with others. The Chukchee, who hunted reindeer along the Bering Strait, used their fingers to count. The question *How many?* is translated "How many fingers?" Their word for *five* is "hand," for *ten*, "both hands," and for *twenty*, "man"—meaning both hands and both feet.

Native Americans also contributed to European culture. The French learned how to trap and to survive in the forest. English families learned to grow local foods such as corn. Cultural exchange also took place between enslaved Africans and their owners. The Africans learned English and used European tools. African music and foods entered the daily lives of slave owners.

Immigrant Contributions This give-and-take happens every time immigrants come to a country. When Russian and Ukrainian settlers came to Canada's Prairie Provinces, they brought a kind of hardy wheat from their home country. Farmers soon learned that it grew well in Canada's climate. These immigrants helped the region become the leading wheat-growing area in Canada today. Members of other ethnic groups have made important contributions to American and Canadian cultures, too. An **ethnic group** is a group of people who share a common language, history, and culture.

✓ **Reading Check** **What are two examples of cultural exchange?**

Cultural Patterns Today

The United States and Canada share similar cultural patterns and histories because both of them were once British colonies. Both of their cultures have also been shaped by immigration. With huge amounts of land to be cultivated, or worked on in order to raise crops, the governments of the United States and Canada first encouraged immigration to increase the work force. With the Industrial Revolution, the end of slavery, and the rise of cities, the demand for workers was great.

Today, the United States and Canada continue to attract immigrants because they are wealthy nations with stable governments. Many immigrants come seeking political asylum, religious freedom, or economic opportunities. Others come to escape famine, disease, or overcrowding in their homelands. They all come looking to improve their lives.

Fitting In   When immigrants move from their homeland to another country, they often have to make difficult decisions. As immigrants build a life in a new country, they must learn different laws and customs. Often they need to learn a new language, too. Some immigrants work hard to keep up the customs of their home culture as they settle in. Many feel torn between their cultural heritage and their new life.

For instance, when he was 14 years old, Herman immigrated to the United States from Guyana, a country in South America. Five years later, someone asked him if he felt Guyanese or American. He said, "I'm in between. Deep down inside, where I was born, that's what I am. You can't change a tiger['s] stripe."

Others, however, try to put as much of their old life behind them as they can. When Louisa and her husband immigrated to Saskatchewan, Canada, from Hong Kong, they were eager to start their new lives:

> **It takes time to adapt to a new environment. It is sometimes difficult for one to change one's life abruptly. However, it is the reality that we must fit in. We are determined to succeed in overcoming the difficulties and to live a Canadian way of life.**
>
> —*Louisa, a Chinese immigrant*

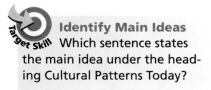

Identify Main Ideas Which sentence states the main idea under the heading Cultural Patterns Today?

Celebrating Cultures
The dancers below march in a parade during Carnival Miami in Florida. The photo on the left is a busy street in Chinatown in Vancouver, British Columbia. **Analyze Images** *In what ways do the photographs below show how immigrants have blended their traditional cultures with their new cultures?*

Play Ball!
Baseball is widely considered to be the "national pastime" of the United States. It is also a popular sport in Canada. One professional baseball team in Canada competes against American teams in the major leagues. **Conclusions** *How does professional baseball link the United States and Canada both culturally and economically?*

Maintaining Traditions Almost all immigrants cling to some of the things that remind them of their former homes. Many large cities in the United States and Canada have areas where certain ethnic groups live or conduct business, such as Chinatown in Vancouver and Little Havana in Miami.

Of course, people maintain traditions in their own homes as well. Think about your family or your friends' families. Do they use special phrases from the language they learned from their parents or grandparents? Do they eat special foods? Customs give people a sense of identity. They also enrich life in both the United States and Canada.

Cultural Ties The United States and Canada are historically and economically linked. They share a border, a continent, and have felt Britain's influence on their history and language. Although the population of the United States is nearly ten times larger than that of Canada, the people are very much alike.

At least three fourths of people in both countries live in urban areas. Most Canadians live within 200 miles (320 kilometers) of the United States' border. Canadians and Americans dress alike and eat similar foods. The majority of both Canadians and Americans are either Roman Catholic or Protestant. Both nations have long life expectancies and high rates of literacy, or the ability to read and write. Canadians and Americans often read the same books and magazines, listen to the same music, and watch many of the same movies and television shows.

Economic Ties With vast resources and strong economies, both the United States and Canada have a high standard of living. A standard of living is a measure of the amount of goods, services, and leisure time people have. Their economies are linked, too. The total amount of trade that takes place each year between the United States and Canada is larger than it is between any other two countries. Changes in business trends in the United States are quickly reflected in the Canadian business sector. The two nations trade in manufactured goods, forestry products, and food items. They also trade heavily in energy, such as oil, coal, and electricity.

In addition, millions of Canadians travel to the United States each year. Nearly two million Canadians visit Florida alone, spending more than a billion dollars there. Most of these tourists, known as Snowbirds, come to escape Canada's long, cold winters. Likewise, most of Canada's tourists are American. Americans can travel to Canada almost as easily as they would to a different state.

✓ **Reading Check** What cultural characteristics do the United States and Canada have in common?

Tourists visit the Grand Canyon (upper photo) and Quebec City (lower photo).

Section 1 Assessment

Key Terms

Review the key terms at the beginning of this section. Use each term in a sentence that explains its meaning.

Target Reading Skill

State the main ideas in Section 1.

Comprehension and Critical Thinking

1. (a) Recall Describe how Native American cultures reflected their environments.

(b) Analyze How did the arrival of Europeans affect Native American cultures?

2. (a) List Note the similarities between the United States and Canada.

(b) Explore the Main Idea How are the economies of the United States and Canada linked?

(c) Draw Conclusions The economy of which country—the United States or Canada—is more dependent on the other's?

Writing Activity

Write a poem about a custom that is important to your family or the family of a friend. Start by listing words or phrases that describe the details of the family custom.

> **Writing Tip** After you write a first draft of the poem, read it aloud. Circle words that do not offer a clear picture of the custom. Replace them with more lively words.

"Today we're going to brainstorm," Ms. King told her social studies class. She drew a large circle at the center of the chalkboard, and inside it she wrote *Cultures of the United States.* "This is our topic. Now, give me the names of some important culture groups in our country."

The ideas flew fast. "European settlers!" "Before them, Native Americans." "Hispanics!" "African Americans!" "Asians!" Ms. King put each group in its own circle and connected it with a line to the center circle.

"Great start! Now give me details about each of these groups," she urged her students. "What ideas did Europeans bring here?"

She made several small circles and connected them to the large circle, saying, *"European settlers."* She filled in the circles as the students brainstormed the topic: *democracy . . . architecture . . . English language . . . banking . . . measurements . . . medicine. . . .*

By the time she finished, the chalkboard looked like a spider web. In fact, the connected circles made what is sometimes called a *web diagram.* It is also known as a *concept web.*

A concept web is a type of *graphic organizer,* a diagram that puts information into a graphic, or visual, form to make it easier to understand.

Learn the Skill

Like an outline, a concept web begins with a main topic and adds subtopics and details. Follow the steps below to learn about concept webs.

1 **Identify a main topic.** A main topic generally has at least two subtopics. Identify the subtopics.

2 **Draw a circle at the center of the concept map.** Label it with the main topic.

3 **For each subtopic, draw a circle.** Label the circles. Attach them to the main circle with lines to show that the subtopics are related to the main topic.

4 **If necessary, divide the subtopics even further.** Some subtopics have subtopics of their own. To show this, draw more circles, label them, and attach them to the circle with the subtopics.

Practice the Skill

Suppose you want to write a paper about your culture. Refer to the steps on the previous page and the concept web below to see how you might organize your thoughts.

1 Your topic is My Culture. You know that many factors affect a person's culture. Those factors will be your subtopics.

2 The concept web below shows My Culture in an oval at the center.

3 The ovals connected to the center show that religion, family history, languages, and the celebration of special occasions are parts of a person's culture.

4 Add supporting details that relate to family history and the other subtopics. These details go in the empty ovals shown below.

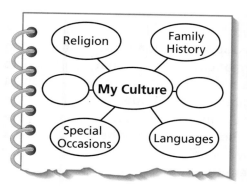

Today, many people can trace their family's history through photographs. This family has photographs of their grandfather (from top to bottom) as a baby, as a young man, with his wife and children, and with his grandson.

Apply the Skill

Choose a part of the text in Section 1. Using the steps for this skill, make a concept web that shows the main idea, subtopics, and details.

Prepare to Read

Objectives

In this section you will
1. Learn about the people of the United States.
2. Find out about the culture of the United States.

Taking Notes

As you read this section, look for details about the cultural diversity of the United States. Copy the chart below and record your findings in it.

Causes	Event	Effects
• • •	The U.S. is culturally diverse	• • •

Target Reading Skill

Identify Supporting Details The main idea of a paragraph or section is supported by details that give further information about it. These details may explain the main idea or give examples or reasons. As you read, note the details that explain the main idea in this section: "The United States is a diverse nation."

Key Terms

- **reservation** (rez ur VAY shun) *n.* an area of land set aside for a special purpose
- **treaty** (TREE tee) *n.* a formal agreement, usually between two or more nations

---

The Statue of Liberty

This view of life in the United States comes from an immigrant arriving in Ellis Island in 1920:

> **I feel like I had two lives. You plant something in the ground, it has its roots, and then you transplant it where it stays permanently. That's what happened to me. . . . All of a sudden, I started life new, amongst people whose language I didn't understand. . . . [E]verything was different . . . but I never despaired, I was optimistic. . . . [T]his is the only country where you're not a stranger, because we are all strangers. It's only a matter of time who got here first.**
>
> —*Lazarus Salamon, a Hungarian immigrant*

The People of the United States

The population of the United States has been growing steadily since the first national census was taken in 1790. About 4 million people lived in the nation then. Today, more than 280 million people live in the United States.

Despite the vast size of the United States, its people share many common attitudes and traditions. These experiences help bring Americans together. At the same time, Americans are a diverse mix of races, ethnicities, and religions.

The First People   Today's Native Americans are descendents of the first people to live in the Americas. Most experts believe that the first Americans migrated from Asia across the Bering Strait thousands of years ago. Gradually, the human population spread south across North America.

When European settlers arrived in North America, they often came into conflict with the Native Americans who were living there. As Europeans moved west, they forced the local Indians to move to land already occupied by other Native American groups.

The United States government pursued a general policy of supporting white settlement. They established **reservations,** or federal lands set aside for Native Americans, and forced Native Americans to relocate.

Conflict With Settlers   From 1778 to 1871, the United States government wrote and signed hundreds of **treaties,** or formal agreements, with American Indian groups. In these treaties, Native Americans agreed to interact peacefully with settlers. They also agreed to give up much of their land. In return, the federal government promised to pay for that land and to protect them.

Most of these treaties were broken, often because settlers wanted to expand onto reservation lands. When settlers violated these treaties, Native Americans fought back. They were fighting not only for their land but for their resources and way of life. Native Americans fought more than 1,000 battles throughout the West between 1861 and 1891.

Native Americans Today   In the 1960s, Native Americans began to seek economic and political equality. Several groups, including the American Indian Movement (AIM), formed to work for better living conditions and equal rights. They called on the government to address their concerns. The United States has since passed a series of reforms, giving money and land to Native American groups. Today, about 2.5 million people in the United States are Native American.

Fighting For Civil Rights
Dennis Banks, a leader in the American Indian Movement (AIM), leads a protest in South Dakota. **Draw Inferences** *Why do you think Banks chose Mount Rushmore as the site for the protest?*

Identify Supporting Details

Which details in the paragraph at the right tell about diversity?

Immigrants The United States has always been a nation of immigrants. However, the first major wave of immigration took place from 1830 to 1890. These immigrants were mainly Protestants from England, Scotland, Scandinavia, and Germany who came to farm the land. They adapted fairly easily to the American ways of life because of their similar backgrounds. These ethnic groups would continue to come to the United States in large numbers until World War I.

The first large influx of Chinese immigrants came in 1849, during the California Gold Rush. More Chinese arrived in the 1860s to lay track for the transcontinental railroad. They had a more difficult time than Europeans adjusting to life in the United States. Widespread unemployment and fierce competition for gold led to violence and discrimination against many Asian immigrants.

A Second Wave of Immigrants The second major wave of immigration took place from 1880 to 1920. Unlike the first wave, these immigrants went to work in factories, mills, and mines. Immigrants from southern and eastern Europe dominated the second wave: Jews from Russia and Poland, Roman Catholics from Poland and Italy, and some of the Greek Orthodox faith. Like the Asian immigrants before them, they dressed differently, ate different foods, and spoke different languages. They often worked in poor conditions for low wages.

■ Graph Skills

Thousands of people attend the annual Ninth Avenue International Food Festival in New York City. The festival features food from nearly 30 countries along the mile-long celebration. **Identify** Where do most immigrants to the United States come from? **Draw Conclusions** What languages might the immigrants from those regions speak?

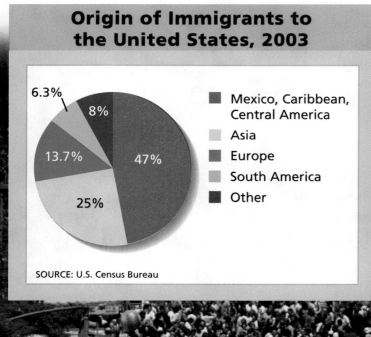

Origin of Immigrants to the United States, 2003

6.3%
8%
13.7%
47%
25%

- Mexico, Caribbean, Central America
- Asia
- Europe
- South America
- Other

SOURCE: U.S. Census Bureau

The writings of Zora Neale Hurston, Ralph Waldo Emerson, and Sandra Cisneros (from far left) reflect the diversity of the books that Americans read.

Immigrants Today   Non-Europeans form the largest immigrant groups coming to the United States today. Most immigrants arrive from Asia and Latin America. The hard work of these immigrants, and of those before them, have helped develop the United States agriculturally, industrially, and economically. They also helped create a culturally diverse nation.

✓ **Reading Check**   **Where do most immigrants arrive from today?**

United States Culture

Have you ever eaten bagels, tacos, dim sum, or spaghetti? Have you listened to music at a Caribbean carnival or watched a dragon parade on Chinese New Year? Diverse foods, books, music, and pastimes all enrich the lives of Americans.

Literature   A distinctly American literature emerged in the nineteenth century, as Ralph Waldo Emerson and others wrote about politics and nature. By the twentieth century, America's diversity had begun to influence its literature. Playwright Eugene O'Neill had an Irish background, while Zora Neale Hurston wrote novels about what it was like to be African American. Traditions such as Native American folk tales and slave narratives also gained importance. American literature is now more varied than ever before, reflecting the diversity in today's culture.

Musical Traditions   In addition to diverse literature, Americans listen to and create many different kinds of music, from classical to popular. Popular music includes country, rap, rock, reggae, and jazz. Although it has its roots in African rhythms, jazz developed in the South, in places like New Orleans, Louisiana. African American singers and musicians, such as Louis Armstrong and Duke Ellington, made jazz popular around the world.

Pianist and composer Duke Ellington and trumpeter Louis Armstrong rehearse their first recording together in a New York City recording studio in 1946.

Probably the most popular style of music to originate in the United States is rock-and-roll. A combination of rhythm and blues, gospel, and country music, rock music first became popular in the 1950s. It created a sensation all over the country and quickly spread from the United States to Europe and Asia. It remains one of the most popular musical styles throughout the world today.

Sports Many Americans watch and participate in sports activities. Sports in North America go all the way back to Native American groups who played a form of lacrosse. In the late 1800s, sports such as tennis, hiking, and golf grew in popularity. Organized team sports also began to develop a following near the end of the 1800s.

Three major sports were invented in the United States: baseball, basketball, and football. Baseball soon became the national pastime, producing sports heroes like Babe Ruth in the early 1900s. Today, baseball's popularity has spread to Japan, the Caribbean, Russia, Mexico, and Central America.

Basketball was invented in 1891 and quickly gained popularity in schools and colleges throughout the country.

 **Reading Check** **Which major sports were invented in the United States?**

 Section 2 Assessment

Key Terms
Review the key terms at the beginning of this section. Use each term in a sentence that explains its meaning.

Target Reading Skill
State the details that support the main idea on page 87 that the United States is diverse.

Comprehension and Critical Thinking
1. (a) Explain How did the United States government support white settlement in the West?

(b) Draw Inferences Why did the government send Native Americans to live on land that was not considered valuable?

(c) Analyze Information How were Native Americans at a disadvantage in their conflict with white settlers?

2. (a) Note When did American literature begin to have a distinct voice?

(b) Identify Causes When and how did American literature become more diverse?

(c) Synthesize Information How has the immigrant experience influenced American culture?

Writing Activity
Write an entry in your journal explaining how the literature and music of the United States reflect diverse cultures. When you write a journal entry, you can let your ideas flow without stopping to edit what you write.

For: An activity on Ellis Island
Visit: PHSchool.com
Web Code: lhd-4302

The Canadian Mosaic

Prepare to Read

Objectives

In this section you will
1. Find out about the people of Canada.
2. Learn about Canadian culture.

Taking Notes

As you read this section, look for details that show why Canadians consider their society to be a mosaic. Copy the concept web below and record your findings in it.

Target Reading Skill

Identify Main Ideas
Identifying main ideas can help you remember the most important ideas that you read. Sometimes, the main ideas are not stated directly. All the details in a section add up to a main idea, but you must state the main idea yourself. Carefully read the details in the two paragraphs below. Then, state the main idea of these paragraphs.

Key Terms

- **melting pot** (MELT ing paht) *n.* a country in which many cultures blend together to form a single culture
- **reserve** (rih ZURV) *n.* an area of land set aside by the government

A crowd celebrates Canada Day.

Over the years, Canada has been as welcoming to immigrants as the United States. However, one important difference between the countries is the way in which they view immigration. The United States considers itself to be a **melting pot,** or a country in which all cultures blend together to form a single culture. In this view, immigrants are encouraged to adopt American ways. Canadians view immigration in a slightly different way, as one Canadian journalist explains:

> **Canadians believe . . . in a mosaic of separate pieces, with each chunk becoming part of the whole physically but retaining its own separate identity, color, and tastes. This certainly makes for an interesting mix. Importantly, it provides Canadians with an identity peg, one major way to see themselves as different from Americans, as they must. And as they are.**
>
> —*Andrew H. Malcolm*

Find out more about Quebec's French culture.

The People of Canada

Today, Canada has a population of more than 31 million people. Many of them are immigrants. At first, Canada's leaders preferred Christian European settlers. At times, laws set limits on immigrants who were Jews, Asians, or Africans. But that has changed. Today, people of all ethnic groups move to Canada.

French Canadians Sometimes, the ties among Canadians are not as strong as those among Americans. People in the United States rarely talk about forming independent states or countries. Some Canadian groups do. French Canadians in Quebec are concerned about preserving their heritage. Special laws promote French culture and language. Street and advertising signs are written in both French and English. But many French Canadians want Quebec to become a separate country. To show their determination, they have license plates that read *Je me souviens,* or "I remember." This phrase refers to remembering their French heritage.

First Nations Canada's indigenous peoples, called First Nations, also want to preserve their culture. They are trying to fix past problems by working with existing governments.

In Canada, as in the United States, early European settlers took over the native peoples' lands. Many indigenous peoples were sent to **reserves**, or areas that the government set aside for them, similar to reservations in the United States. Others were denied equal rights. Recently, laws have been passed allowing First Nations to use their own languages in their schools.

Graph Skills

Canada is an ethnically diverse country. **Identify** Where do most immigrants to Canada come from? **Compare and Contrast** Compare the Origin of Immigrants to Canada chart here with the similar chart on page 86. How are they similar? How do they differ?

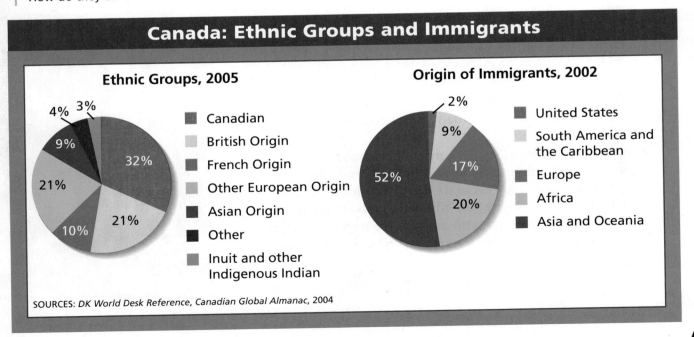

Canada: Ethnic Groups and Immigrants

Ethnic Groups, 2005

- 3% — Canadian 32%
- 4%
- 9% — British Origin
- 21% — French Origin
- 10% — Other European Origin
- 21% — Asian Origin
- Other
- Inuit and other Indigenous Indian

Origin of Immigrants, 2002

- 2% — United States
- 9% — South America and the Caribbean
- 17% — Europe
- 52% — Africa
- 20% — Asia and Oceania

SOURCES: *DK World Desk Reference, Canadian Global Almanac,* 2004

Inuits Canada's Inuits (IN oo its) lived in the Arctic for centuries as nomadic hunters and gatherers. They had excellent survival skills and were fine craftworkers. They made everything they needed using available materials, such as snow, stone, animal bones, and driftwood. Modern technology, however, allows them to buy the clothes and tools they used to make. Many Inuits have lost their traditional skills. As a result, some feel they are losing their identity.

Immigrants Because Britain and France were the first countries to colonize Canada, most Canadians were of British or French descent by the late 1800s. By the 1920s, many immigrants came from central and eastern Europe to farm the prairies in the west. But when the Depression hit in 1929, there was no longer a need for as many workers. The government restricted immigration.

After World War II, the economy began to grow again. With the need for more workers, millions of immigrants came to Canada. Many of them were from Africa, Asia, and Latin America and settled mainly in large urban areas. For example, many Asian immigrants settled in Vancouver and Toronto. Since World War II, Canada's population has more than doubled. Much of that growth is because of immigrants and their children.

✓ Reading Check **How has technology changed the way that Inuits live?**

Remembering Canada's History
The community of Chemainus, British Columbia, is famous for its collection of 35 larger-than-life historical murals. **Analyze Images** *How does this mural honor the role that the country's indigenous peoples have played in Canada's history?*

Identify Main Ideas In one sentence, state the topic that all the details in the paragraph at the left are about.

Playing hockey on an outdoor ice rink

Canadian Culture

Canada has made a special effort to encourage people to be Canadian and to express their ethnic heritage at the same time. One cultural issue does unite most Canadians: They feel that the United States has too much influence on their culture. Even today, Canadians search for ways to express their unique culture.

Canadian writers have long been famous for their work. From Lucy Maud Montgomery's *Anne of Green Gables* to writers of today, such as Margaret Atwood and Alice Munro, Canadian literature is popular throughout the world.

Canadian singers have made contributions to cultural life as well. Popular Canadian singers include Shania Twain and Céline Dion. Many singers maintain their ties to Canada even though their jobs often require them to be elsewhere. Since the 1960s, the Canadian recording industry has become a billion-dollar business.

Another billion-dollar industry in Canada is sports. Ice hockey is Canada's national sport. Every year, hockey teams from the United States and Canada compete for the Stanley Cup, a Canadian prize. Hockey serves not only as a national pastime but also as an important symbol of national identity.

 **Reading Check** **Which industries bring billions of dollars into the Canadian economy?**

Section 3 Assessment

Key Terms
Review the key terms at the beginning of this section. Use each term in a sentence that explains its meaning.

Target Reading Skill
State the main ideas in Section 3.

Comprehension and Critical Thinking
1. (a) List What are two languages spoken in Canada?

(b) Identify the Main Idea In what ways do French Canadians try to preserve their culture and language?

(c) Draw Conclusions Why do many French Canadians want Quebec to be an independent country?

2. (a) Explain How do Canadians try to express their culture?

(b) Make Generalizations Why do Canadians worry about the influence of the United States on their culture?

Writing Activity
Write a brief paragraph explaining why you think ice hockey developed in Canada.

For: An activity on immigrants
Visit: PHSchool.com
Web Code: lhd-4303

Review and Assessment

◆ Chapter Summary

Section 1: A Heritage of Diversity and Exchange

- Both the United States and Canada contain a wide variety of cultures.
- Immigrants have shaped the histories and cultures of the United States and Canada.
- The United States and Canada are important to each other for many reasons, including the cultural and economic ties that they share.

Section 2: The United States: A Nation of Immigrants

- The United States government fought many battles with Native Americans, pushing them westward.
- Millions of immigrants came to the United States to work on farms and railroads and in factories, mills, and mines.
- Diverse foods, literature, music, and sports help enrich life in the United States.

Section 3: The Canadian Mosaic

- Many immigrants come to Canada in search of a better life.
- First Nations, Inuits, and immigrants all add to the diversity of Canadian life.
- Canadians have made many contributions to the worlds of literature, music, and sports.

Quebec City

◆ Key Terms

Copy the lists of vocabulary words and definitions side by side on a sheet of paper. Then, draw a line from each term to its correct definition.

1. cultural diversity
2. cultural exchange
3. reservation
4. melting pot
5. ethnic group
6. treaty
7. reserve

A an area of land set aside for a special purpose

B an area of land set aside by the Canadian government

C a variety of cultures

D people who share a language, history, and culture

E a formal agreement

F the process in which different cultures share ideas and ways of doing things

G a country in which all cultures blend together to form a single culture

Review and Assessment (continued)

◆ Comprehension and Critical Thinking

8. (a) Explain Why did the United States and Canada first encourage immigration?
(b) Identify Causes Why do the United States and Canada continue to attract immigrants today?
(c) Identify Frame of Reference Why do some immigrants find it challenging to balance their cultural heritage with their new environment?

9. (a) Recall How do Canadians contribute to Florida's economy?
(b) Predict In what ways would Florida's economy be affected if these tourists vacationed somewhere else?

10. (a) Recall Why did most of the first wave of immigrants adapt fairly easily to life in the United States?
(b) Draw Conclusions Why was the second wave of immigrants discriminated against when the first wave of immigrants largely was not?

11. (a) Explain How does American society influence American music?
(b) Analyze What is it about jazz or rock-and-roll music that makes them uniquely American?

12. (a) Explain How are First Nations preserving their culture?
(b) Compare and Contrast Why is Canada characterized as a mosaic rather than as a melting pot?
(c) Identify Point of View Why is it important for Canadians to see themselves as different from Americans?

◆ Skills Practice

Using Graphic Organizers In the Skills for Life activity in this chapter, you learned how to use graphic organizers. You also learned that graphic organizers put information into a visual form.

Review the steps you followed to learn this skill. Then reread Cultural Patterns Today, beginning on page 78. Create a concept web about peoples' reasons for choosing to immigrate to the United States and Canada.

◆ Writing Activity: Math

In pairs or teams, research the different ethnic or cultural groups that are represented in your state. Calculate the results in percentage form. Then display the information as a circle graph. Write a brief summary of your findings.

MAP MASTER™
Skills Activity

Place Location For each Native American group listed below, write the letter from the map that shows its location.

1. Miami
2. Chippewa
3. Cherokee
4. Iroquois
5. Pueblo
6. Cheyenne
7. Comanche
8. Huron

Go Online
PHSchool.com Use Web Code lhp-4333 for an interactive map.

Native American Groups

Standardized Test Prep

Test-Taking Tips

Some questions on standardized tests ask you to analyze a passage to find a main idea. Read the passage below. Then follow the tips to answer the sample question.

> One Toronto radio station broadcasts in thirty languages. . . . In many Vancouver neighborhoods the street signs are in . . . English and Chinese. Toronto's city government routinely prepares its annual property tax notices in six languages: English, French, Chinese, Italian, Greek, and Portuguese.

TIP Before reading the answer choices, think of a main idea that would cover each sentence in the passage. Then match your idea to one of the answer choices.

Pick the letter that best answers the question.

What is the main idea of this passage?

A Toronto's city government prepares tax notices in many languages.

B The Chinese are an important ethnic group in Toronto.

C Many people in Toronto are bilingual, or speak two languages.

D Toronto has a diverse mix of people and ethnic groups.

TIP Read all of the answer choices before making a final choice. You can't be sure you have the right answer until you have read each one.

Think It Through You can rule out answer A, because it applies only to one of the sentences in the passage. You can rule out answer B because though it may be true, the Chinese are only one of the ethnic groups mentioned in the passage. Both answers C and D sound like they might be correct. Read answer C carefully. It isn't right because though the passage describes many languages, it does not say that most people in Toronto are bilingual. The correct answer is D.

Practice Questions

Use the tips above and other tips in this book to help you answer the following questions.

1. When two groups of people share ideas and ways of doing things, they are practicing
   A trade.
   B cultural exchange.
   C cultural diversity.
   D immigration.

2. What kind of standard of living do the United States and Canada have?
   A Both countries have low standards of living.
   B Both countries have high standards of living.
   C The United States has a high standard of living, while Canada's is low.
   D Canada has a high standard of living, while that of the United States is low.

3. Which group in Canada often talks about forming an independent country?
   A the Chippewa
   B the British
   C the French Canadians
   D the Inuit

Read the passage below, and then answer the question that follows.

> Culture here has been shaped by a history of British colonization. It has also been shaped by immigrants who have come here from all over the world, bringing their cultures with them. Music, literature, and sports are important parts of the culture.

4. Based on what you have read, which country could this passage be describing?
   A either the United States or Canada
   B the United States
   C Canada
   D neither the United States nor Canada

Use Web Code **lha-4303** for a **Chapter 3 self-test**.

4 The United States

Chapter Preview

This chapter will introduce you to the four regions of the United States.

Country Databank
The Country Databank provides data on each of the fifty states.

Section 1
The Northeast
An Urban Center

Section 2
The South
The Growth of Industry

Section 3
The Midwest
Leaving the Farm

Section 4
The West
Using and Preserving Resources

**Target
Reading Skill**

Comparison and Contrast In this chapter you will focus on using comparison and contrast to help you sort out and analyze information.

▶ Members of the California National Guard display an American flag.

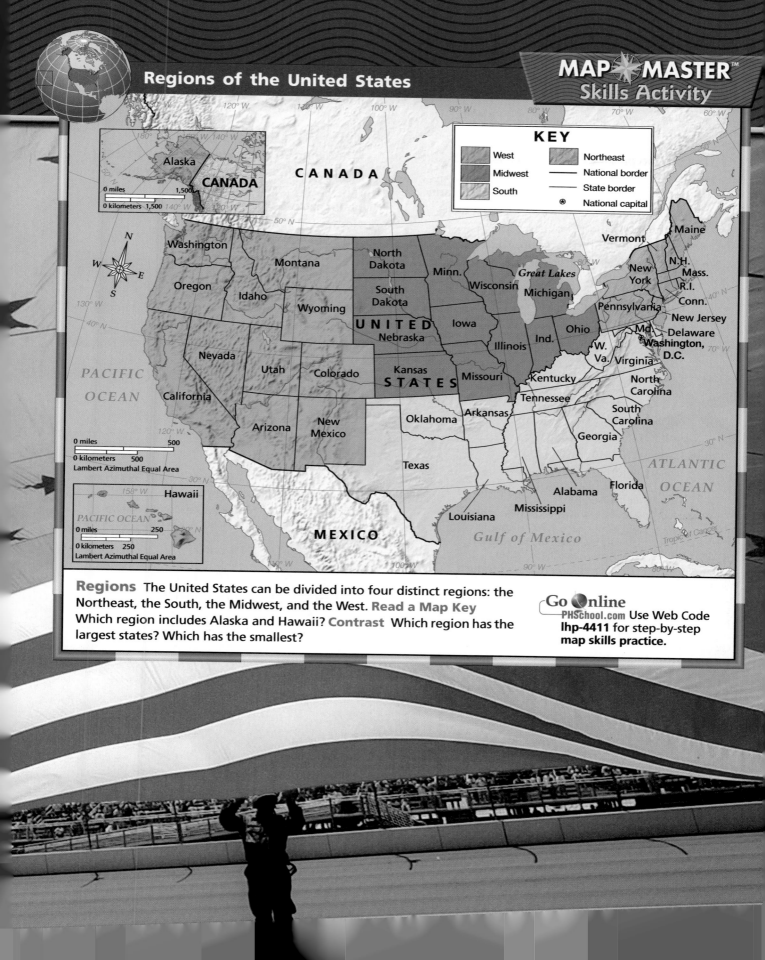

Regions of the United States

MAP MASTER™
Skills Activity

KEY

- West
- Midwest
- South
- Northeast
- National border
- State border
- ⊛ National capital

Regions The United States can be divided into four distinct regions: the Northeast, the South, the Midwest, and the West. **Read a Map Key** Which region includes Alaska and Hawaii? **Contrast** Which region has the largest states? Which has the smallest?

Go Online
PHSchool.com Use Web Code
lhp-4411 for step-by-step
map skills practice.

Guide for Reading

This section provides an introduction to the fifty states that make up the United States.

- Look at the map on the previous page, and then read the information below to learn about each state.
- Analyze the data to compare the states.
- What are the characteristics that most of the states share?
- What are some of the key differences among the states?

Viewing the Video Overview

View the World Studies Video Overview to learn more about each of the states. As you watch, answer this question:

- What are the four major regions of the United States, and what natural resources does each region contribute to the economy of the country?

DISCOVERY CHANNEL SCHOOL Video
Explore the geography of the United States.

Alabama

Year of Statehood	1819
Capital	Montgomery
Land Area	50,744 sq mi; 131,427 sq km
Population	4,447,100
Ethnic Group(s)	71.1% white; 26.0% African American; 1.7% Hispanic; 0.7% Asian; 0.5% Native American; 0.7% other
Agriculture	cotton, greenhouse products, peanuts
Industry	pulp, paper, chemicals, electronics

Alaska

Year of Statehood	1959
Capital	Juneau
Land Area	571,951 sq mi; 1,481,353 sq km
Population	626,932
Ethnic Group(s)	69.3% white; 15.6% Native American; 4.1% Hispanic; 4.0% Asian; 3.5% African American; 2.1% other
Agriculture	greenhouse products, barley, oats
Industry	petroleum, tourism, fishing

Geological formations of limestone, called tufa, in Mono Lake, California

Arizona

Year of Statehood	1912
Capital	Phoenix
Land Area	113,635 sq mi; 294,315 sq km
Population	5,130,632
Ethnic Group(s)	75.5% white; 25.3% Hispanic; 5.0% Native American; 3.1% African American; 1.8% Asian; 11.7% other
Agriculture	cotton, lettuce, cauliflower
Industry	manufacturing, construction, tourism

Arkansas

Year of Statehood	1836
Capital	Little Rock
Land Area	52,068 sq mi; 134,856 sq km
Population	2,673,400
Ethnic Group(s)	80.0% white; 15.7% African American; 3.2% Hispanic; 0.8% Asian; 0.8% Native American; 1.6% other
Agriculture	poultry, cattle, rice, soybeans
Industry	manufacturing, agriculture, tourism, forestry

California

Year of Statehood	1850
Capital	Sacramento
Land Area	155,959 sq mi; 403,934 sq km
Population	33,871,648
Ethnic Group(s)	59.5% white; 32.4% Hispanic; 10.9% Asian; 6.7% African American; 1.0% Native American; 17.1% other
Agriculture	poultry, cattle, milk
Industry	agriculture, tourism, apparel

Colorado

Year of Statehood	1876
Capital	Denver
Land Area	103,718 sq mi; 268,630 sq km
Population	4,301,261
Ethnic Group(s)	82.8% white; 17.1% Hispanic; 3.8% African American; 2.2% Asian; 1.0% Native American; 7.3% other
Agriculture	poultry, cattle, corn, wheat
Industry	manufacturing, construction

Introducing **The United States**

Connecticut

Year of Statehood	1788
Capital	Hartford
Land Area	4,845 sq mi; 12,549 sq km
Population	3,405,565
Ethnic Group(s)	81.6% white; 9.1% African American; 9.4% Hispanic; 2.4% Asian; 0.3% Native American; 4.3% other
Agriculture	nursery stock, mushrooms, vegetables, sweet corn
Industry	manufacturing, retail trade, government

Delaware

Year of Statehood	1787
Capital	Dover
Land Area	1,954 sq mi; 5,061 sq km
Population	783,600
Ethnic Group(s)	74.6% white; 19.2% African American; 4.8% Hispanic; 2.1% Asian; 0.3% Native American
Agriculture	poultry, soybeans, potatoes, corn
Industry	chemicals, agriculture, finance

An alligator at Everglades National Park, Florida

Florida

Year of Statehood	1845
Capital	Tallahassee
Land Area	53,927 sq mi; 139,671 sq km
Population	15,982,378
Ethnic Group(s)	78.0% white; 16.8% Hispanic; 14.6% African American; 1.7% Asian; 0.3% Native American; 3.1% other
Agriculture	poultry, cattle, citrus fruits
Industry	tourism, agriculture, manufacturing

Georgia

Year of Statehood	1788
Capital	Atlanta
Land Area	57,906 sq mi; 149,977 sq km
Population	8,186,453
Ethnic Group(s)	65.1% white; 28.7% African American; 5.3% Hispanic; 2.1% Asian; 0.3% Native American; 2.5% other
Agriculture	poultry, cattle, peanuts, cotton
Industry	services, manufacturing, retail trade

Hawaii

Year of Statehood	1959
Capital	Honolulu
Land Area	6,423 sq mi; 16,636 sq km
Population	1,211,537
Ethnic Group(s)	41.6% Asian; 24.3% white; 9.4% Native Hawaiian or Pacific Islander; 7.2% Hispanic; 1.8% African American; 0.3% Native American; 1.3% other
Agriculture	sugar, pineapples
Industry	tourism, defense, sugar

Idaho

Year of Statehood	1890
Capital	Boise
Land Area	82,747 sq mi; 214,315 sq km
Population	1,293,953
Ethnic Group(s)	91.0% white; 7.9% Hispanic; 1.4% Native American; 0.9% Asian; 0.4% African American; 4.3% other
Agriculture	poultry, cattle, potatoes
Industry	manufacturing, agriculture, tourism

Illinois

Year of Statehood	1818
Capital	Springfield
Land Area	55,584 sq mi; 143,963 sq km
Population	12,419,293
Ethnic Group(s)	73.5% white; 15.1% African American; 12.3% Hispanic; 3.4% Asian; 0.2% Native American; 5.8% other
Agriculture	livestock, corn, soybeans, wheat
Industry	services, manufacturing, travel

Indiana

Year of Statehood	1816
Capital	Indianapolis
Land Area	35,867 sq mi; 92,896 sq km
Population	6,080,485
Ethnic Group(s)	87.5% white; 8.4% African American; 3.5% Hispanic; 1.0% Asian; 0.3% Native American; 1.6% other
Agriculture	livestock, corn, soybeans, wheat
Industry	manufacturing, services, agriculture

Iowa

Year of Statehood	1846
Capital	Des Moines
Land Area	55,869 sq mi; 144,701 sq km
Population	2,926,324
Ethnic Group(s)	93.9% white; 2.8% Hispanic; 2.1% African American; 1.3% Asian; 0.3% Native American; 1.3% other
Agriculture	livestock, poultry, grain, corn
Industry	agriculture, communications, construction

Winner of the Indianapolis 500 race in Indiana

Introducing **The United States**

Kansas

Year of Statehood	1861
Capital	Topeka
Land Area	81,815 sq mi; 211,901 sq km
Population	2,688,418
Ethnic Group(s)	86.1% white; 7.0% Hispanic; 5.7% African American; 1.7% Asian; 0.9% Native American; 3.4% other
Agriculture	livestock, poultry, wheat, sorghum
Industry	manufacturing, finance, insurance

Kentucky

Year of Statehood	1792
Capital	Frankfort
Land Area	39,728 sq mi; 10,896 sq km
Population	4,041,769
Ethnic Group(s)	90.1% white; 7.3% African American; 1.5% Hispanic; 0.7% Asian; 0.2% Native American; 0.6% other
Agriculture	poultry, cattle, tobacco, corn
Industry	manufacturing, services, finance

Louisiana

Year of Statehood	1812
Capital	Baton Rouge
Land Area	43,562 sq mi; 112,826 sq km
Population	4,468,976
Ethnic Group(s)	63.9% white; 32.5% African American; 2.4% Hispanic; 1.2% Asian; 0.6% Native American; 0.7% other
Agriculture	poultry, soybeans, sugar cane
Industry	wholesale and retail trade, tourism

Maine

Year of Statehood	1820
Capital	Augusta
Land Area	30,862 sq mi; 76,933 sq km
Population	1,274,923
Ethnic Group(s)	96.9% white; 0.7% Asian; 0.7% Hispanic; 0.6% Native American; 0.5% African American; 0.2% other
Agriculture	poultry, potatoes, aquaculture
Industry	manufacturing, agriculture, fishing

Maryland

Year of Statehood	1788
Capital	Annapolis
Land Area	9,774 sq mi; 25,315 sq km
Population	5,296,486
Ethnic Group(s)	64.0% white; 27.9% African American; 4.3% Hispanic; 4.0% Asian; 0.3% Native American; 1.8% other
Agriculture	poultry, greenhouse and nursery products
Industry	manufacturing, biotechnology

Massachusetts

Year of Statehood	1788
Capital	Boston
Land Area	7,840 sq mi; 20,306 sq km
Population	6,349,097
Ethnic Group(s)	84.5% white; 6.8% Hispanic; 5.4% African American; 3.8% Asian; 0.2% Native American; 3.7% other
Agriculture	cranberries, greenhouse products, vegetables
Industry	services, trade, manufacturing

Michigan

Year of Statehood	1837
Capital	Lansing
Land Area	56,804 sq mi; 147,122 sq km
Population	9,938,444
Ethnic Group(s)	80.2% white; 14.2% African American; 3.3% Hispanic; 1.8% Asian; 0.6% Native American; 1.3% other
Agriculture	poultry, corn, wheat, soybeans
Industry	manufacturing, services, tourism, agriculture

Minnesota

Year of Statehood	1858
Capital	St. Paul
Land Area	79,610 sq mi; 206,190 sq km
Population	4,919,479
Ethnic Group(s)	89.4% white; 3.5% African American; 2.9% Asian; 2.9% Hispanic; 1.1% Native American; 1.3% other
Agriculture	livestock, poultry, corn, soybeans
Industry	agribusiness, forest products, mining

Mississippi

Year of Statehood	1817
Capital	Jackson
Land Area	46,907 sq mi; 121,489 sq km
Population	2,844,658
Ethnic Group(s)	61.4% white; 36.3% African American; 1.4% Hispanic; 0.7% Asian; 0.4% Native American; 0.5% other
Agriculture	cattle, poultry, cotton, rice
Industry	warehousing/distribution, services

Missouri

Year of Statehood	1821
Capital	Jefferson City
Land Area	68,886 sq mi; 178,415 sq km
Population	5,595,211
Ethnic Group(s)	84.9% white; 11.2% African American; 2.1% Hispanic; 1.1% Asian; 0.4% Native American; 0.9% other
Agriculture	livestock, poultry, soybeans, corn
Industry	agriculture, manufacturing, aerospace

Detroit, Michigan

Introducing **The United States**

Horses grazing in Montana

Montana

Year of Statehood	1889
Capital	Helena
Land Area	145,552 sq mi; 376,980 sq km
Population	902,195
Ethnic Group(s)	90.6% white; 6.2% Native American; 2.0% Hispanic; 0.5% Asian; 0.3% African American; 0.7% other
Agriculture	cattle, wheat, barley, sugar beets
Industry	agriculture, timber, mining, tourism

Nebraska

Year of Statehood	1867
Capital	Lincoln
Land Area	76,872 sq mi; 199,098 sq km
Population	1,711,263
Ethnic Group(s)	89.6% white; 5.5% Hispanic; 4.0% African American; 1.3% Asian; 0.9% Native American; 2.8% other
Agriculture	livestock, poultry, corn, sorghum
Industry	agriculture, manufacturing

Nevada

Year of Statehood	1864
Capital	Carson City
Land Area	109,826 sq mi; 284,449 sq km
Population	1,998,257
Ethnic Group(s)	75.2% white; 19.7% Hispanic; 6.8% African American; 4.5% Asian; 1.3% Native American; 8.4% other
Agriculture	hay, alfalfa seed, potatoes
Industry	tourism, mining, manufacturing

New Hampshire

Year of Statehood	1788
Capital	Concord
Land Area	8,968 sq mi; 23,227 sq km
Population	1,235,786
Ethnic Group(s)	96.0% white; 1.7% Hispanic; 1.3% Asian; 0.7% African American; 0.2% Native American; 0.6% other
Agriculture	dairy products, nursery and greenhouse products
Industry	tourism, manufacturing

New Jersey

Year of Statehood	1787
Capital	Trenton
Land Area	7,417 sq mi; 19,210 sq km
Population	8,414,350
Ethnic Group(s)	72.6% white; 13.6% African American; 13.3% Hispanic; 5.7% Asian; 0.2% Native American; 5.4% other
Agriculture	poultry, nursery and greenhouse products, tomatoes
Industry	pharmaceuticals, telecommunications

New Mexico

Year of Statehood	1912
Capital	Santa Fe
Land Area	121,356 sq mi; 314,312 sq km
Population	1,819,046
Ethnic Group(s)	66.8% white; 42.1% Hispanic; 9.5% Native American; 1.9% African American; 1.1% Asian; 17.1% other
Agriculture	cattle, hay, onions, chilies
Industry	government, services, trade

New York

Year of Statehood	1788
Capital	Albany
Land Area	47,214 sq mi; 122,284 sq km
Population	18,976,457
Ethnic Group(s)	67.9% white; 15.9% African American; 15.1% Hispanic; 5.5% Asian; 0.4% Native American; 7.1% other
Agriculture	cattle, poultry, apples, grapes
Industry	manufacturing, finance, communications

North Carolina

Year of Statehood	1789
Capital	Raleigh
Land Area	48,711 sq mi; 126,161 sq km
Population	8,049,313
Ethnic Group(s)	72.1% white; 21.6% African American; 4.7% Hispanic; 1.2% Native American; 2.3% other
Agriculture	livestock, poultry, tobacco, cotton
Industry	manufacturing, agriculture, tourism

The Exploris museum in Raleigh, North Carolina

Introducing **The United States**

North Dakota

Year of Statehood	1889
Capital	Bismarck
Land Area	68,976 sq mi; 178,648 sq km
Population	642,200
Ethnic Group(s)	92.5% white; 4.9% Native American; 1.2% Hispanic; 0.6% African American; 0.6% Asian; 0.4% other
Agriculture	cattle, spring wheat, durum, barley
Industry	agriculture, mining, tourism

Ohio

Year of Statehood	1803
Capital	Columbus
Land Area	40,948 sq mi; 106,055 sq km
Population	11,353,140
Ethnic Group(s)	85.0% white; 11.5% African American; 1.9% Hispanic; 1.2% Asian; 0.2% Native American; 0.8% other
Agriculture	livestock, poultry, corn, hay
Industry	manufacturing, trade, services

Oklahoma

Year of Statehood	1907
Capital	Oklahoma City
Land Area	68,667 sq mi; 177,848 sq km
Population	3,450,654
Ethnic Group(s)	76.2% white; 7.9% Native American; 7.6% African American; 5.2% Hispanic; 1.4% Asian; 4.6% other
Agriculture	livestock, poultry, wheat, cotton
Industry	manufacturing, mineral and energy exploration

Oregon

Year of Statehood	1859
Capital	Salem
Land Area	95,997 sq mi; 248,632 sq km
Population	3,421,399
Ethnic Group(s)	86.6% white; 8.0% Hispanic; 1.6% African American; 3.0% Asian; 1.3% Native American; 4.4% other
Agriculture	cattle, poultry, greenhouse products
Industry	manufacturing, services, trade, finance

Pennsylvania

Year of Statehood	1787
Capital	Harrisburg
Land Area	44,817 sq mi; 116,076 sq km
Population	12,281,054
Ethnic Group(s)	85.4% white; 10.0% African American; 3.2% Hispanic; 1.8% Asian; 0.1% Native American; 1.5% other
Agriculture	livestock, poultry, corn, hay
Industry	agribusiness, manufacturing, health care

Rhode Island

Year of Statehood	1790
Capital	Providence
Land Area	1,045 sq mi; 2,707 sq km
Population	1,048,319
Ethnic Group(s)	85.0% white; 8.7% Hispanic; 4.5% African American; 2.3% Asian; 0.5% Native American; 5.1% other
Agriculture	nursery products, turf, vegetables
Industry	services, manufacturing

South Carolina

Year of Statehood	1788
Capital	Columbia
Land Area	30,109 sq mi; 77,982 sq km
Population	4,012,012
Ethnic Group(s)	67.2% white; 29.5% African American; 2.4% Hispanic; 0.9% Asian; 0.3% Native American; 1.0% other
Agriculture	poultry, tobacco, cotton, soybeans
Industry	tourism, agriculture, manufacturing

South Dakota

Year of Statehood	1889
Capital	Pierre
Land Area	75,885 sq mi; 196,542 sq km
Population	754,844
Ethnic Group(s)	88.7% white; 8.3% Native American; 1.4% Hispanic; 0.6% African American; 0.6% Asian; 0.5% other
Agriculture	livestock, poultry, corn, soybeans
Industry	agriculture, services, manufacturing

Congaree Swamp National Monument, South Carolina

Tennessee

Year of Statehood	1796
Capital	Nashville
Land Area	41,217 sq mi; 106,752 sq km
Population	5,689,283
Ethnic Group(s)	80.2% white; 16.4% African American; 2.2% Hispanic; 1.0% Asian; 0.3% Native American; 1.0% other
Agriculture	cattle, poultry, tobacco, cotton
Industry	manufacturing, trade, services

Texas

Year of Statehood	1845
Capital	Austin
Land Area	261,797 sq mi; 678,054 sq km
Population	20,851,820
Ethnic Group(s)	71.0% white; 32.0% Hispanic; 11.5% African American; 2.7% Asian; 0.6% Native American; 11.8% other
Agriculture	livestock, poultry, cotton
Industry	manufacturing, trade, oil and gas extraction

Introducing **The United States**

Utah

Year of Statehood	1896
Capital	Salt Lake City
Land Area	82,144 sq mi; 212,753 sq km
Population	2,233,169
Ethnic Group(s)	89.2% white; 9.0% Hispanic; 1.7% Asian; 1.3% Native American; 0.8% African American; 4.9% other
Agriculture	poultry, hay, corn, wheat, barley
Industry	services, trade, manufacturing

Vermont

Year of Statehood	1791
Capital	Montpelier
Land Area	9,250 sq mi; 23,958 sq km
Population	608,827
Ethnic Group(s)	96.8% white; 0.9% Asian; 0.5% African American; 0.4% Native American; 1.2% other
Agriculture	dairy products, apples, maple syrup
Industry	manufacturing, tourism, agriculture

Rower in Seattle, Washington

Virginia

Year of Statehood	1788
Capital	Richmond
Land Area	39,594 sq mi; 102,548 sq km
Population	7,078,515
Ethnic Group(s)	72.3% white; 19.6% African American; 0.7% Hispanic; 3.7% Asian; 0.3% Native American; 0.1% Native Hawaiian or Pacific Islander; 2.0% other
Agriculture	cattle, poultry, tobacco
Industry	services, trade, government

Washington

Year of Statehood	1889
Capital	Olympia
Land Area	66,544 sq mi; 172,349 sq km
Population	5,894,121
Ethnic Group(s)	81.8% white; 7.5% Hispanic; 5.5% Asian; 3.2% African American; 1.6% Native American; 4.3% other
Agriculture	cattle, poultry, apples, potatoes
Industry	technology, aerospace, biotechnology

West Virginia

Wisconsin

Year of Statehood	1863
Capital	Charleston
Land Area	24,078 sq mi; 62,362 sq km
Population	1,808,344
Ethnic Group(s)	95.0% white; 3.2% African American; 0.7% Hispanic; 0.5% Asian; 0.2% Native American; 0.2% other
Agriculture	apples, peaches, hay, tobacco
Industry	manufacturing, services, mining

Year of Statehood	1848
Capital	Madison
Land Area	54,310 sq mi; 140,663 sq km
Population	5,363,675
Ethnic Group(s)	88.9% white; 5.7% African American; 3.6% Hispanic; 1.7% Asian; 0.9% Native American; 1.6% other
Agriculture	cattle, poultry, corn, hay
Industry	services, manufacturing, trade

Wyoming

Year of Statehood	1890
Capital	Cheyenne
Land Area	97,100 sq mi; 251,489 sq km
Population	493,782
Ethnic Group(s)	92.1% white; 6.4% Hispanic; 2.3% Native American; 0.8% African American; 0.6% Asian; 2.6% other
Agriculture	cattle, wheat, beans, barley
Industry	mineral extraction, oil, natural gas, tourism and recreation

SOURCE: U.S. Census; *World Almanac,* 2003
Note: Percentages may not total 100% due to rounding. The Hispanic population may be any race and is dispersed among racial categories.

Wisconsin dairy farm

Assessment

Comprehension and Critical Thinking

1. Compare and Contrast Compare the physical sizes and the population sizes of California and Rhode Island.

2. Draw Conclusions Are there characteristics that most of the states share? Explain.

3. Compare and Contrast What are some key differences among the states?

4. Categorize What are the major products of the South and the Midwest?

5. Make Generalizations Based on the data, make a generalization about industry in the United States.

6. Make a Timeline Create a timeline showing the year of statehood for 15 states.

Keeping Current

Access the **DK World Desk Reference Online** at **PHSchool.com** for up-to-date information about the United States.

Go Online
PHSchool.com
Web Code: lhe-4401

The Northeast
An Urban Center

Prepare to Read

Objectives

In this section, you will
1. Learn how the large cities of the Northeast contribute to the economy of the United States.
2. Find out how the Northeast has been a port of entry for many immigrants.

Taking Notes

As you read this section, look for details about Boston, Philadelphia, and New York City. Copy the chart below, and record your findings in it.

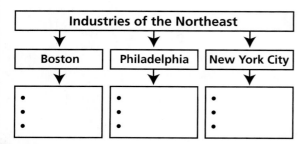

Industries of the Northeast
↓ ↓ ↓
Boston | Philadelphia | New York City

Target Reading Skill

Compare and Contrast Comparing and contrasting can help you sort out and analyze information. When you compare, you examine the similarities between things. When you contrast, you look at the differences between things. As you read this section, compare and contrast the large cities of the Northeast.

Key Terms

- **commute** (kuh MYOOT) *v.* to travel to work
- **megalopolis** (meg uh LAHP uh lis) *n.* a number of cities and suburbs that blend into one very large urban area
- **population density** (pahp yuh LAY shun DEN suh tee) *n.* the average number of people per square mile or square kilometer

Rush hour in a New York City subway station

For more than a century, life in New York City has been crowded. One hundred years ago, horse-drawn carriages caused traffic jams. Today, more than 3 million riders squeeze into New York's subway cars every day. Others travel the many miles of bus lines or catch one of the city's 12,000 taxis. And many people drive their own cars through the city's busy streets.

New York City is not unique. Washington, D.C., Boston, Massachusetts, and Philadelphia, Pennsylvania, are also crowded. In these big cities, thousands of people **commute,** or travel to work, each day. Many drive to work from suburbs that are far from the city's center. Even people who live in the city must travel from one area to another to work.

A Region of Cities

A nearly unbroken chain of cities runs from Boston to New York to Washington, D.C. This coastal region of the Northeast is a megalopolis (meg uh LAHP uh lis). A **megalopolis** is a region where the cities and suburbs have grown so close together that they form one big urban area. Find this area on the map below.

The Northeast is the most densely populated region of the United States. **Population density** is the average number of people per square mile (or square kilometer). The population density of New Jersey is 10 times greater than the density of Kentucky.

The Northeast's economy is based on its cities. Many were founded in colonial times, along rivers or near the Atlantic Ocean. These cities began as transportation and trade centers. Today, manufacturing, finance, communications, and government employ millions of urban northeasterners.

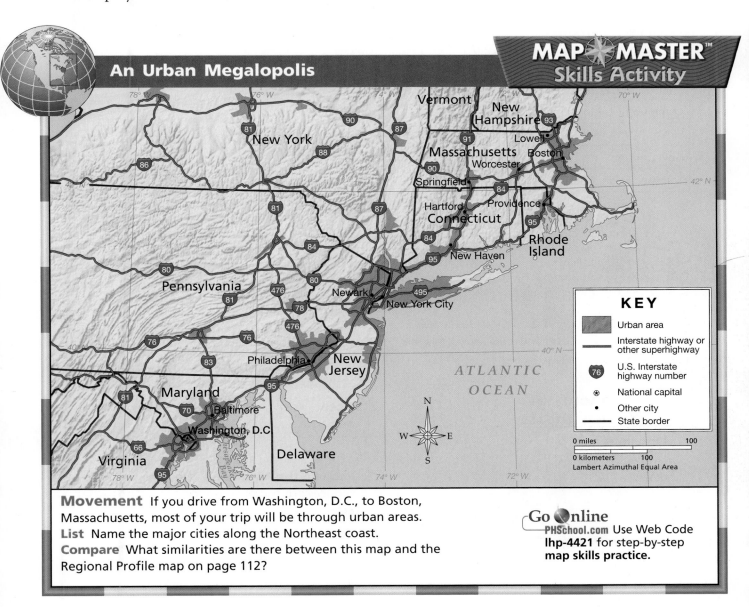

An Urban Megalopolis

MAP MASTER™
Skills Activity

KEY

Urban area

Interstate highway or other superhighway

U.S. Interstate highway number

National capital

Other city

State border

0 miles 100
0 kilometers 100
Lambert Azimuthal Equal Area

Movement If you drive from Washington, D.C., to Boston, Massachusetts, most of your trip will be through urban areas.
List Name the major cities along the Northeast coast.
Compare What similarities are there between this map and the Regional Profile map on page 112?

Go Online
PHSchool.com Use Web Code
lhp-4421 for step-by-step
map skills practice.

The Northeast

Although it is the nation's smallest region, the Northeast is the most heavily populated region in the United States. It has many large and old cities. New York is the center of international trade and finance, while Philadelphia was the birthplace of the Declaration of Independence and the United States Constitution. With so many people living in such a small area, services are an important part of the Northeast's economy. As you study the graphs and map, think about how population density affects an area's economy.

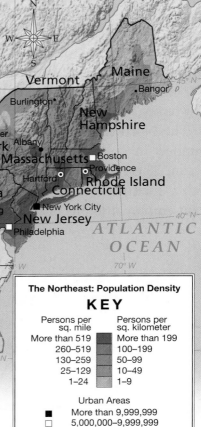

The Northeast: Population Density

KEY

Persons per sq. mile	Persons per sq. kilometer
More than 519	More than 199
260–519	100–199
130–259	50–99
25–129	10–49
1–24	1–9

Urban Areas
- ■ More than 9,999,999
- □ 5,000,000–9,999,999
- ◉ 1,000,000–4,999,999
- • 500,000–999,999
- · Less than 500,000
- — National border
- — State border

Types of Services

Community, business, personal
Financial, insurance, real estate
Government
Transportation, utilities, communication

Northeast Population Density, 2000

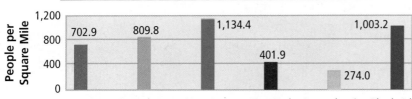

People per Square Mile

- Connecticut 702.9
- Massachusetts 809.8
- New Jersey 1,134.4
- New York 401.9
- Pennsylvania 274.0
- Rhode Island 1,003.2

SOURCE: *New York Times Almanac,* 2006

Economy of the Northeast

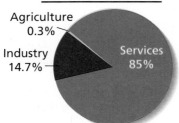

- Agriculture 0.3%
- Industry 14.7%
- Services 85%

SOURCE: Bureau of Economic Analysis

Map and Chart Skills

1. **Note** Which state has the highest population density overall?
2. **Infer** Why did most major northeastern cities develop along the coast?
3. **Explore the Main Idea** Why do you think services are the most important economic activity in this region?

Use Web Code **lhe-4411** to access the **DK World Desk Reference Online.**

Boston In colonial times, the city of Boston was called the "hub of the universe." Boston remains an important city in the Northeast. It is a city filled with history. The American Revolution began when British troops marched from Boston to Concord in 1775. You can still visit buildings that date from before the American Revolution, including Paul Revere's house, which is the oldest building in the downtown area. Yet you will find that Boston is a very modern city, too.

The Boston area is known worldwide for its leading research centers, including dozens of colleges and universities. Cambridge (KAYM brij) is the home of Harvard, which was founded in 1636 and is the oldest university in the United States. Cambridge is also home to the Massachusetts Institute of Technology (MIT).

Boston is noted for its medical, science, and technology centers as well. Some of the best medical schools and hospitals in the country are located in Boston. Many medical firsts took place here, including the use of anesthesia (an es THEE zhuh) during surgery. Boston's universities and scientific companies often work together to carry out research and to design new products.

Boston's outdoor market, Haymarket, is one of the city's most famous attractions.

Philadelphia Many people consider Philadelphia to be the "cradle of the nation" because, like Boston, it was an important city in our nation's early history. It was once the capital of the country. It was in Philadelphia that America's founders wrote the Declaration of Independence and the Constitution. By the late 1700s, Philadelphia had become the political, financial, and commercial center of the nation. Home to the country's leading seaport until it was surpassed by New York's in the 1820s, Philadelphia quickly became a major shipbuilding center as well.

Today, Philadelphia is an industrial center. It is located on the Delaware River. Important land and water transportation routes pass through there. Ships, trucks, and trains bring in raw materials from other parts of Pennsylvania and from all over the world. Many factories process food, produce medical supplies, and manufacture chemicals. Hundreds of products are then shipped out for sale. In addition, Philadelphia has become a center of the health care industry, due to its several medical, dental, and pharmacology schools.

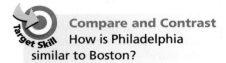

DISCOVERY CHANNEL SCHOOL Video
Learn about the Minutemen in the American Revolution.

Target Skill
Compare and Contrast
How is Philadelphia similar to Boston?

The Skyscraper

After the Civil War, the United States grew rapidly. People streamed into the cities to fill jobs in new factories and offices. To create more office and living space, architects used new technology to build taller and taller structures. By the 1930s, the skylines of all major American cities were dominated by tall skyscrapers. The Empire State Building, shown at right, was built in 1931. At 1,252 feet (382 meters), it is the tallest skyscraper in New York City.

Rockefeller Center, New York City
Most modern skyscrapers wear a glass skin of windows.

High-speed elevators travel as fast as 1,400 feet (426 meters) a minute.

The outside of the building is covered with ten million bricks.

60,000 tons of steel were used to make the skeleton that supports the building.

About ten minutes is all it takes for the fittest runners to race up the 1,576 steps from the lobby to the 86th floor, in the Fleet Empire State Run-Up.

More than 200 steel and concrete piles support the 365,000-ton building.

Construction workers
Workers rest during the construction of New York City's Chrysler Building. Built in 1930, the building's owner hoped it would be the tallest in the world—but even taller buildings were soon built.

ANALYZING IMAGES
How does the structure of this building allow more offices in less space?

New York City The largest, wealthiest, and most influential city in the United States is New York City. More than 8 million people live there, making it one of the 10 largest cities in the world. The city covers an area of about 300 square miles (800 square kilometers) on islands and the mainland around the mouth of the Hudson River. Tunnels and bridges connect the various parts of the city.

New York is the center of fashion, publishing, advertising, and the arts in the United States. New York's Broadway is known for its plays and musicals, Fifth Avenue for its shopping, and Wall Street for its finance.

New York City is our nation's "money capital." About 350,000 New Yorkers work for banks and other financial institutions. The headquarters of many of the country's wealthiest corporations are in New York. The New York Stock Exchange is on Wall Street. Noted for its skyscrapers, New York City's skyline is recognized by people around the world.

On September 11, 2001, the city became a target of terrorists, who crashed two planes into the towers of the World Trade Center. The World Trade Center held government agencies and businesses that were involved in international trade. Nearly 3,000 people were killed as a result of the attack.

View From the Top
More than 30 million tourists visit New York City each year. Among the city's biggest tourist attractions are the theaters on 42nd Street (lower photo) and Central Park, which lies in the midst of a maze of skyscrapers (upper photo).
Identify Effects *What effect does tourism have on New York's economy?*

✓ Reading Check **Which city is considered the financial capital of the United States?**

Ports of Entry

Louis Waldman came to the United States in 1909, when he was seventeen years old. He landed at the Ellis Island immigration station in New York harbor:

> ❝Behind me was the bustling harbor with its innumerable boats, the sight of which made me seasick all over again. Facing me were the tall buildings of lower Manhattan, buildings which were more magnificent and higher than any I had ever imagined, even in my wildest dreams. . . .❞
>
> —*Russian immigrant Louis Waldman*

From 1892 to 1954, millions of immigrants came to the United States through Ellis Island. Today, Ellis Island is a national monument.

Although New York was the main port of entry, Boston and Philadelphia were also important gateways for immigrants. In the 1700s, more German immigrants entered the country through Philadelphia than through any other port. In the 1800s, many Irish immigrants entered through both Philadelphia and Boston.

After arriving in these port cities, many immigrants stayed and built new lives. Today, all three cities are rich in ethnic diversity. To get a real sense of this ethnic diversity, just look at the names in the phonebooks of these big cities.

✓ **Reading Check** **Where is Ellis Island located?**

Immigrants arrive at Ellis Island in 1920.

Section 1 Assessment

Key Terms
Review the key terms at the beginning of this section. Use each term in a sentence that explains its meaning.

Target Reading Skill
What are two ways that the cities of the Northeast are similar? What are two ways that they are different?

Comprehension and Critical Thinking
1. (a) Recall How many people live in New York City?

(b) Compare How does the population density of the Northeast compare with densities of other regions of the country?

(c) Cause and Effect How does population density affect the ways people live and work?

2. (a) Recall What city was the main port of entry for European immigrants in the 1800s?

(b) Identify the Main Idea Why might immigrants have chosen to live in the Northeast?

(c) Cause and Effect How have immigrants affected the culture of the Northeast?

Writing Activity
Which city described in this section are you most interested in learning more about? Make a list of things you would like to learn about this city. Then write a brief paragraph explaining why you want to learn these things.

For: An activity on mass transit systems
Visit: PHSchool.com
Web Code: lhd-4401

Prepare to Read

Objectives

In this section, you will
1. Learn how the South's land is important to its economy.
2. Read about how the growth of industry is changing the South.

Taking Notes

As you read this section, look for details about the growth of industry and how it has affected the economy. Copy the table below, and record your findings in it.

Industry	Products	Effects on Economy

Target Reading Skill

Use Signal Words Signal words point out relationships among ideas or events. Certain words, such as *however* or *like,* can signal a comparison or contrast. As you read this section, notice the contrast between what the South's economy was based on 50 years ago and what it is based on today. What signal words indicate the contrast?

Key Terms

- **petrochemical** (pet roh KEM ih kul) *n.* a substance such as plastic or paint that is made from petroleum
- **industrialization** (in dus tree ul ih ZAY shun) *n.* the process of building new industries in an area dominated by farming
- **Sun Belt** (sun belt) *n.* an area of the United States stretching from the southern Atlantic coast to the California coast

In 1895, at the age of fifteen, Catherine Evans Whitener had no idea that she was about to make history. Her friends and family liked the cotton bedspreads she made so much that she began to display them on her front porch in Dalton, Georgia. Her first sale earned her $2.50. After a large store placed an order for 24 bedspreads, an industry was born.

As interest in her work grew, Whitener began to train other girls to help produce the bedspreads. In 1917, she and her brother formed the Evans Manufacturing Company. Their company and others like it employed some 10,000 workers during the Great Depression. So many bedspreads were sold to travelers in the Dalton area that the highway through the town became known as "Bedspread Alley."

Catherine Evans Whitener

The Land of the South

There are many different ways that people in the South can make a living. The South's particular geography and climate make many of these jobs possible.

The region has a warm climate, and most parts of it receive plenty of rain. The wide coastal plains along the Atlantic Ocean and the Gulf of Mexico have rich soil. In addition, the South has a long growing season. There are between 200 and 290 frost-free days every year. Together, these features make much of the South an excellent place for growing crops such as cotton, rice, tobacco, and sugar cane and raising animals.

REGIONAL PROFILE

Focus on Culture

The South

The South's economy has been shifting from agriculture to services and manufacturing. The attraction of new jobs, along with the promise of a warm climate, has brought people to the region. Descendants of African Americans who left the South after the Civil War are returning in large numbers, and Hispanics from Mexico and Central American immigrants are arriving. As you study the map and charts, think about how changes in population can affect a region's culture.

The South: Land Use
KEY

Forestry
Livestock raising
Commercial farming
Manufacturing and trade
Limited economic activity
National border
State border

African American Migration by Region, 1990–2000

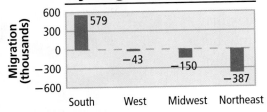

South	579
West	−43
Midwest	−150
Northeast	−387

SOURCE: Population Reference Bureau

Hispanic Population of the South, 2002

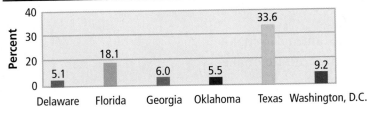

Delaware	5.1
Florida	18.1
Georgia	6.0
Oklahoma	5.5
Texas	33.6
Washington, D.C.	9.2

SOURCE: *New York Times Almanac,* 2006

Map and Chart Skills

1. **Identify** The black migration to the South is mainly from what region of the United States?
2. **Explain** What southern states have the largest Hispanic populations?
3. **Analyze** In what ways do you think the culture of the South is changing as its people and economy change?

Go Online
PHSchool.com

Use Web Code lhe-4412 to access the **DK World Desk Reference Online.**

Farming One of the most important parts of the South's economy is farming. For years, the South's major crop was cotton. By the 1950s, bedspread factories in Georgia alone consumed 500,000 bales of cotton every year. Many southern farmers once depended on cotton as their only source of income. Today, cotton still brings much money to the South, especially to Alabama, Mississippi, and Texas, but King Cotton no longer rules this region. In the 1890s, the boll weevil (bohl WEE vul), a kind of beetle, began to attack cotton plants in the South. Over the next 30 years, it destroyed cotton crops across the region. Without money from cotton, many farmers went bankrupt. Today, most southern farmers raise more than one crop.

Growing Conditions Some of these crops need special growing conditions. Citrus fruits require year-round warmth and sunshine. Florida has plenty of both. More oranges, tangerines, grapefruits, and limes are grown here than in any other state. Rice needs warm, moist growing conditions. Farmers in Arkansas, Louisiana, and Mississippi take advantage of their climate by growing rice along the coast of the Gulf of Mexico and in the Mississippi River valley.

Agricultural Products Some areas of the South have become famous for their agricultural products. Georgia has taken one of its products as its nickname—the Peach State. Georgia is also known for its peanut and pecan crops. Texans raise more cattle than do farmers in any other state. All of these items are just a sample of the diversity of southern agriculture.

The Cotton Crop
Although cotton (below) is no longer the South's major crop, it is still important to the region's economy.
Identify Effects *How did boll weevils (above) affect the South's economy and way of farming?*

Offshore Drilling
The rig provides a platform for oil drilling in the Gulf of Mexico. **Draw Conclusions** *Why is drilling for oil an important industry in the South?*

Drilling and Mining   In some parts of the South, what is under the soil is as important as what grows in it. In Louisiana, Oklahoma, and Texas, companies drill for oil and natural gas. These can be used as fuel and made into **petrochemicals,** which are substances, such as plastics, paint, nylon, and asphalt, that come from petroleum. In Alabama, Kentucky, West Virginia, and Tennessee, miners dig for coal. Southern states are leading producers of minerals such as salt, sulfur, and zinc. The South also produces many important building materials, including crushed stone, construction sand and gravel, and cement.

Fishing and Forestry   Many people in the South make a living in fishing and forestry. The Chesapeake Bay area of Maryland and Virginia is famous for its shellfish, including clams, crabs, and scallops. Mississippi leads the nation in catfish farming. However, the South's fishing industry is strongest in Louisiana, Texas, and Florida. The timber industry is active in most of the southern states. Softwood trees like southern pine are turned into lumber or paper. People use hardwood trees to make furniture. North Carolina has the nation's largest hardwood furniture industry.

✓ Reading Check   **Name two kinds of crops that need special growing conditions.**

Southern Cities and Industries

Some people still think of the South as it was in the early 1900s—a slow-moving, mostly rural region. But over the past 50 years, this region has gone through many changes. Although the South's rural areas are still important to its economy, most people in the South today live in cities. Some work in factories or in high-technology firms. Others work in tourism or in one of the other service industries in this region's growing economy. This change from an agriculture-based economy to an industry-based economy is called **industrialization.**

Textiles   One of the most important industries in the South is the textile industry. Textile mills make cloth. They were originally built in this region to use the South's cotton. Today, many mills still make cotton cloth. Others now make cloth from synthetic, or human-made, materials. The textile industry is strongest in Georgia, the Carolinas, and Virginia.

Technology   One expanding set of industries is in the field of high technology. For example, workers develop computers and other electronics and figure out better ways to use them. Some centers of high technology are Raleigh-Durham, North Carolina, and Austin, Texas.

Another high-technology industry is the aerospace business. In Cape Canaveral, Florida, Houston, Texas, and Huntsville, Alabama, people work for the National Aeronautics and Space Administration (NASA). Some people train as astronauts, while others run the space shuttle program. Atlanta, Georgia, is now a center for the cable television industry.

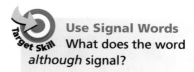

Use Signal Words What does the word *although* signal?

Space Camp
Every year, people attend United States Space Camp in Huntsville, Alabama. As one student (left) sits in the cockpit of a space shuttle, other students (right) experiment with the feeling of being in outer space.
Analyze Images *How do these photographs reflect the high-technology industry?*

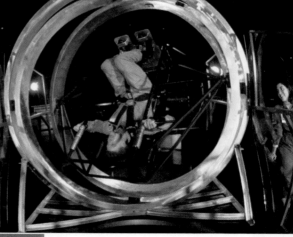

Explore Miami's
Little Havana

Transportation and Tourism A big part of the South's economy depends on moving goods and people into and out of the region. Most of the South's largest cities play important roles in this transportation industry. Miami, Florida, and New Orleans, Louisiana, are major ports. Miami is a center for goods and people going to and from Central and South America. New Orleans is a gateway between the Gulf of Mexico and the Mississippi River system. It is also an important port for oil tankers.

Some of the people the transportation industry brings to the South come to stay. Thousands come to work in the South's new industries. Thousands more choose to move to the South because of its climate. The South is part of the Sun Belt. The **Sun Belt** is the broad area of the United States that stretches from the southern Atlantic coast to the coast of California. It is known for its warm weather. The population of the Sun Belt has been rising for the past few decades. Some arrivals are older adults who want to retire to places without cold, snowy winters. Others come to take advantage of both the weather and the work that the Sun Belt offers.

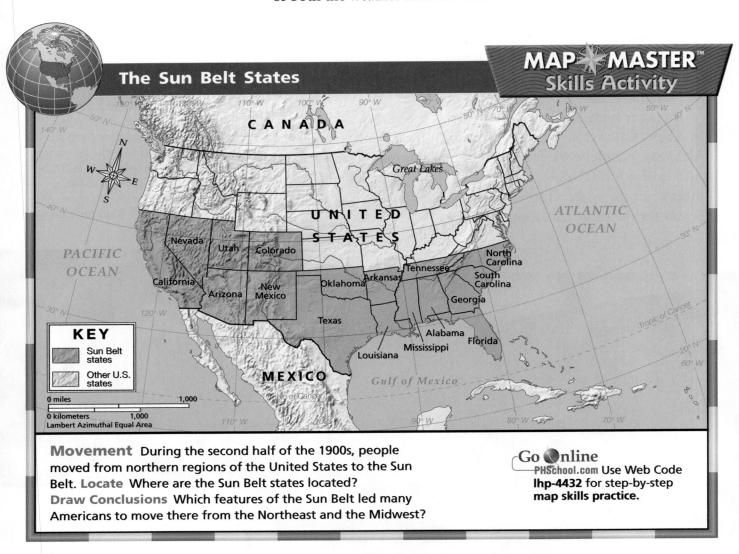

The Sun Belt States

MAP MASTER™
Skills Activity

KEY

Sun Belt states

Other U.S. states

0 miles 1,000
0 kilometers 1,000
Lambert Azimuthal Equal Area

Movement During the second half of the 1900s, people moved from northern regions of the United States to the Sun Belt. **Locate** Where are the Sun Belt states located?
Draw Conclusions Which features of the Sun Belt led many Americans to move there from the Northeast and the Midwest?

Go Online
PHSchool.com Use Web Code
lhp-4432 for step-by-step map skills practice.

Warm weather also brings to the South people who only plan to visit. These people fuel the region's tourist industry. In winter, tourists flock to the sunny beaches of Florida and the Gulf Coast. In the summer, they hike in the mountains of the Appalachians and Ozarks. Southern historic cities such as Charleston, South Carolina, or New Orleans, Louisiana, draw tourists at any time of the year. In states throughout the South, there are always fun and exciting things to see and to do.

The Nation's Capital The city of Washington is not in a state. Instead, it is in the District of Columbia, which lies between the states of Maryland and Virginia. This area of land was chosen in 1790 as the site for the nation's capital. Located on the shore of the Potomac River, Washington, D.C., is a planned city. Many people consider Washington to be one of the most beautiful cities in the world. It has wide avenues, grand public buildings, and dramatic monuments, including the Supreme Court, the Library of Congress, the Washington Monument, and the Lincoln Memorial. The city's major avenues are named after the states. As the nation's capital, Washington is home to the nation's leaders and to hundreds of foreign diplomats.

Tourists on a paddleboat near the Jefferson Memorial in Washington, D.C.

 **Reading Check** **Where is the city of Washington located?**

 Section 2 Assessment

Key Terms
Review the key terms at the beginning of this section. Use each term in a sentence that explains its meaning.

Target Reading Skill
Review the section Fishing and Forestry on page 120. Find the word that signals contrast in relation to the fishing industry.

Comprehension and Critical Thinking
1. (a) List Name five of the southern states.
(b) Draw Conclusions How have the geography and climate of the South shaped its economy?

(c) Summarize In what ways has the South's economy changed since the 1800s?
2. (a) Recall Why has the population of the Sun Belt been increasing?
(b) Explain Why have many people in the South moved from rural to urban areas?
(c) Identify Cause and Effect How has the South's economy affected this population growth?

Writing Activity
Suppose that you work in an advertising firm in Atlanta, Georgia; Houston, Texas; or Miami, Florida. Create an advertisement persuading people to move to your city or state. It can be designed for a newspaper or a magazine. It can also be for radio, television, or the Internet.

Go Online
PHSchool.com

For: An activity on oil
Visit: PHSchool.com
Web Code: lhd-4402

Understanding Circle Graphs

Chris walked across the playground with his new friend Kyung, who had just moved to Florida from Korea. Kyung looked up at the sun.

"It's really hot here. Does the entire United States get weather like this?"

"Let me think," said Chris. "In the Northwest it rains a lot, and I don't think it gets quite as hot as here. Arizona and New Mexico do, for sure. The Midwest has some really hot summers but freezing-cold winters. And then there's arctic Alaska—the summers don't get too hot there, even though the sun shines all night long. The United States gets a lot of different weather."

Boston meteorologist Mish Michaels

Meteorologists collect an amazing variety of weather information from all over the country. One way they present data on temperatures, rainfall, and other weather information is to put it into graphs.

Learn the Skill

Follow the steps below to learn how to read and interpret a circle graph.

1. **Study the elements of the circle graph.** Read the title of the graph and all the labels. Make sure that you understand the purpose of the graph.

2. **Study the information shown in the graph.** The full circle represents 100 percent, or all, of something. Identify what the circle represents.

3. **Compare the portions within the graph.** Each division of the circle represents a certain percentage, or portion, of the whole. The portions should always add up to 100 percent. Notice which piece is the biggest—that is, the highest percentage. Which piece is the smallest?

4. **Draw conclusions from the graph.** Draw conclusions about the topic of the graph. Your conclusion should attempt to explain any differences or similarities in the sizes of the pieces of the circle.

Practice the Skill

Refer to the circle graph on the right and follow the steps for interpreting it.

1 After reading the title and labels of the graph, what do you think is its purpose?

2 What does the full circle represent—the circle is 100 percent of what?

3 What does each colored portion of the graph represent? Which is the largest portion? Which is the smallest portion?

4 Write a conclusion statement about the graph. Explain the meaning of the differences in the sizes of the portions.

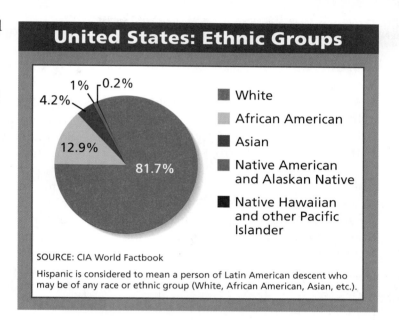

United States: Ethnic Groups

- 0.2%
- 1%
- 4.2%
- 12.9%
- 81.7%

■ White
■ African American
■ Asian
■ Native American and Alaskan Native
■ Native Hawaiian and other Pacific Islander

SOURCE: CIA World Factbook

Hispanic is considered to mean a person of Latin American descent who may be of any race or ethnic group (White, African American, Asian, etc.).

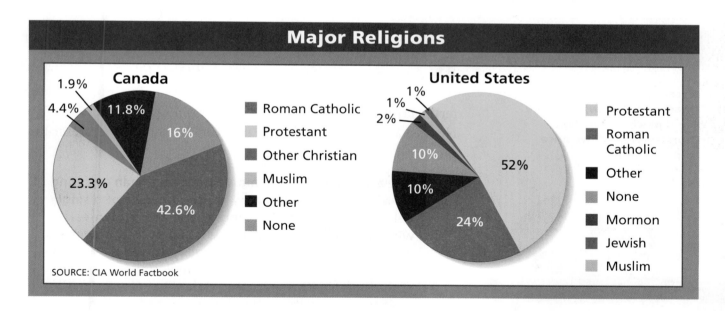

Major Religions

Canada

- 1.9%
- 4.4%
- 11.8%
- 16%
- 23.3%
- 42.6%

■ Roman Catholic
■ Protestant
■ Other Christian
■ Muslim
■ Other
■ None

SOURCE: CIA World Factbook

United States

- 1%
- 1%
- 2%
- 10%
- 10%
- 52%
- 24%

■ Protestant
■ Roman Catholic
■ Other
■ None
■ Mormon
■ Jewish
■ Muslim

Apply the Skill

Study the two circle graphs above. Following the steps in this skill, write a conclusion statement about each graph. Then compare the graphs and write a conclusion about their similarities and differences.

The Midwest
Leaving the Farm

Prepare to Read

Objectives

In this section, you will
1. Read about how technology is changing life on farms.
2. Learn how changes in farming are affecting the development of cities.

Taking Notes

As you read this section, look for details that show how changes in agriculture have caused cities to grow. Copy the chart below, and record your findings in it.

CAUSES	EVENT	EFFECTS
•	Changes in agriculture	•
•		•
•		•

Target Reading Skill

Identify Contrasts When you contrast two or more situations, you examine how they differ. In this section you will read about family farms and corporate farms. Although they both rely on technology, they differ in how they use it. As you read, list all of the differences between family farms and corporate farms.

Key Terms

- **mixed-crop farm** (mikst krahp fahrm) *n.* a farm that grows several different kinds of crops
- **recession** (rih SESH un) *n.* a decline in business activity and economic prosperity
- **corporate farm** (KAWR puh rit fahrm) *n.* a large farm that is run by a corporation, or an agricultural company

Present-day harvesting machines (below) work the land much faster than horse-driven plows once did (bottom).

Nebraska is one of several states in the middle of the country that make up the Midwest. Nebraska is a land of vast prairies and fertile farmland. Willa Cather's 1913 novel *O Pioneers!* is set on a Nebraska farm. A daughter of pioneers herself, Cather describes the farmland in great detail:

" There are few scenes more gratifying than a spring plowing in that country, where the furrows of a single field often lie a mile in length, and the brown earth, with such a strong, clean smell, and such a power of growth . . . in it, yields itself eagerly to the plow; rolls away from the shear, not even dimming the brightness of the metal, with a soft, deep sigh of happiness. . . . The grain is so heavy that it bends toward the blade and cuts like velvet. "

—*Willa Cather,* O Pioneers!

Farming in the Midwest has changed since Cather's time. Tractors have replaced horse-drawn farm equipment. Electricity and roads have been brought out to rural farms. Today, technology continues to change the way people farm the land.

REGIONAL PROFILE

Focus on Economics

The Midwest

As in other regions of the country, the economy of the Midwest has come to rely more on manufacturing and services than it does on agriculture. Transportation is one example of an important service that strengthens the Midwest's economy. As you study the map and charts, consider the importance of this service to the entire nation.

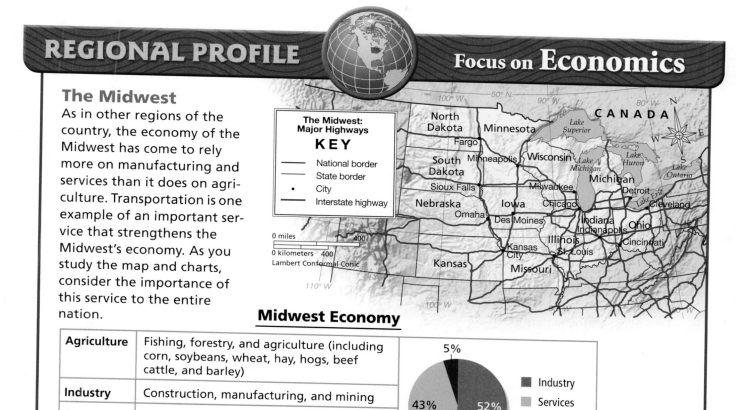

The Midwest: Major Highways

KEY

—— National border
—— State border
• City
—— Interstate highway

0 miles 400
0 kilometers 400
Lambert Conformal Conic

Midwest Economy

Agriculture	Fishing, forestry, and agriculture (including corn, soybeans, wheat, hay, hogs, beef cattle, and barley)
Industry	Construction, manufacturing, and mining
Services	Community, business, and personal services; finance; government and trade; transportation, communication, and utilities

- Industry — 5%
- Services — 43%
- Agriculture — 52%

SOURCE: U.S. Bureau of Economic Analysis

Chicago, Major Transportation Hub

Airport	O'Hare Airport is the nation's busiest. A plane takes off every minute.
Railroads	More than seven railroads serve Chicago, the nation's rail center.
Highways	I-90 from Seattle, I-80 from New York, I-55 from the South all cross in Chicago.
Rivers and waterways	The Chicago River, Chicago Canal, and Lake Michigan carry commercial shipping traffic.

SOURCE: Chicago Department of Aviation

Map and Chart Skills

1. **Explain** Which sector of the Midwest economy is the biggest?
2. **Infer** There is a general trend for people to move from rural to urban areas. Do you think this is true in the Midwest as well? Explain why.
3. **Analyze** What feature of its geographic setting makes the Midwest an important area for transportation?

Use Web Code **Ihe-4413** for **DK World Desk Reference Online.**

Technology Changes Farm Life

The Midwest is often called the heartland because it is the agricultural center of our nation. The soil is rich, and the climate is suitable for producing corn, wheat, soybeans, and livestock. Inventions such as the steel plow, the windmill, and barbed wire helped settlers carve out farms on the plains. Drilling equipment helped to make wells deep enough to reach water. These tools also helped make farms productive. Technological advances continue to improve farming techniques today.

Family Farms Decline   Until the 1980s, small family farms were common in the Midwest. Many of these farms were mixed-crop farms. On a **mixed-crop farm,** several different kinds of crops are grown. This was a sensible way for farmers to work. If one crop failed, the farm had others to fall back on.

In the 1960s and 1970s, family farms prospered. The world population was rising, and demand for American farm products was high. Farmers felt that they could increase their business if they enlarged their farms. To build bigger farms, farmers bought more land and equipment. But all of this cost money. Many farmers borrowed money from local banks.

In the early 1980s, there was a countrywide **recession** (rih SESH un), or a downturn in business activity. The demand for farm products decreased. Then, interest rates on bank loans increased. As a result, many farmers were not able to make enough money to pay their loans. Some families sold their farms. More than one million American farmers have left the land since 1980.

■ Graph Skills

In the early 1900s, about one-third of the workers in the United States worked on farms, such as the Illinois farm shown below. **Describe** What is the pattern of the number of farm workers shown in the graph? **Analyze Information** What does the information on the graph tell you about farming today?

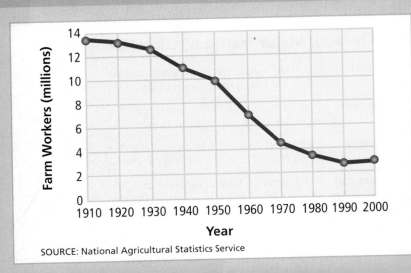

Number of U.S. Farm Workers, 1910–2000

SOURCE: National Agricultural Statistics Service

Corporate Farms Rise A small number of agricultural companies bought many of these family farms. When these agricultural companies combine several small family farms into one large farm, it is called a **corporate farm.** Large corporations can afford to buy the expensive land and equipment that modern farming requires. These large farms are run efficiently and make a profit.

Corporate farmers rely on machines and computers to do much of the work. This means that corporate farms employ fewer workers. Kansas offers a good example of corporate farming, since it has fewer workers and larger farms. In Kansas, 90 percent of the land is farmland, but fewer than 1 percent of the people are farmers. Most of the people in Kansas live and work in cities such as Wichita.

Small family farms do still exist in the Midwest. But most of them struggle to earn enough money for supporting a family. Family farmers usually need to have another job as well. Many people look to the cities for more job opportunities.

✓ Reading Check **Why did so many families sell or leave their farms?**

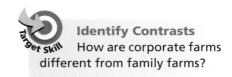

Identify Contrasts
How are corporate farms different from family farms?

Cities Develop in the Midwest

Many Midwestern cities began as centers of transportation and processing. Farmers from the surrounding area would send their harvests and livestock to nearby cities to be processed and shipped east. The largest processing city was Chicago, Illinois.

Chicago Located on Lake Michigan, Chicago was surrounded by prairies and farms in the mid-1800s. Farmers sent corn, wheat, cattle, and hogs to the mills and meat-packing plants in the city. Here the raw materials were turned into foods and shipped east by way of the Great Lakes. When railroads were built, Chicago really boomed. By the late 1800s, it had become a steel-making and manufacturing center. What was one of the most important manufactured products made in Chicago? You probably guessed it: farm equipment.

Today, Chicago is the biggest city in the heartland. It is known for its ethnic diversity and lively culture. It is the hub of major transportation routes including highways, railroads, airlines, and shipping routes. Chicago is also the home of the first steel skyscraper—the Home Insurance Company Building—and many other architectural wonders. For a bird's-eye view of Chicago, go to the top of the Sears Tower, one of the tallest buildings in the world.

Links Across The World

Higher and Higher Until 1996, Chicago's Sears Tower, at 1,454 feet (443 meters), was the world's tallest building. The photo below shows the view from the Sears Tower. The twin Petronas Towers in Malaysia then held the title. In 2004, the Taipei 101 building in Taipei, Taiwan, gained the title of world's tallest building, topping out at 1,671 feet (509 meters). Today, even taller skyscrapers are being planned in cities around the world.

Major Rail Routes of the Late 1800s

KEY
- Major railroads
- National border
- State border
- • City or town

0 miles 500
0 kilometers 500
Lambert Azimuthal Equal Area

Human-Environment Interaction In the late 1800s, the midwestern cities that grew the fastest were the ones located on railroad routes. Chicago became a railroad junction—a place where a number of railroad lines meet. **List** Locate Chicago on the map and list how many railroad routes met there.
Draw Conclusions Why was Chicago's location important to its becoming a railroad junction?

Go Online
PHSchool.com Use Web Code
lhp-4443 for step-by-step
map skills practice.

Detroit and St. Louis Two other large cities in the Midwest are Detroit, Michigan, and St. Louis, Missouri. They have both played an important role in the country's history. Why do you think Detroit is called the Motor City? You will find the head-quarters of America's automobile manufacturers here. General Motors, Ford, and Daimler Chrysler have their main offices and factories in the city.

Covered wagons, not cars, used to roll through St. Louis. Located on the Mississippi River, this city was the starting point for pioneers heading west. Its location on the banks of the Mississippi River made it an important city in the days before railroads. Today, a huge stainless steel arch beside the river marks St. Louis as the Gateway to the West. St. Louis is also a banking and commercial center.

DISCOVERY CHANNEL SCHOOL Video
Find out about the powerful Mississippi River.

Inside the Mall of America in Minnesota

The Twin Cities   Minneapolis is the largest city in Minnesota, followed by St. Paul. Together, they are known as the Twin Cities because they are next to each other on the Mississippi River. The Twin Cities were once the flour-milling center of the United States. Pillsbury and Company was founded there in 1872. Today, publishing, medical, computer, and art businesses flourish there. The city's suburbs have replaced hundreds of square miles of fertile land once used for farming.

✓ Reading Check   **Where was the world's first skyscraper located?**

 Section 3 Assessment

Key Terms
Review the key terms at the beginning of this section. Use each term in a sentence that explains its meaning.

Target Reading Skill
What are two ways that farming in the 1960s and 1970s was different from farming since the 1980s?

Comprehension and Critical Thinking
1. (a) Explain Why is the Midwest called the nation's heartland?

(b) Explore the Main Idea Why did family farmers face hard times in the 1980s?
(c) Predict What do you think the future holds for family farmers?
2. (a) Recall How did some midwestern cities get their starts?
(b) Identify Effects How did railroads affect the growth of midwestern cities?
(c) Draw Inferences How might Chicago's location affect its growth today?

Writing Activity
Suppose that you are a farmer and you have decided to sell your farm and move to a city. Write a letter to a friend explaining your decision.

Go Online PHSchool.com
For: An activity on the automobile industry
Visit: PHSchool.com
Web Code: lhd-4403

Prepare to Read

Objectives

In this section you will
1. Learn about the natural resources of the West.
2. Read about the challenges facing the urban West.

Taking Notes

As you read this section, look for ways that natural resources are used and conserved in the West. Copy the table below, and record your findings in it.

Resources of the West	
Using Resources	**Conserving Resources**
•	•
•	•
•	•

Target Reading Skill

Make Comparisons Comparing two or more situations enables you to see how they are alike. As you read this section, compare how different parts of the West use and manage resources. Write the information in your Taking Notes table.

Key Terms

- **forty-niner** (FAWRT ee NY nur) *n.* the nickname for a miner who took part in the California Gold Rush of 1849
- **responsible development** (rih SPAHN suh bul dih VEL up munt) *n.* balancing the needs of the environment, community, and economy
- **mass transit** (mas TRAN sit) *n.* a system of subways, buses, and commuter trains used to transport large numbers of people

From colonial days to the present, Americans have been drawn westward. Over time, explorers and settlers have pushed out the farthest boundaries of the western frontier. In the 1780s, the frontier was considered to be the land as far west as the Mississippi River. Twenty years later, it included all of the land to the Rocky Mountains. By the 1850s, the frontier was the region that we now think of as the West—the land from the Rocky Mountains to the Pacific Ocean. By the 1900s, it also included Alaska and Hawaii.

Although the boundaries of the West have changed dramatically over the years, one factor has remained the same: People are attracted westward by the promise of the land.

Rocky Mountains, Colorado

Natural Resources of the West

For well over 400 years, people have been drawn to the West by its wealth of natural resources. The Spanish had already settled in the Southwest when the Pilgrims arrived in New England in the 1620s. After Lewis and Clark's exploration of the Louisiana Territory in the early 1800s, more people moved westward.

REGIONAL PROFILE

Focus on Geography

The West

Water is an important resource of the West—more important even than gold. Farmers have always needed large quantities of water to irrigate their lands. Today, as large cities and their populations grow, people are demanding more and more water for every-day use. Study the map and charts, and think about how water availability and use are shaping this region.

California Cropland

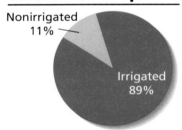

Nonirrigated 11%

Irrigated 89%

SOURCE: National Agriculture Statistics Service

Leading Hydroelectric Power-Producing States, 2006

States	Thousands of Megawatt Hours
Washington	14,650
Oregon	7,854
California	8,088
New York*	4,173
Alabama*	1,913
Idaho	1,736
Tennessee*	1,557

SOURCE: Energy Information Administration, US Department of Energy
*not a western state

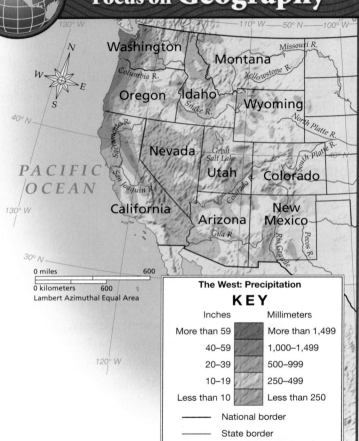

The West: Precipitation

KEY

	Inches		Millimeters
	More than 59		More than 1,499
	40–59		1,000–1,499
	20–39		500–999
	10–19		250–499
	Less than 10		Less than 250

—— National border
—— State border

0 miles 600
0 kilometers 600
Lambert Azimuthal Equal Area

Map and Chart Skills

1. **Locate** Which areas of the West receive the most rain?
2. **Identify** What state produces the most hydroelectric power?
3. **Analyze** There is a category of law devoted to water use. What issues might be addressed by lawyers who specialize in water use?

Use Web Code lhe-4414 to access the **DK World Desk Reference Online**.

Mineral Resources Before gold was discovered in California, Native Americans and Spanish settlers lived in the region. With the California Gold Rush, the population exploded. The sleepy port of San Francisco boomed into a prosperous city. Its population grew from 800 people in 1848 to 25,000 just two years later. The first miners and prospectors of the Gold Rush were called **forty-niners** because they arrived in 1849. They arrived, bought supplies, and headed off to the Sierra Nevada expecting to strike it rich. Few of them succeeded, but many remained in the West.

A gold strike in 1858 in Colorado led to the founding of the city of Denver. Similar events took place in Nevada, Idaho, and Montana in the 1860s. Further discoveries of valuable minerals, including silver and copper, drew more and more people to the West. A mining town formed around each new discovery.

All of these new settlers needed homes, and the timber to build them with was in large supply in the the Pacific Northwest. After the Civil War, logging camps, sawmills, and paper mills sprang up in Washington, Oregon, and northern California. At first, the resources of the West seemed unlimited. The use of these resources created wealth and many jobs. However, it also brought with it new challenges.

Learn more about the California Gold Rush.

The Cost of Mining
Merchants and traders supplied miners with food, clothing, and tools. Supplies were hauled from the river ports to the mining camps by wagons and mules. This caused increased prices. With the population boom and the difficulty of getting supplies up to the camps, the cost of living for miners was high. **Conclude** *Was trying to strike it rich worth the amount of time, effort, and money needed? Explain your answer.*

The Cost of Mining

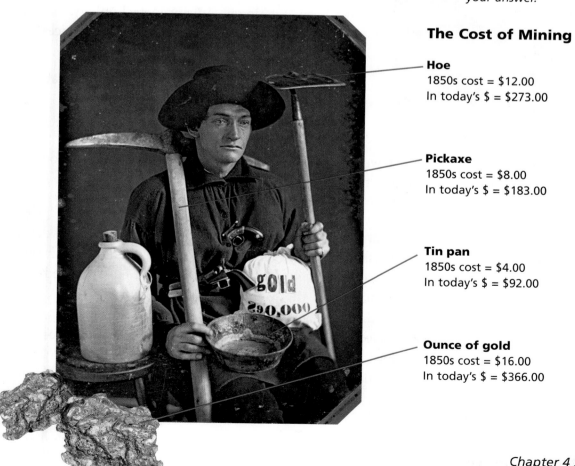

Hoe
1850s cost = $12.00
In today's $ = $273.00

Pickaxe
1850s cost = $8.00
In today's $ = $183.00

Tin pan
1850s cost = $4.00
In today's $ = $92.00

Ounce of gold
1850s cost = $16.00
In today's $ = $366.00

Managing Resources California's population continued to grow after the Gold Rush. To meet the demand for new houses, loggers leveled many forests. Engineers built dams to pipe water through the mountains to coastal cities. Next to the dams, they built hydroelectric plants. Cities like San Francisco got water and power this way, but the dams flooded whole valleys of the Sierras.

To save parts of the West as natural wilderness, Congress created several national parks and forests. Yet these parks are not trouble-free. California's Yosemite (yoh SEM uh tee) National Park now gets so many visitors that it suffers from traffic jams and air pollution in the summer. Some of the scenic views in Montana's Glacier National Park are also reduced by hazy skies.

Some westerners are working on **responsible development,** or balancing the needs of the environment, the community, and the economy. For example, Yosemite now limits the number of campers in the park. Dam building has stopped. In addition, some logging companies are working to preserve the environment by planting new trees to replace the ones that have been cut down. Advanced technology, such as power plants with better pollution-control devices, can help meet energy and environmental needs.

✓ **Reading Check** **What caused California's population to grow in the 1800s?**

Old Faithful is the best-known geyser in Yellowstone National Park, Wyoming.

The Urban West

Most westerners today are not miners, farmers, or loggers. Rather, they live and work in cities. Their challenge is to figure out how to use natural resources wisely.

Portland, Oregon "Your town or mine?" two land developers asked each other in 1845. They were at the same site and predicted the development of a major port city. Located near the junction of the Willamette and Columbia rivers, how could they fail? Francis W. Pettygrove of Portland, Maine, won the coin toss. He named the site after his hometown in the East.

Portland became a trade center for lumber, fur, grain, salmon, and wool. In the 1930s, new dams produced cheap electricity. Portland attracted many manufacturing industries.

Seattle, Washington   The port city of Seattle was founded in the early 1850s. It was named after a Native American leader who helped the area's first settlers. Seattle has grown into a bustling city of more than half a million people.

Years of unchecked growth eventually led to problems. In the 1960s, a group of local citizens started a campaign to revitalize the local economy. A bridge was built across Lake Washington to help residents commute. Sewage was cleaned up from Lake Washington, and many neighborhood parks were created. The group also kept Pike Place Market from being destroyed. It is the oldest continuously run market in the country. Farmers have sold their crops and produce there since 1907.

San Jose, California   Urban sprawl is a local challenge in San Jose. The area around San Jose was once known for its beautiful orchards and farms. Now it is called Silicon Valley because it is a part of the computer industry.

San Jose's most valuable resource is now its people. They come from all parts of the world. The greater population density has created crowded freeways and air pollution. To counter these problems, San Jose has built a light-rail mass transit system. A **mass transit** system replaces individual cars with energy-saving buses or trains.

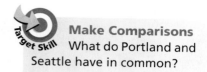

Make Comparisons
What do Portland and Seattle have in common?

■ Graph Skills

The Internet boom of the 1990s saw between 7,000 and 10,000 Internet companies start up. It began to decline dramatically by the beginning of 2000.
Describe In what year did the most Internet companies shut down?
Predict If the number of company shutdowns continues, what would be the effect on urban sprawl?

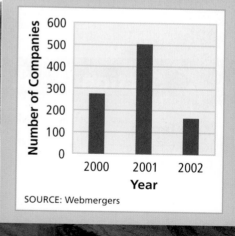

Internet Company Shutdowns

SOURCE: Webmergers

The Hollywood sign hovers over Los Angeles, California, and is a reminder that the city is home to the entertainment industry. Cameramen (lower photo) shoot a movie on a local set.

Los Angeles, California Los Angeles is another California city whose people are its greatest resource. It has grown from a small Mexican village in the 1780s to the second-most-populated city in the United States. The Gold Rush and the building of the transcontinental railroad helped the city grow.

By the 1920s, the movie, petroleum, and manufacturing industries all brought more people to the city. Today, Los Angeles is a center for banking and aircraft manufacturing. But, it is most noted for its entertainment industry. In addition to the Hollywood movie industry, the headquarters of many of the country's recording companies and radio and television networks are located here. Many broadcasts are in foreign languages, especially Spanish. Hispanics are the largest ethnic group in the city, followed by Asians.

✓ **Reading Check** Why did San Jose need a mass transit system?

Section 4 Assessment

Key Terms
Review the key terms at the beginning of this section. Use each term in a sentence that explains its meaning.

Target Reading Skill
Compare Los Angeles today to what it was like in the 1780s.

Comprehension and Critical Thinking
1. (a) Recall What event took place in California in 1849?
(b) Identify Cause and Effect How did that event lead to the formation of towns and cities?

(c) Infer How did the population explosion affect the West's natural resources?
2. (a) Explain How did Portland, Oregon, get its name?
(b) Summarize What natural resources made Portland a good location for a city?
(c) Predict How might these resources be protected today?

Writing Activity
What natural resources are there in your community? In what ways do people use these natural resources? Write a paragraph describing the natural resources in your area and how they are used.

Go Online
PHSchool.com

For: An activity on Denver
Visit: PHSchool.com
Web Code: lhd-4404

Review and Assessment

◆ Chapter Summary

Section 1: The Northeast
- A chain of cities runs from Boston, Massachusetts, to Washington, D.C.
- The Northeast is the most densely populated region of the United States.
- Many immigrants entered the United States through one of the ports in the Northeast.

Section 2: The South
- The South's warm climate and abundant rainfall make it suitable for growing many crops.
- Drilling, mining, fishing, and forestry are important industries in the South.
- Many people have moved from rural towns to the cities for better job opportunities.

Section 3: The Midwest
- Technology has changed the way that American farms operate.
- Many small family farms have closed because they are unprofitable.
- Many Midwestern cities got their start as places that processed and shipped farm products.

Section 4: The West
- The West has a wide array of natural resources.
- Managing these natural resources is an important task for people in the West.
- People are some of the urban West's most valuable resources.

Haymarket in Boston, Massachusetts

◆ Key Terms

Use each key term below in a sentence that shows the meaning of the term.

1. commute
2. megalopolis
3. population density
4. petrochemical
5. industrialization
6. Sun Belt
7. mixed-crop farm
8. recession
9. corporate farm
10. forty-niner
11. mass transit

◆ Comprehension and Critical Thinking

12. (a) List What are some of the large cities in the Northeast?
(b) Compare and Contrast Choose two of the Northeast's cities. How are they similar? How have they developed differently?

13. (a) Locate Which city in the Northeast was attacked by terrorists in 2001?
(b) Draw Conclusions Why might terrorists have targeted that city in particular?

14. (a) Explain What features make the South a good place for farming?
(b) Identify What was the South's most important crop until the 1900s?
(c) Predict How might farming in the South have been different without the boll weevil?

15. (a) Recall How do people in the South make a living other than by farming?
(b) Draw Conclusions How is Georgia important to the textile industry?

16. (a) Summarize How did the recession in the 1980s affect farmers?
(b) Compare and Contrast How are mixed-crop farming and corporate farming different?

17. (a) Name What are the main natural resources of the West?
(b) Summarize How have people used these natural resources?
(c) Compare and Contrast How has the way people manage natural resources in the West changed since the 1800s?

◆ Skills Practice

Understanding Circle Graphs In the Skills for Life activity in this chapter, you learned that information can be given in the form of circle graphs.

Review the steps you followed to learn this skill. Then reread the Regional Profile of the Midwest on page 127. Study the Midwest Economy circle graph on that page. Identify what percentage of the graph each part represents. Use the information in the circle graph to draw conclusions about the economy of the Midwest.

◆ Writing Activity: Science

Suppose that you are the science reporter for a newspaper covering the history of farming on the plains. Write a brief report about how advances in science and technology have contributed to successfully farming the land.

MAP★MASTER™ Skills Activity

Place Location Write the letter from the map that shows its location.
1. Boston
2. New York City
3. Washington, D.C.
4. Atlanta
5. Chicago
6. St. Louis
7. Portland
8. Los Angeles

Go Online
PHSchool.com Use Web Code **lhp-4444** for an **interactive map.**

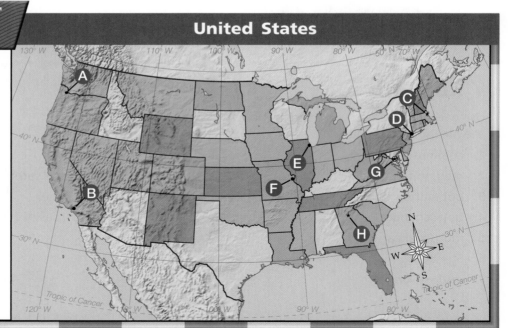

United States

Standardized Test Prep

Test-Taking Tips

Some questions on standardized tests ask you to analyze graphs. Study the graph below. Then follow the tips to answer the sample question.

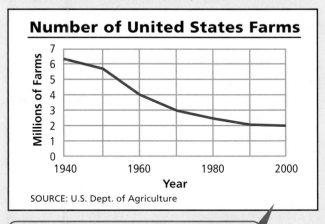

Number of United States Farms

SOURCE: U.S. Dept. of Agriculture

> **TIP** When you study a graph, read the title to understand its subject. Then study information on the left side and bottom of the graph.

Based on this graph, it is clear that the

A size of farms has decreased since the 1940s.

B size of farms increased during the last half of the 1900s.

C number of farms steadily decreased during the last half of the 1900s.

D number of farms probably will increase during the first twenty years of the present century.

> **TIP** Restate the question to make sure you understand what it is asking. "Based on the graph, what conclusion can you draw about United States farms?"

Think It Through Read the title of the graph. You can eliminate A and B because they are about the *size* of American farms. What does the graph show about the *number* of farms? The number line goes down after 1940, but there is no indication that the number of farms will increase in the 2000s. The correct answer is C.

Practice Questions

Use the tips above and other tips in this book to help you answer the following questions.

1. The most densely populated region of the United States is the

A South. **B** Midwest.

C Northeast. **D** West.

2. What caused San Francisco to grow into a large city?

A the Gold Rush

B hydroelectricity

C the logging industry

D Lewis and Clark's expedition

3. The Midwest's largest city is

A Detroit, Michigan. **B** St. Louis, Missouri.

C Minneapolis, Minnesota. **D** Chicago, Illinois.

Study the graph below, and then answer the question that follows.

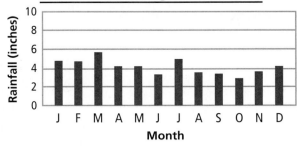

Atlanta, Georgia: Rainfall

SOURCE: *The World Almanac*, 2001

4. In which month is the average temperature highest in Atlanta? How much rain falls in that month?

A March; 5.5 inches **B** May; 6 inches

C July; 6 inches **D** September; 3 inches

Go Online
PHSchool.com

Use Web Code **lha-4404** for a **Chapter 4 self-test**

From **Childtimes**

By Eloise Greenfield and Lessie Jones Little, with material by Pattie Ridley Jones

Prepare to Read

Background Information

How much do people know about the lives of their grandparents or their parents as children? Suppose someone wanted to write a history of his or her family. How could he or she find information?

You can learn a great deal from seeing how a single family lives through several generations. Every family history reflects the history of the place where that family lives. The following excerpts come from a memoir, or a story of personal experience, written by a mother, a daughter, and a grandmother. The book tells the story of their family, as well as the growth of their hometown, Parmele, North Carolina.

Objectives

In this section you will

1. Learn how and why the town of Parmele changed over three generations.

2. Identify elements that the memoirs of the three generations have in common.

About the Selection

Childtimes: A Three-Generation Memoir was published in 1979 by Thomas Y. Crowell.

✓ **Reading Check**

How did the town of Parmele get its name?

Pattie Frances Ridley Jones—born in Bertie County, North Carolina, December 15, 1884

Parmele, North Carolina

Towns build up around work, you know. People go and live where they can find jobs. And that's how Parmele got started.

At first, it was just a junction, a place where two railroads crossed. Two Atlantic Coast Line railroads, one running between Rocky Mount and Plymouth, and one running between Kinston and Weldon. Didn't too many people live around there then, and those that did were pretty much spread out.

Well, around 1888, a Yankee named Mr. Parmele came down from New York and looked the place over, and he saw all those big trees and decided to start a lumber company. Everybody knew what that meant. There were going to be jobs! People came from everywhere to get work. I was right little at that time, too little to know what was going on, but everybody says it was something to see how fast that town grew. All those people moving in and houses going up. They named the town after the man who made the jobs, and they called it *Pomma-lee*.

The lumber company hired a whole lot of people. They hired workers to lay track for those little railroads they call tram roads that they were going to run back and forth between the town and the woods. They hired lumberjacks to chop the trees down and cut them up into logs, and load them on the tram cars. They hired men to build the mill and put the machinery in, and millworkers to run the machines that would cut the logs into different sizes and dry them and make them nice and smooth. . . .

Lessie Blanche Jones Little—born in Parmele, North Carolina, October 1, 1906

Parmele

I used to hear Papa and Mama and their friends talking about the lumber mill that had been the center of life in Parmele before I was born, but there wasn't any mill when I was growing up. The only thing left of it was the sawdust from all the wood they had sawed there. The sawdust was about a foot thick on the land where the mill had been. I used to love to walk on it. It was spongy, and it made me feel like I was made of rubber. I'd take my shoes off and kind of bounce along on top of it. But that was all that was left of the mill.

My Parmele was a train town. The life of my town moved around the trains that came in and out all day long. About three hundred people lived in Parmele, most of them black. There were three black churches, a Baptist, a Methodist, and a Holiness, and one white church. Two black schools, one white. There wasn't even one doctor, and not many people would have had the money to pay one, if there had been. If somebody got down real bad sick, a member of the family would go by horse and buggy to a nearby town and bring the doctor back, or sometimes the doctor would ride on his own horse.

Most of the men and women in Parmele earned their living by farming. Some did other things like working at the tobacco factory in Robersonville, but most worked on the farms that were all around in the area, white people's farms usually. When I was a little girl, they earned fifty cents a day, a farm day, sunup to sundown, plus meals. After they got home, they had all their own work to do, cooking and cleaning, laundry, chopping wood for the woodstove, and shopping. . . .

A steam engine pulls a train through the countryside.

Parmele had trains coming in and going out all day long. Passenger trains and freight trains. There was always so much going on at the station that I wouldn't know what to watch. People were changing trains and going in and out of the cafe and the restaurant. They came from big cities like New York and Chicago and Boston, and they were all wearing the latest styles. Things were being unloaded, like furniture and trunks and plows and cases of fruit and crates of clucking chickens, or a puppy, or the body of somebody who had died and was being brought back home. And every year around the last two weeks in May, a special train would come through. It had two white flags flying on the locomotive, and it was carrying one hundred carloads of white potatoes that had been grown down near <u>Pamlico Sound</u>, where everybody said the soil was so rich they didn't even have to fertilize it.

The train station was a gathering place, too. A lot of people went there to relax after they had finished their work for the day. They'd come downtown to pick up their mail, or buy a newspaper, and then they'd just stand around laughing and talking to their friends. And on Sundays fellas and their girls would come all the way from other towns, just to spend the afternoon at the Parmele train station. . . .

It was hard for Papa to find work. Not long after Sis Clara died, we moved to Mount Herman, a black section of Portsmouth, Virginia. Papa worked on the docks there, and even though he didn't make much money, the work was steady. But when we moved back to Parmele, it was hard for him to find any work at all. . . .

Eloise Glynn Little Greenfield—born in Parmele, North Carolina, May 17, 1929

Daddy Makes a Way

When I was three months old, Daddy left home to make a way for us. He went North, as thousands of black people had done, during slavery and since. They went North looking for safety, for justice, for freedom, for work, looking for a good life. Often one member of a family would go ahead of the others to make a way—to find a job and a place to live. And that's what my father did.

In the spring of 1926, Daddy had graduated from high school, Parmele Training School. He had been offered a scholarship by Knoxville College in Tennessee, but he hadn't taken it. He and Mama had gotten married that fall, and now they had Wilbur and me to take care of. Mama had been teaching school since her graduation from Higgs, but she had decided to stop.

Pamlico Sound (PAM lih koh sownd) *n.* a long body of water off the coast of North Carolina that separates the Hatteras Islands from the mainland

Reading Check

What kind of work did Eloise's father do before he went to Washington, D.C.?

Sharecroppers in the South

Nineteen twenty-nine was a bad time for Daddy to go away, but a worse time for him not to go. The <u>Great Depression</u> was about to begin, had already begun for many people. All over the United States, thousands of people were already jobless and homeless.

In Parmele, there were few permanent jobs. Some seasons of the year, Daddy could get farm work, harvesting potatoes and working in the tobacco fields. Every year, from August to around Thanksgiving, he worked ten hours a day for twenty-five cents an hour at a tobacco warehouse in a nearby town, packing tobacco in huge barrels and loading them on the train for shipping. And he and his father were house movers. Whenever somebody wanted a house moved from one place to another, Daddy and Pa would jack it up and attach it to a windlass, the machine that the horse would turn to move the house. But it was only once in a while that they were called on to do that.

So, one morning in August 1929, Mama went with Daddy to the train station and tried to hold back her tears as the Atlantic Coast Line train pulled out, taking him toward Washington, D.C. Then she went home, sat in the porch swing, and cried.

In Washington, friends helped Daddy find a room for himself and his family to live in, and took him job hunting. He found a job as a dishwasher in a restaurant, and in a few weeks, he had saved enough money for our train fare.

Great Depression (grayt dee PRESH un) *n.* an economic collapse that began in 1929 and lasted throughout the 1930s, causing many people to lose their jobs

Review and Assessment

Thinking About the Selection

1. **(a) Recall** Why was the town located where it was? What caused the town to first begin to grow?
(b) Identify Why did building a sawmill attract more people to Parmele? How did they earn a living after the mill closed?
(c) Evaluate How did the life of a young person in Parmele compare with your own?
2. **(a) Respond** What do these memoirs tell you about how hard life in Parmele was at different time periods?

(b) Infer What aspect of their parents' lives most shaped the lives of these women when they were young girls?
(c) Compare and Contrast What do the three narrators have in common? How are they different?

Writing Activity

Write a Memoir Write a memoir of your own childhood. Use the point of view of yourself as an older person. Talk about the forces that have most shaped your life.

About the Author

Eloise Greenfield (b. 1929) was born in Parmele, North Carolina. She has received dozens of awards and honors for her more than thirty books of poetry, biography, and fiction. Greenfield's fiction often depicts strong, loving African American families and contains positive messages for all of her readers. She currently lives in Washington, D.C.

Chapter
5 Canada

Chapter Preview

This chapter will introduce you to the provinces and territories of Canada.

Country Databank
The Country Databank provides data of each of the provinces and territories in Canada.

 **Target Reading Skill**

Context In this chapter, you will focus on using context to help you understand unfamiliar words. Context includes the words, phrases, and sentences surrounding the word.

▶ **Lighthouse in Peggy's Cove, Nova Scotia, Canada**

MAP MASTER™
Skills Activity

KEY
— National border
— Provincial or territorial border
⊛ National capital
★ Provincial or territorial capital
• Other city

0 miles 1,000
0 kilometers 1,000
Lambert Azimuthal Equal Area

Regions Canada is politically divided into ten provinces and three territories. **Locate** Describe the relative locations of Quebec, Saskatchewan, and British Columbia. **Draw Conclusions** Which of the three provinces do you think Europeans settled first? Explain your answer.

Go Online
PHSchool.com Use Web Code **lhp-4511** for step-by-step **map skills practice.**

Guide for Reading

This section provides an introduction to the ten provinces and three territories that make up Canada.

- Look at the map on the previous page, and then read the information below to learn about each province and territory.
- Analyze the data to compare the provinces and territories.
- What are the characteristics that most of the provinces and territories share?
- What are some of the key differences among the provinces and territories?

Viewing the Video Overview

View the World Studies Video Overview to learn more about each of the provinces and territories. As you watch, answer these questions:

- Why do most Canadians live in the southern part of the country?
- What factors influenced where the big cities of Canada developed?

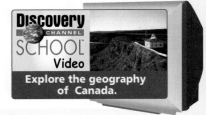

DISCOVERY CHANNEL
SCHOOL Video
Explore the geography of Canada.

Alberta

Capital	Edmonton
Land Area	247,999 sq mi; 642,317 sq km
Population	3,101,561
Language(s)	English, Chinese, German, French
Agriculture	livestock, wheat, canola, dairy products, barley, poultry, potatoes, nurseries, vegetables, eggs, sugar beets, honey
Industry	manufacturing, construction, oil production and refinery

British Columbia

Capital	Victoria
Land Area	357,214 sq mi; 925,186 sq km
Population	4,118,141
Language(s)	English, Chinese, Punjabi, German, French
Agriculture	nurseries, livestock, dairy products, vegetables, poultry, fruit, potatoes, ginseng, canola, wheat
Industry	forestry, wood and paper, mining, tourism, agriculture, fishing, manufacturing

Odyssium is Edmonton, Alberta's space and science center.

Manitoba

Capital	Winnipeg
Land Area	213,728 sq mi; 553,556 sq km
Population	1,150,038
Language(s)	English, German, French
Agriculture	wheat, livestock, canola, dairy products, potatoes, barley, poultry, eggs, nurseries, vegetables, corn, honey
Industry	manufacturing, agriculture, food industry, mining, construction

New Brunswick

Capital	Fredericton
Land Area	27,587 sq mi; 71,450 sq km
Population	756,939
Language(s)	English, French
Agriculture	potatoes, dairy products, poultry, nurseries, livestock, eggs, fruit
Industry	manufacturing, fishing, mining, forestry, pulp and paper, agriculture

Newfoundland and Labrador

Capital	St. John's
Land Area	144,362 sq mi; 373,872 sq km
Population	531,820
Language(s)	English, French
Agriculture	dairy products, eggs, nurseries, vegetables, potatoes, hogs
Industry	mining, manufacturing, fishing, logging and forestry, electricity production, tourism

Northwest Territories

Capital	Yellowknife
Land Area	456,789 sq mi; 1,183,085 sq km
Population	40,071
Language(s)	English, French, Inuktitut
Agriculture	potatoes, hay, nurseries, livestock
Industry	construction, mining, utilities, services, tourism

Nova Scotia

Capital	Halifax
Land Area	20,594 sq mi; 53,338 sq km
Population	943,497
Language(s)	English, French
Agriculture	dairy products, poultry, livestock, nurseries, fruit, eggs, vegetables
Industry	manufacturing, fishing and trapping, mining, agriculture, pulp and paper

Snowy owl

Introducing Canada

Nunavut

Capital	Iqaluit
Land Area	747,533 sq mi; 1,936,113 sq km
Population	29,016
Language(s)	Inuktitut, English
Industry	mining, tourism, shrimp and scallop fishing, hunting and trapping, arts and crafts production

Ontario

Capital	Toronto
Land Area	354,340 sq mi; 917,741 sq km
Population	11,977,360
Language(s)	English, French, Chinese, Italian, German, Portuguese, Polish, Spanish, Punjabi
Agriculture	livestock, dairy products, nurseries, vegetables, poultry, soybeans, corn, tobacco, eggs, fruit, wheat, ginseng, maple products
Industry	manufacturing, construction, agriculture, forestry, mining

Prince Edward Island

Capital	Charlottetown
Land Area	2,185 sq mi; 5,660 sq km
Population	135,294
Language(s)	English, French
Agriculture	potatoes, dairy products, livestock, vegetables
Industry	agriculture, tourism, fishing, manufacturing

Cape Tryon on Prince Edward Island

Quebec

Capital	Quebec
Land Area	594,860 sq mi; 1,365,128 sq km
Population	7,432,005
Language(s)	French, English, Italian
Agriculture	dairy products, livestock, poultry, vegetables, corn, nurseries, maple products, fruit, potatoes, soybeans, barley, tobacco, wheat
Industry	manufacturing, electric power, mining, pulp and paper, transportation equipment

Saskatchewan

Capital	Regina
Land Area	251,866 sq mi; 591,670 sq km
Population	1,001,224
Language(s)	English, German, Cree, Ukrainian, French
Agriculture	wheat, livestock, canola, barley, lentils, dairy products, poultry, potatoes, nurseries, eggs, honey
Industry	agriculture, mining, manufacturing, electric power, construction, chemical production

Musicians in Montreal, Quebec

Yukon Territory

Capital	Whitehorse
Land Area	186,661 sq mi; 474,391 sq km
Population	29,552
Language(s)	English, German, French
Agriculture	nurseries, vegetables, poultry
Industry	mining, tourism

SOURCES: *CIA World Factbook, 2002; World Almanac, 2003; Canadian Global Almanac, 2003, Canada Census, 2001*

Assessment

Comprehension and Critical Thinking

1. Compare and Contrast Compare Nunavut and Ontario based on physical size and population size.

2. Draw Conclusions What characteristics do the three territories share?

3. Contrast How has geographic location affected the populations and industries of Canada's provinces and territories?

4. Categorize What are the major products in Canada?

5. Infer What can you infer about Nunavut if there are no agricultural products listed?

6. Make a Bar Graph Create a bar graph showing the population of the provinces and territories of Canada.

Keeping Current

Access the **DK World Desk Reference Online** at PHSchool.com for up-to-date information about Canada.

Go Online
PHSchool.com

Web Code: lhe-4501

Section 1

Ontario and Quebec
Bridging Two Cultures

Prepare to Read

Objectives

In this section you will
1. Read about the seat of the Canadian government in Ontario.
2. Learn about the French cultural influence in Quebec.

Taking Notes

As you read this section, look for ways that people in Quebec are preserving and celebrating their culture. Copy the concept web below, and record your findings in it.

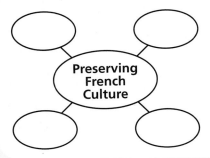

Target Reading Skill

Use Context Clues When you come across an unfamiliar word, you can often figure out its meaning from clues in the context. The context refers to the surrounding words, phrases, and sentences. Sometimes the context will define the word. In this example, the phrase in italics explains what a tariff is: Both countries charged tariffs, or *fees*, on imported goods.

Key Terms

- **federation** (fed ur AY shun) *n.* a union of states, groups, provinces, or nations
- **Francophone** (FRANG koh fohn) *n.* a person who speaks French as his or her first language
- **Quiet Revolution** (KWY ut rev uh LOO shun) *n.* a peaceful change in the government of Quebec
- **separatist** (SEP ur uh tist) *n.* a person who wants Quebec to become an independent country

The Macdonald-Cartier Bridge

Much of the border between Ontario and Quebec is formed by the Ottawa River. The Macdonald-Cartier Bridge stretches across the river, connecting the two provinces. The bridge is named for two Canadian political leaders, one an English speaker and one a French speaker. While the bridge links the two provinces, its very name characterizes the differences between the provinces—people in Ontario speak English primarily, while people in Quebec mostly speak French.

In spite of this significant distinction, Ontario and Quebec have much in common. They are home to Canada's two largest cities—Toronto, Ontario, and Montreal, Quebec. They are the two most populous provinces in Canada. Canada's capital, Ottawa, is located in Ontario. But government functions spill over into the city of Hull, Quebec, located on the other end of the Macdonald-Cartier Bridge. Hull is considered Ottawa's "sister city" because a number of federal government office buildings dot its landscape.

Ontario

The province of Ontario is perhaps Canada's most diverse province geographically. Located on the United States border, it reaches from Hudson Bay in the north to the Great Lakes in the south. Ontario's northern region is part of the Canadian Shield, the region of ancient rock that covers about half of Canada. The Canadian Shield has rocky terrain, rugged winters, and is sparsely populated. Ontario's southern lowlands have milder winters and warm summers. About one third of Canada's entire population lives in this southern area.

Canada's Federal Government

Canada is a **federation,** or union, of 10 provinces and 3 territories. In the Canadian federation, each province has its own government. Each of these governments shares power with Canada's central government, located in Ottawa.

Although Canada's formal head of state is the monarch of Britain, Canada has complete power over its own government. The head of state, represented by the governor general, performs mainly ceremonial duties, such as hosting politicians from other countries, supporting charitable causes, and honoring the achievements of Canadians. Unlike the United States, in which the president is head of state as well as head of government, Canada has a separate head of government, called the prime minister. The prime minister leads the government and is part of Canada's central legislature—the Canadian Parliament.

Ottawa Ottawa has been a capital city since the middle of the nineteenth century, when Upper and Lower Canada—present-day Ontario and Quebec—formed the Province of Canada. Ottawa was selected as the capital because it was located on the border of the two territories. In 1867, Nova Scotia and New Brunswick joined Ontario and Quebec to become the Dominion of Canada, an autonomous, or self-governing, member of the British Empire.

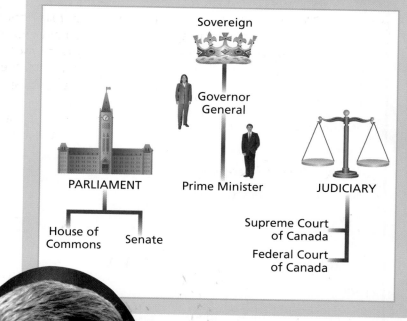

The Canadian Government

Sovereign

Governor General

PARLIAMENT

Prime Minister

JUDICIARY

House of Commons — Senate

Supreme Court of Canada

Federal Court of Canada

Diagram Skills

In the Canadian government structure, the executive, or prime minister, proposes laws; the legislature, Parliament, adopts laws; and the judiciary interprets laws. Stephen Harper, shown at left, was elected as Canadian prime minister in 2006. **Identify** Name the two houses of Parliament. **Contrast** How does Canada's head of state differ from the President of the United States?

Ontario

Canada separated from England very gradually. It went from a dependent colony of England, to a dominion, and finally to an independent nation with ties to Great Britain through the British Commonwealth of Nations. As you study the map and charts, compare and contrast Canada's government with that of the United States.

The House of Commons

Province or Territory	Seats
Alberta	28
British Columbia	36
Manitoba, Saskatchewan	14
New Brunswick	10
Newfoundland and Labrador	7
Northwest Territories, Nunavut, Yukon Territory	1
Nova Scotia	11
Ontario	106
Prince Edward Island	4
Quebec	75

SOURCE: *Canadian Global Almanac*, 2003

Structure of Government

	Canada	United States
Head of State (ceremonial)	Queen of England Governor General (the Queen's representative)	President (elected by the voters)
Head of Government (political)	Prime Minister (PM, the leader of the majority party in the House of Commons)	President
Legislature	Parliament • House of Commons (elected by the voters) • Senate (appointed by PM)	Congress • House of Representatives (elected) • Senate (elected)
Districts	Provinces and territories	States

Map and Chart Skills

1. **Note** Where is most of Ontario's population located?

2. **Explain** How does population affect the number of seats a province or territory has in the House of Commons?

3. **Analyze** What is the difference in the roles of the voters in Canada and in the United States?

Use Web Code **lhe-4511** for **DK World Desk Reference Online.**

Toronto Each of Canada's provinces has a capital. Toronto is the capital of Ontario. It is also Canada's largest city and its commercial and financial center. Founded in 1793, Toronto was first known as York. Its location on Lake Ontario made it a major trade and transportation center. Toronto has come to be identified by its Canadian National (CN) Tower, which, at 1,815 feet (553 meters), is the world's tallest freestanding structure.

Toronto has matured into a cultural mosaic with a very diverse population—nearly half of its residents are foreign-born. After World War II, a large number of Europeans immigrated to Canada, with many settling in Toronto.

The most recent wave of immigrants included a large number of Asians. About 10 percent of Toronto's residents are of Chinese ethnicity. British, Italian, First Nations, Portuguese, East Indian, Greek, German, Ukrainian, Polish, and French are among the other ethnic groups that make up Toronto's population.

✓ **Reading Check** **Where is Canada's federal government located?**

Toronto Cityscape
The CN Tower (right) dominates Toronto's skyline. The large aerial photo taken from the tower shows Rogers Centre (formerly the SkyDome), home of the Toronto Blue Jays baseball team. It was the first domed stadium built with a roof that opens and closes.
Draw Conclusions *Why would a domed stadium be needed in Toronto?*

DISCOVERY CHANNEL **SCHOOL** Video
Learn about Toronto: Canada's largest city

French Culture in Quebec

French culture first reached Quebec in the 1500s, when Jacques Cartier (zhahk kahr tee AY), a French explorer, sailed along the St. Lawrence River and landed in a village called Stadacona (stad uh KOH nuh). The Iroquois, the native people of the area, inhabited the village. Today, the site of that village is the city of Quebec, capital of the province of Quebec.

Cartier claimed the region we now know as Quebec for France and named it Canada. Great Britain, however, was also interested in the region. French and British forces fought for the land in four separate wars over a period of nearly 80 years. The last of the battles were part of the French and Indian War. In 1759, the British captured the city of Quebec. Within four years, France surrendered all of its North American land east of the Mississippi River to the British.

Despite Great Britain's victory, tens of thousands of French colonists remained in the region, and their descendants make up the majority of Quebec's population today. They are called **Francophones** (FRANG koh fohnz), or people who speak French as their first language. In Quebec's largest city, Montreal, and its surrounding areas, more than 65 percent of the population are Francophones.

French Influence in Quebec
French culture reached Quebec hundreds of years ago, and it still exists in the capital city today.
Analyze Images *How can the influence of French culture be seen in this street in Quebec City?*

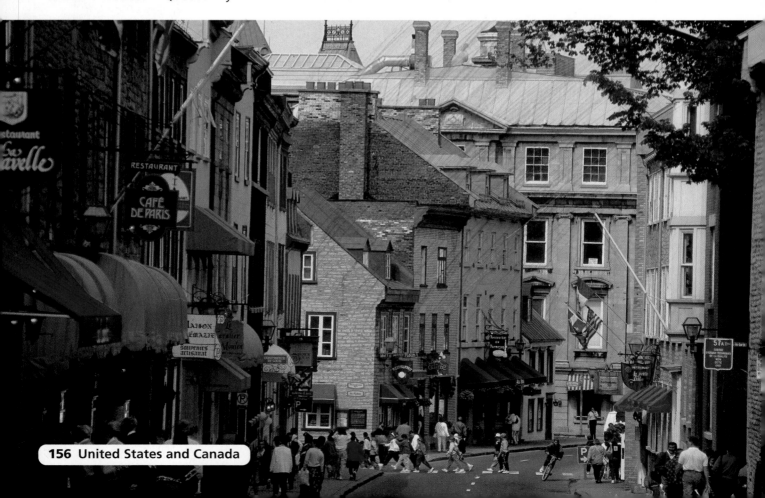

Francophones Seek Rights

In the 1960s, many Francophones began to express concern that their language and culture might die, because English was spoken in the schools and at work. They also believed that opportunities for Francophones in Quebec were not equal to those for English speakers. For the most part, Francophones got jobs with lower pay. So they set out to create change, in a movement that was similar to the civil rights movement in the United States in the 1960s. In 1960, the Liberal party, which supported Francophones, came to power in Quebec. Prime Minister Jean Lesage led the government in creating better job opportunities for Francophones and in modernizing education and health care in Quebec. This change in the government became known as the **Quiet Revolution** because great changes were brought about peacefully.

Disagreement on Separation
A Quebec resident (left) displays her opposition to separation. Other people carrying signs calling for independence and sovereignty rally to support the split from Canada (above). **Analyze Images** *What evidence is there that the woman at the left is against the Separatist Movement?*

The Separatist Movement   During the Quiet Revolution, the separatist movement began to grow. **Separatists** are people who want to see Quebec break away from the rest of Canada and become an independent country. French-Canadian separatists saw important victories in the 1970s as French became the official language of Quebec and the children of immigrants to the province were required to learn French. But still, Quebec remained a province of Canada.

Not everyone in Quebec supported the idea of separation from Canada. In 1980, the provincial government held a referendum. In a referendum, voters cast ballots for or against an issue. This referendum asked voters whether Quebec should become a separate nation. A majority voted no.

In 1995, Quebec held another referendum. Again, Quebec's people voted to remain part of Canada. But this time the margin was very slim—50.6 percent voted against separation while 49.4 percent voted for it. Since then, separatists have lost power and positions in government, but they vow that they will continue to fight for Quebec's independence.

Use Context Clues If you do not know what a referendum is, look for a context clue. Here, the sentence following *referendum* is a definition of the term. What is a referendum?

Quebec

Like much of Canada, Quebec's early history was shaped by two countries—Great Britain and France. Unlike the rest of the nation, however, French influence has remained particularly strong in Quebec. The province's recent history reflects the importance of the French legacy in the region. As you study the map, chart, and timelines, think about how history and culture have interacted in Quebec throughout its history.

Languages Spoken in Montreal

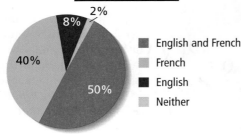

- 2%
- 8%
- 40%
- 50%

- ■ English and French
- ■ French
- ■ English
- ■ Neither

SOURCE: *Canadian Global Almanac, 2003*

Quebec: Population Density

KEY

Persons per sq. mile	Persons per sq. kilometer
More than 129	More than 49
25–129	10–49
1–24	1–9
Less than 1	Less than 1

Urban Areas
- ⊙ More than 999,999
- ● 500,000–999,999
- • Less than 500,000

— National border
— Provincial or territorial border

0 miles 400
0 kilometers 400
Lambert Azimuthal Equal Area

Early Canadian History

1608 Samuel de Champlain builds a fort at Quebec for the French fur trade.

1663 King Louis XIV declares New France a royal colony.

1754 French and Indian War pits the British against the French.

| 1600 | 1650 | 1700 | 1750 | 1800 |

1610 English explorer Henry Hudson charts Hudson Bay.

1670 Hudson's Bay Company is set up in England.

1763 The Treaty of Paris ends French control of Canada.

Recent Quebec History

1968 Interest grows in a separate French-speaking province.

1976 Parti Québécois (PQ) takes power under Premier René Lévesque.

1980 In a referendum, Quebec votes to stay a part of federal Canada.

| 1965 | 1970 | 1975 | 1980 |

1977 French becomes the official language of Quebec.

Map and Chart Skills

1. **Identify** Where is most of Quebec's population located?
2. **Infer** How do the place names on the map reflect early Canadian history?
3. **Analyze** What effect do you think the language law had on those who wanted Quebec to be a separate country?

Use Web Code **lhe-4521** for **DK World Desk Reference Online.**

Celebrating Quebec's Culture One of the ways in which Quebec's people celebrate their culture is through festivals. The Quebec Winter Carnival lasts 17 days. Fantastic ice sculptures adorn Quebec City, and canoe races take place among the ice floes in the St. Lawrence River.

Another Quebec festival honors St. Jean-Baptiste (zhahn bah TEEST), or John the Baptist, the patron saint, or special guardian, of French Canadians. This festival is held June 24. All over the province, people celebrate with bonfires, firecrackers, and street dances.

French style and cooking flourish in Quebec—with Quebec variations. Sugar pie, for example, uses maple sugar from the province's forests. Quebec also has French architecture. The people of Quebec take pride in preserving their lively culture.

✓ **Reading Check** **What is the official language of Quebec?**

An ice slide sculpture at Quebec City's Winter Carnival

Section 1 Assessment

Key Terms
Review the key terms at the beginning of this section. Use each key term in a sentence that explains its meaning.

Target Reading Skill
Find the word *autonomous* on page 153. Use context to figure out its meaning. What clue helped you figure out its meaning?

Comprehension and Critical Thinking
1. (a) Identify Who is the head of state in Canada?

(b) Contrast How does the head of state differ from the head of government?
(c) Analyze What are the possible benefits of this kind of system?
2. (a) Recall How many people in and around Montreal are Francophones?
(b) Make Generalizations Why are French-Canadians concerned with preserving their heritage?
(c) Summarize What has the Canadian government done to meet the demands of French-Canadians?

Writing Activity
You have read that some people in Quebec want to remain a part of Canada while others want Quebec to become a separate country. Write a paragraph giving your opinion on the subject. Be sure to give reasons for your point of view.

For: An activity on Quebec
Visit: PHSchool.com
Web Code: lhd-4501

The Prairie Provinces
Canada's Breadbasket

Prepare to Read

Objectives

In this section you will
1. Learn why many immigrants came to the Prairie Provinces in the 1800s.
2. Read about how Canadians celebrate their cultural traditions.

Taking Notes

As you read this section, looks for details about European immigration to the Prairie Provinces. Copy the chart below, and record your findings in it.

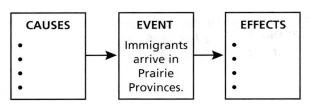

Target Reading Skill

Interpret Nonliteral Meanings Literal language means exactly what it says. Nonliteral language uses images to communicate an idea. Sometimes nonliteral language communicates a point more vividly than literal language. In this section, you will read about "Canada's Breadbasket." When you see these words, ask yourself: How does nonliteral language make a point about the Prairie Provinces region?

Key Terms

- **descent** (dee SENT) *n.* a person's ancestry
- **immunity** (ih MYOO nuh tee) *n.* a natural resistance to disease

Sheets of floating ice in Hudson Bay

One day in 1821, after a difficult journey, about 200 Swiss immigrants reached Hudson Bay in northern Canada. They wanted to become farmers in the region that now includes Saskatchewan (sas KACH uh wahn), Alberta, and Manitoba. Stories of good land and an excellent climate attracted the settlers to the vast plains. But no shelter, food, or supplies awaited them. The settlers survived only because the native people of the region, the Saulteaux (sawl TOH), helped them.

The winters were harsh. In summer they had to put up with drought, floods, and swarms of grasshoppers. With few trees on the plains, people built homes out of prairie sod—strips of grass with thick roots and soil attached. They cut it into blocks, which they piled up to make walls in the same way that American settlers did in the Midwest. "Soddies" were cheap, but if it rained, the roofs leaked. Few settlers had farming experience, and they did not anticipate such hardships.

The Prairie Provinces

Manitoba, Saskatchewan, and Alberta are located on the largest prairie in the world, stretching across the three provinces and down into the central United States. As a result, they are often called the Prairie Provinces. These provinces occupy lands where indigenous peoples have lived for thousands of years.

A Way of Life Ends The Cree and Saulteaux were among the indigenous peoples who lived on the plains in present-day Manitoba. The Cree, Blackfoot, and Assiniboine (uh SIN uh boyn) lived in present-day Alberta. The Chipewyan (chip uh WY un) and Sioux, also called Dakota, are native to Saskatchewan.

These native peoples were deeply connected to the plants and animals of their lands. Buffalo, in particular, were the foundation of their daily lives. Buffalo meat provided food, and buffalo hides were made into clothing. Regina, now the capital of Saskatchewan, was once a place the Cree called *Wascana*, which means "pile of bones." Here people made buffalo bones into tools. Despite their dependence on the buffalo, however, native peoples only used what they needed. Huge numbers of buffalo remained.

In the late 1870s, however, that changed. People of European **descent,** or ancestry, moved into the region and began killing off the buffalo herds that blanketed the region. People killed the buffalo both for sport and for their hides. In a few years, nearly all the buffalo were gone. At the same time, the government of Canada began to take over the indigenous peoples' land. Most agreed to give up their land and live on reserves. The ways of life of many indigenous peoples in the Plains region of North America had come to an end.

A Buffalo Hunt
By the 1730s, Plains Indians were able to trade for horses. **Analyze Images** *How did horses help the Plains Indians to hunt buffalo more effectively?*

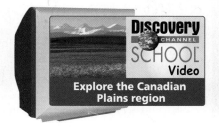

Explore the Canadian Plains region

Prairie Provinces

Canada is the world's second-largest exporter of wheat, after the United States. Although the size of farms in Canada is growing larger, there are fewer of them. Farmers take advantage of science and new technology to increase their crop production. But the new methods are expensive, so corporate farms are replacing small family farms. As you study the map and charts, think about where the food you eat comes from.

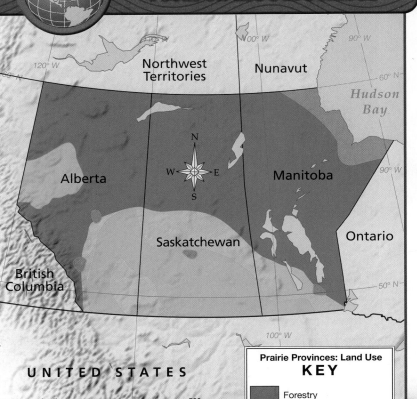

Prairie Provinces: Land Use
KEY

- Forestry
- Livestock raising
- Commercial agriculture
- Manufacturing and trade
- Limited economic activity
- National border
- Provincial or territorial border

0 miles 500
0 kilometers 500
Lambert Azimuthal Equal Area

Number of Farms in Prairie Provinces

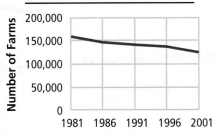

SOURCE: Statistics Canada

Average Size of Farms in Prairie Provinces

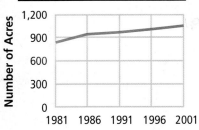

SOURCE: Statistics Canada

Percent of Canadian Grains Grown in Prairie Provinces

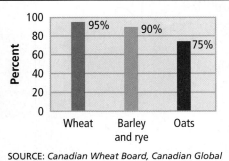

SOURCE: *Canadian Wheat Board, Canadian Global Almanac,* 2004

Map and Chart Skills

1. **Identify** What important crops are grown in the Prairie Provinces?

2. **Note** How much larger was a Prairie Province farm in 2001 than in 1981?

3. **Draw Conclusions** How is it possible that the number of farms has decreased but the Prairie Provinces produce most of Canada's wheat, barley, rye, and oats?

Use Web Code **Ihe-4511** for **DK World Desk Reference Online.**

Increasing Immigration The population of the indigenous peoples also began to shrink. This happened, in part, because European immigrants brought diseases to which the Plains Indians did not have **immunity**, or natural resistance. At the same time, the European population swelled. The settlers were eager to farm the prairie. The Canadian government encouraged people to settle on the Plains. Newcomers would help the economy grow. In the late 1800s and early 1900s, Canada advertised free land in European newspapers. The advertisements worked, and immigration increased. From 1900 to 1910, the population of Alberta alone increased by more than 500 percent.

Until the early 1900s, nearly all Canadians were indigenous peoples or people of French or British descent. That quickly changed. German, French, Belgian, Ukrainian, Hungarian, and Scandinavian immigrants all came to the Prairie Provinces. These immigrants farmed, mined, ranched, and participated in the fur trade.

Links to
Science

Sanctuary Visitors to Saskatchewan's Grasslands National Park see some of North America's last untouched prairies. Ancient grasses called wheat grass, spear grass, and sage blow in the wind. The park is also home to 12 endangered and threatened species. They include hawks, burrowing owls, and short-horned lizards (below).

Prairie wheat grows in Saskatchewan, Canada.

Farming the Land Many of the European immigrants who arrived became wheat farmers. In 1886, the completion of the Canadian Pacific Railway allowed settlers to reach the Prairie Provinces more easily. Better transportation also meant that wheat could be carried more quickly from farms to Canadian ports and then to the rest of the world. The wheat economy of Canada boomed.

Today, more than three fourths of Canada's farmland is in the Prairie Provinces. Wheat is still the major crop. Every year since the mid-1930s, Saskatchewan has produced more than half of Canada's wheat crop. This has helped Canada to become one of the world's leading exporters of wheat. It is no wonder then, that the region is known as Canada's Breadbasket. Although corporate farming is increasing, there are still more family-run farms in Canada than there are in the United States.

✓ **Reading Check** **Why is this region known as Canada's Breadbasket?**

Target Skill Interpret Nonliteral Meanings
What does the phrase *Canada's Breadbasket* mean?

Harvesting Wheat
This farmer harvests wheat near Saskatoon, Saskatchewan. Saskatchewan has more farmland than any other Canadian province. It is also Canada's largest producer of wheat. **Compare** *What part of the United States is similar to this part of Canada? Explain why.*

Celebrating Traditions

Each year, cities of the Prairie Provinces celebrate their ethnic or cultural heritage. In Calgary, Alberta, the Calgary Stampede commemorates the area's ranching legacy. This ten-day rodeo event has been held in Calgary since 1912. It offers a large variety of events such as chuck-wagon races, cow-milking contests, and bull riding. For ten days every July, the city of Edmonton, Alberta, celebrates the gold rush with its Klondike Days. Popular events include the raft race and the sourdough pancake breakfast. (During the gold rush many prospectors ate sourdough bread and biscuits).

Festival du Voyageur is held each February in Winnipeg, the capital of Manitoba. It honors the French Canadian fur-trading heritage of the area and features traditional food, arts and crafts, and exhibits. And in Weyburn, Saskatchewan, residents pay tribute to wheat as the area's most important crop with the Weyburn Wheat Festival. A great deal of fun at this festival comes from harvesting competitions and plant shows. The smell of fresh-baked bread from outdoor ovens adds to the atmosphere.

Rodeo events take place during the Calgary Stampede in Calgary, Alberta.

 **Reading Check** **Which Canadian festival celebrates ranching?**

Section 2 Assessment

Key Terms
Review the key terms at the beginning of this section. Use each key term in a sentence that explains its meaning.

Target Reading Skill
Find the phrase "buffalo herds that blanketed the region" on page 161. Explain in your own words what it means.

Comprehension and Critical Thinking
1. (a) List Which three provinces make up the Prairie Provinces?
(b) Explain What attracted thousands of European immigrants to the Canadian Prairie Provinces?

(c) Identify Effects How did the lives of indigenous people in the Canadian plains change after Europeans arrived?
2. (a) Recall Name two ways that Canadians celebrate their cultural heritage.
(b) Identify Effects How have European immigrants influenced the life and culture of the Prairie Provinces?
(c) Draw Conclusions What do you think were the advantages and disadvantages of moving to the Canadian plains in the 1800s?

Writing Activity
Suppose that it is the year 1900, and you work for Canada's government. The government will give 160 acres of land to people willing to come to the Prairie Provinces to start farms. Make a poster advertising free land. Describe conditions that would make settlers want to come.

For: An activity on Saskatchewan
Visit: PHSchool.com
Web Code: lhd-4502

Prepare to Read

Objectives

In this section you will
1. Find out about the people and cultures of the Canadian West.
2. Learn what the economy and culture of British Columbia are like.

Taking Notes

As you read this section, look for details about the history of British Columbia. Copy the table below, and record your findings in it.

Events in British Columbian History	
10,000 years ago	
1700s	
1800s	
Today	

Target Reading Skill

Use Context Clues When you come across an unfamiliar word, you can sometimes figure out its meaning by using context—the surrounding words, phrases, and sentences. Sometimes the meaning of a word may not be clear until you have read an entire passage. However, you can infer the meaning of the unfamiliar word using general context clues and evaluating the information in the reading passage.

Key Terms

- **totem pole** (TOHT um pohl) *n.* a tall, carved pole containing the symbols of a particular Native American group, clan, or family
- **boomtown** (boom town) *n.* a settlement that springs up quickly to serve the needs of miners

A visitor starts her day at a tiny coffee shop. All around her, people are speaking Dutch, Japanese, Spanish, German, and English. After having breakfast, the visitor gets into her car. On the radio, she hears country music—sung in French. Driving downtown, she passes street signs in Chinese, Indian men wearing turbans, a Korean travel agency, and a Thai restaurant. Where in the world is she? It may seem like the United Nations. But it is Vancouver (van KOO vur), British Columbia—a truly international city. As the largest city in British Columbia, Vancouver is the province's major center of industry, transportation, commerce, and culture.

**Dancers at Chinese
New Year in Vancouver,
British Columbia**

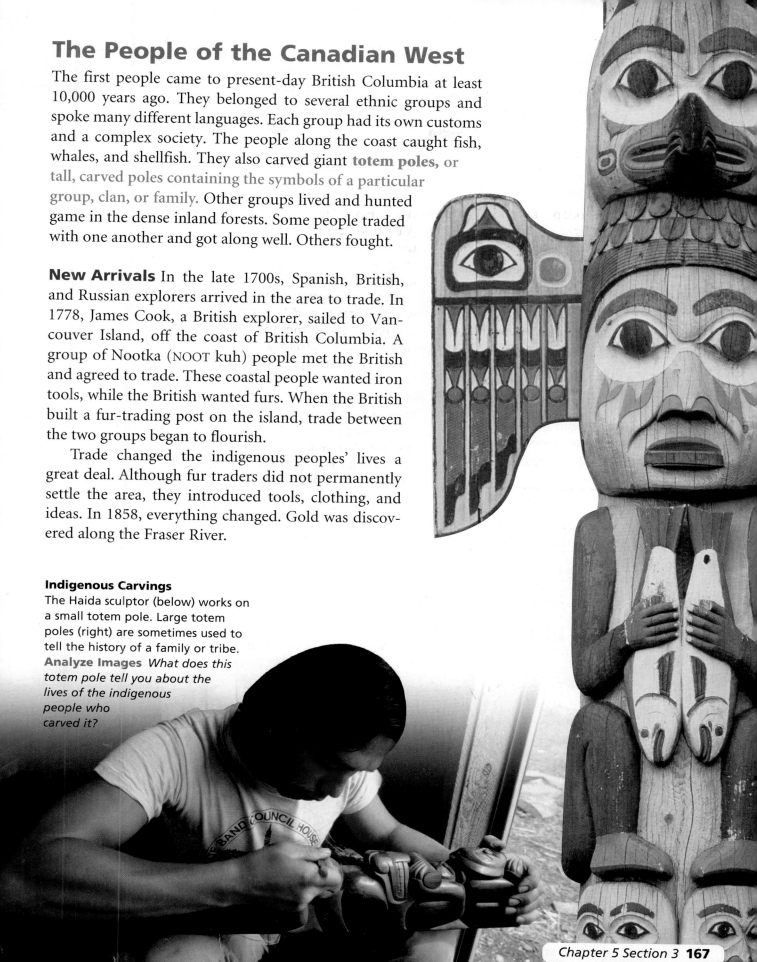

The People of the Canadian West

The first people came to present-day British Columbia at least 10,000 years ago. They belonged to several ethnic groups and spoke many different languages. Each group had its own customs and a complex society. The people along the coast caught fish, whales, and shellfish. They also carved giant **totem poles,** or tall, carved poles containing the symbols of a particular group, clan, or family. Other groups lived and hunted game in the dense inland forests. Some people traded with one another and got along well. Others fought.

New Arrivals In the late 1700s, Spanish, British, and Russian explorers arrived in the area to trade. In 1778, James Cook, a British explorer, sailed to Vancouver Island, off the coast of British Columbia. A group of Nootka (NOOT kuh) people met the British and agreed to trade. These coastal people wanted iron tools, while the British wanted furs. When the British built a fur-trading post on the island, trade between the two groups began to flourish.

Trade changed the indigenous peoples' lives a great deal. Although fur traders did not permanently settle the area, they introduced tools, clothing, and ideas. In 1858, everything changed. Gold was discovered along the Fraser River.

Indigenous Carvings
The Haida sculptor (below) works on a small totem pole. Large totem poles (right) are sometimes used to tell the history of a family or tribe.
Analyze Images *What does this totem pole tell you about the lives of the indigenous people who carved it?*

British Columbia

More than 90 percent of British Columbia is owned by the government, which manages the land and its resources. The government sets certain rules about where and how forests can be cut, and then leases the land to private companies and loggers. More than 260,000 British Columbians depend on forestry for their jobs. British Columbia is the largest single exporter of softwood lumber in the world. As you study the map and charts, think about the importance of the provinces' natural resources.

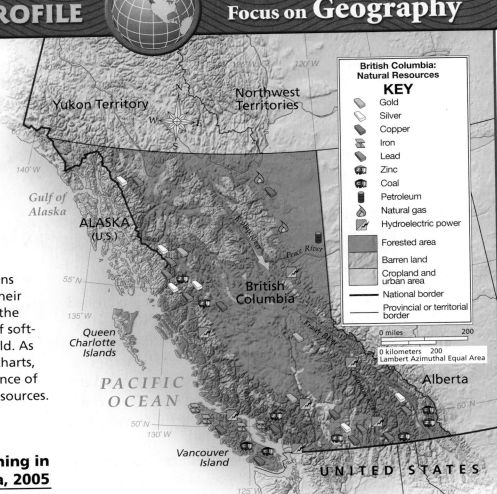

British Columbia: Natural Resources

KEY

- Gold
- Silver
- Copper
- Iron
- Lead
- Zinc
- Coal
- Petroleum
- Natural gas
- Hydroelectric power
- Forested area
- Barren land
- Cropland and urban area
- National border
- Provincial or territorial border

0 miles 200
0 kilometers 200
Lambert Azimuthal Equal Area

Income From Mining in British Columbia, 2005

Mineral	Dollars (millions)
Copper	$1,130
Zinc	$528
Gold	$255
Lead	$87

SOURCE: *Price Waterhouse Coopers, Canada*

Canadian Wood and Paper Products Production

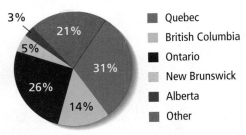

- 3%
- 21%
- 5%
- 31%
- 26%
- 14%

- Quebec
- British Columbia
- Ontario
- New Brunswick
- Alberta
- Other

SOURCE: *Canadian Global Almanac, 2004*

Map and Chart Skills

1. **Identify** Look at the map to describe the location of British Columbia's forests.
2. **Analyze Information** What is the total income British Columbia received in 2005 from mining copper, gold, zinc, and lead?
3. **Draw Conclusions** What do the charts tell you about the importance of forest products to the economy of British Columbia?

 Use Web Code **lhe-4513** for **DK World Desk Reference Online.**

The Gold Rush A few years earlier, the British had established Victoria, a trading village on Vancouver Island. It was a small town of traders and farmers. Then, one Sunday morning in April 1858, an American paddlewheeler entered Victoria's harbor. It dropped off more than 400 men. They carried packs, blankets, spades, pickaxes, knives, and pistols. These rugged-looking characters had come to mine gold in the area. In a single morning, Victoria's population more than doubled.

Within weeks, tens of thousands more miners had arrived. Victoria quickly became a "stumptown"—all of its great trees had been chopped down to build shacks and boats. The town served as a supply center for the miners who were looking for gold on the Fraser River.

Two years later, miners also struck gold in the Cariboo Mountains in eastern British Columbia. Another wave of miners came from China, Europe, and the United States. The region was far from the coast and hard to reach, so the government built a 400-mile (644-kilometer) highway to it. Almost overnight, **boomtowns,** or settlements that were built to serve the needs of the miners, sprang up along the road. When the gold rush was over, many boomtowns died out.

Changes for Indigenous Peoples The thousands of settlers who arrived were taking gold from indigenous people's land—even taking over the land itself. In 1888, the British government took steps to confine some indigenous peoples to a small reserve. The indigenous peoples protested. The reserve was located on land that they had always lived on. How, they asked, could the government now "give" it to them?

Mining for Gold
This photograph, taken in 1900, shows a group of people looking for gold at Pine Creek, British Columbia.
Analyze Information *Why would most people choose to mine gold from creeks and streams rather than by digging deep into the ground?*

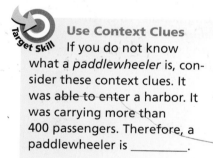

Use Context Clues If you do not know what a *paddlewheeler* is, consider these context clues. It was able to enter a harbor. It was carrying more than 400 passengers. Therefore, a paddlewheeler is _____.

Explore Vancouver, British Columbia's largest city.

Like indigenous peoples throughout Canada, they had little choice. In a few short years, native people had gone from being the great majority to being the smallest minority of the population. They were pushed onto small reserves. The government passed laws banning many of their customs, religions, and languages. Authorities took children from their parents and placed them in government-run schools.

Recently, the indigenous peoples of British Columbia have found new pride in their history and culture. Their art is thriving. They are also demanding political rights and land. As a result, tension has developed between indigenous peoples and other British Columbians. For example, in 1999 the Sechelt Indians were awarded thousands of acres of land northwest of Vancouver and more than $40 million Canadian dollars. Many people felt that these terms were too generous. In July 2002, residents of British Columbia voted to place limits on native land claims.

An indigenous man uses a gaff, an iron hook with a long handle, to catch salmon on the Moricetown Indian Reserve in British Columbia.

The Canadian Pacific Railway British Columbia officially joined Canada in 1871. One of the conditions of joining was that a transcontinental railroad would be built within 10 years. Construction began in 1875, but little progress was made until 1881. That spring, Canadians began work on the enormous project of building a railroad that would stretch from Montreal to Vancouver. The goal of the project was to unite Canada. Look at the physical map of Canada on page 4 and you can see what a huge task this was. There were countless obstacles—soaring mountains, steep valleys, and glaciers. Workers built bridges and blasted long tunnels through the mountains.

The railroad project brought more change to Canada. There were not enough workers available to complete the railway on schedule. Thousands of immigrants, particularly from Ireland and China, came to work on the railroad. Towns grew up along the railroad, and more newcomers moved in. In a few short years, British Columbia changed from a sparsely inhabited region to a settled one, complete with cities.

✓ Reading Check **Why was the Canadian Pacific Railway built?**

Economics and Culture

Although the Canadian Pacific Railroad connects all of Canada, the mountains are a barrier between British Columbia and the rest of the country. Today, most British Columbians live along the coast, west of the mountains. Many of them feel that their economic future lies with other countries more than with the rest of Canada.

The Pacific Rim Many British Columbians feel a link between their province and the Pacific Rim countries—nations that border the Pacific Ocean. One link is British Columbia's diverse people. More than 15 percent have Asian ancestors.

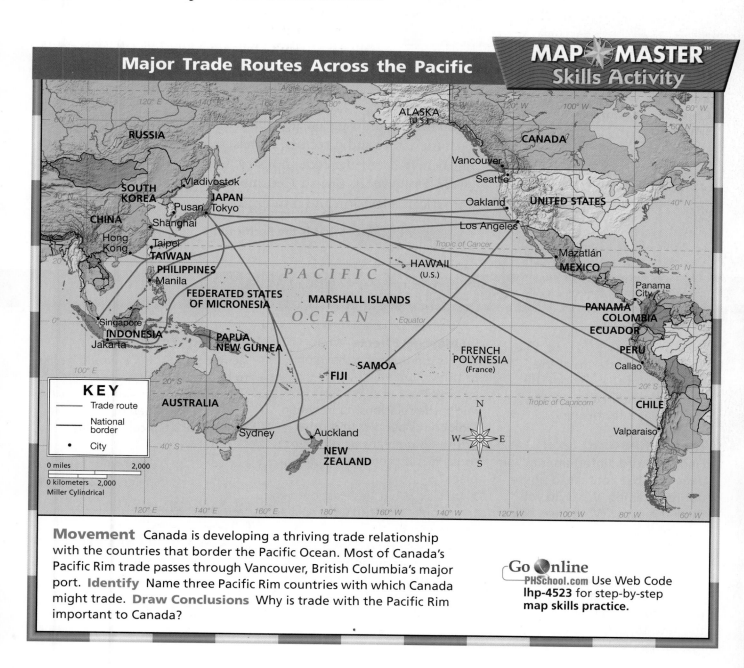

Major Trade Routes Across the Pacific

MAP MASTER™
Skills Activity

KEY
— Trade route
— National border
• City

0 miles 2,000
0 kilometers 2,000
Miller Cylindrical

Movement Canada is developing a thriving trade relationship with the countries that border the Pacific Ocean. Most of Canada's Pacific Rim trade passes through Vancouver, British Columbia's major port. **Identify** Name three Pacific Rim countries with which Canada might trade. **Draw Conclusions** Why is trade with the Pacific Rim important to Canada?

Go Online
PHSchool.com Use Web Code **lhp-4523** for step-by-step map skills practice.

The water in Vancouver's harbor does not freeze. As a result, it's one of Canada's most important ports.

Trade is still another link between British Columbia and the Pacific Rim. Forty percent of the province's trade is with Asian countries. British Columbia wants good relationships with them. As a result, in British Columbian schools, students learn Asian languages. They learn Japanese, Cantonese Chinese, or Mandarin Chinese. Some even learn Punjabi (pun JAH bee), a language of India and Pakistan.

The Film Industry   The television and film industry is another example of British Columbia's strong link to other countries. British Columbia is the third-largest film production center in North America—after New York and Los Angeles. More than 200 productions were filmed in the province in 2002, bringing more than $800 million Canadian dollars to the region.

The film industry creates about 50,000 jobs. The jobs are not just for actors and directors. Hotels, restaurants, and gas stations all benefit from the film industry. Only a two-hour plane ride from Hollywood, British Columbia is a good option for many American television and film projects.

✓ **Reading Check**   **What is the Pacific Rim?**

Section 3 Assessment

Key Terms
Review the key terms at the beginning of this section. Use each key term in a sentence that explains its meaning.

Target Reading Skill
Find the word "international" on page 166. Use context to figure out its meaning. What do you think it means? What clues helped you arrive at a meaning?

Comprehension and Critical Thinking
1. (a) Recall What brought people to British Columbia in the late 1800s?

(b) Identify Effects What effects did this event have on British Columbia?
(c) Link Past and Present How might the relationship between indigenous peoples and other British Columbians be different today if this event hadn't taken place?
2. (a) List What ties exist between the people of British Columbia and the Pacific Rim?
(b) Analyze How does British Columbia's geography contribute to its economic and cultural ties with the Pacific Rim?

Writing Activity
What do you think it would be like to be a gold prospector in one of the gold rushes in Canada? Write a journal entry describing a gold prospector's typical workday.

For: An activity on totem poles
Visit: PHSchool.com
Web Code: lhd-4503

The Atlantic Provinces
Relying on the Sea

Prepare to Read

Objectives
In this section you will
1. Learn what life is like on the Atlantic coast.
2. Discover how maritime industries affect the provinces.

Taking Notes
As you read this section, look for the causes and effects of overfishing. Copy the chart below, and record your findings in it.

Target Reading Skill
Use Context Clues Context, the words and phrases surrounding a word, can help you understand a word you may not know. One context clue to look for is cause and effect. The context clues show how the unfamiliar word is related to the cause or is the result of an action or idea. Clues to look for include *because, since, therefore,* and *so.*

Key Terms
• **exile** (EK syl) *v.* to force someone to leave his or her native land or home
• **maritime** (MA rih tym) *adj.* having to do with navigation or shipping on the sea
• **aquaculture** (AHK wuh kul chur) *n.* the cultivation of fish or water plants

Modern-day Norwegian explorer Helge Ingstad was aboard a ship in 1960 that stopped at a rocky peninsula in Newfoundland. The land formation was similar to what he had seen on ancient maps, and the scenery reminded him of the descriptions in Viking legends. After spotting what appeared to be the outlines of old building foundations, Ingstad believed he might be at the site of the first known Viking settlement in North America. Eight years of archaeological digs proved that Ingstad had unearthed a Viking settlement—possibly the very one that Leif Ericsson reached and named Vinland around the year 1000. Many artifacts were found at the site, including fireplaces, and a pit where iron may have been heated and formed into tools. The Viking settlement is now called L'Anse aux Meadows (lahns oh meh DOH). Viking buildings and artifacts have been reconstructed, and the historic site has become a popular tourist attraction.

From the time of the Vikings until today, the location of the Atlantic Provinces has had a huge influence on the region.

Some historians believe that Leif Ericsson may have landed here at L'Anse aux Meadows about 1,000 years ago.

Discovery CHANNEL
SCHOOL Video
Explore the cultures of the Atlantic Provinces.

Living on the Coast

Today, Newfoundland and Labrador, along with Prince Edward Island, New Brunswick, and Nova Scotia, make up the Atlantic Provinces. These provinces are located in eastern Canada, where they all share at least part of their border with the Atlantic Ocean. Many of the people in these provinces live on the coast. One exception is Prince Edward Island, where the population is evenly spread across the island. The people in the Atlantic Provinces are mainly of English, Irish, Scottish, and French descent.

Newfoundland and Labrador   Five hundred years after the Vikings left their colony in Vinland, John Cabot rediscovered the island in 1497. He called it the *New Found Land.* About 100 years later, the island became England's first overseas colony. It was used mainly as a fishing station until settlers moved there permanently in the early 1600s. In 2001, the province's name officially changed from Newfoundland to Newfoundland and Labrador.

The province of Newfoundland and Labrador is the easternmost part of North America. Because of its location, the province is an important transatlantic transportation and communications center. It was here in 1901 that Guglielmo Marconi (goo lee EL moh mahr KOH nee) received the first wireless telegraph signals from across the Atlantic Ocean. More importantly, the province is located next to the Grand Banks, which at one time were the best fishing grounds in the world.

Target Skill

Use Context Clues
If you do not know what *transatlantic* means, look for a context clue. Use the cause and effect context clue and the surrounding sentences to figure out its meaning. What does *transatlantic* mean?

Northern gannets fly around Avalon Peninsula, Newfoundland and Labrador.

The Atlantic Provinces

Long before the Atlantic Provinces were settled, European fishermen had been coming to the Grand Banks to fish. The abundance and variety of fish astonished them. Since that time, fishing, especially cod fishing, has been a vital part of the region's economy. Because of overfishing, cod fishing was banned in 2003. People in the Atlantic Provinces are beginning to concentrate on other economic activities. As you study the map and charts, think about how a natural resource can affect a region's people and economy.

Atlantic Provinces: Natural Resources
KEY

Gold		Iron		Hydroelectric power	
Silver		Coal		Timber	
Copper		Petroleum		Fish	
—— National border		—— Provincial or territorial border			

Cod Fishing in Newfoundland

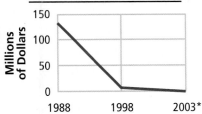

* Cod fishing banned throughout Canada
SOURCES: *The World Today Series: Canada, 2003;
Boston Globe, 2003*

Aquaculture in Newfoundland and Labrador

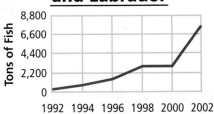

SOURCE: Government of Newfoundland

Economic Activities in the Atlantic Provinces

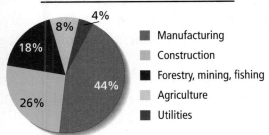

4%
8%
18%
44%
26%

- Manufacturing
- Construction
- Forestry, mining, fishing
- Agriculture
- Utilities

SOURCE: *Canadian Global Almanac,* 2003

Map and Chart Skills

1. **List** What are the Atlantic Provinces' major natural resources?
2. **Analyze** How has aquaculture changed in the past decade?
3. **Predict** How do you think the cod fishing ban will affect the region? How might it help the development of other economic activities?

Use Web Code
lhe-4514 for **DK World Desk Reference Online.**

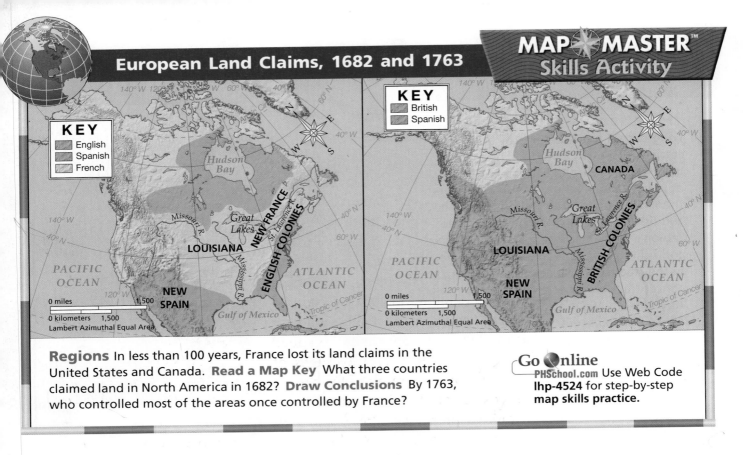

MAP MASTER
Skills Activity

European Land Claims, 1682 and 1763

KEY
- English
- Spanish
- French

KEY
- British
- Spanish

Regions In less than 100 years, France lost its land claims in the United States and Canada. **Read a Map Key** What three countries claimed land in North America in 1682? **Draw Conclusions** By 1763, who controlled most of the areas once controlled by France?

Go Online
PHSchool.com Use Web Code **lhp-4524** for step-by-step map skills practice.

Acadia Eastern Canada was once almost entirely populated by people of French descent. Nova Scotia, New Brunswick, and Prince Edward Island were part of Acadia. Here, in the early 1600s, the French established their first permanent North American settlement. French control of the area, however, did not last long. The English wanted this land, and the two countries fought over it many times. The area shifted from one country's control to the other's more than once. During the fighting, Acadians remained neutral.

In 1755, a time when Britain controlled the area, Britain feared that the French inhabitants of Acadia might secretly be loyal to France. As a result, Acadians were **exiled,** or forced to leave the area. Some exiled Acadians settled in Quebec or New Brunswick, while others moved to France, the West Indies, and other French colonies. Still others moved to present-day Louisiana, then a French settlement, where their descendants today are known as Cajuns. Britain gained permanent control over Acadia in 1763 at the end of the Seven Years' War. Many Acadians returned to the area only to find that the British had taken control of the fertile lands they had once farmed. So they took up fishing and lumbering instead to support themselves.

✓ **Reading Check** When did Britain gain permanent control over Acadia?

Links to
Science

High Tide The Bay of Fundy lies between New Brunswick and Nova Scotia. Its unique funnel shape—narrow with shallow water at the north end of the bay and wide with deep water where the bay opens into the ocean—causes some of the highest tides in the world. Water in the bay can rise as much as 60 feet at high tide. These exceptional tides carry about 100 billion tons of water in and out of the bay each day.

A Maritime Economy

Maritime means related to navigation or commerce on the sea. No term better sums up the focus of life in the Atlantic Provinces. The Atlantic Provinces are often called the Maritime Provinces. Much of the economy there depends on fishing.

In the 1800s, the demand for fishing vessels brought about the growth of the shipbuilding industry. The region led Canada in ship construction through most of the 1800s. The forestry industry in the area kept shipbuilders well supplied. Both industries helped the region's economy boom. Shipbuilding is still a major employer in the region, particularly in Nova Scotia.

Fishing is another major industry. However, the fishing industry has changed. In Newfoundland and Labrador, cod had been the primary catch until cod fishing was partially banned in 1992 and completely banned in 2003. The government banned cod fishing because the waters had been overfished. Tens of thousands of fishing jobs have been lost as a result of the ban.

Today, the province has turned its attention toward other types of fish to make up for loss of revenue from cod. Fish farming, or **aquaculture,** is a growing industry. Mussels are grown on Canada's eastern coast, and salmon farms are operating off the shores of New Brunswick.

Fishing village on Cape Breton Island, Nova Scotia

✓ **Reading Check** **Which Atlantic Province is a leader in the shipbuilding industry?**

Section 4 Assessment

Key Terms

Review the key terms at the beginning of this section. Use each key term in a sentence that explains its meaning.

Target Reading Skill

Find the word *overfished* on page 177. Use context to figure out its meaning. What clue helped you?

Comprehension and Critical Thinking

1. (a) List Name the provinces that make up the Atlantic Provinces.

(b) Explain Where are the Atlantic Provinces located?
(c) Analyze How has the location of Newfoundland and Labrador made it an important communications center?
2. (a) Recall What industries did fishing help to grow in the 1800s?
(b) Summarize How has the fishing industry in the Atlantic Provinces changed in recent years?
(c) Predict What role might the fishing industry play in the Atlantic Provinces' economy in the future?

Writing Activity

Suppose that you are a French farmer living in Acadia in 1755. The British have told you that you must move to Louisiana. Write a paragraph describing how you feel about the move.

For: An activity on Nova Scotia
Visit: PHSchool.com
Web Code: lhd-4504

"Hey, how was your weekend?"

If your friend asked you this question, would you tell him every-thing that happened over the weekend? Of course you wouldn't. You would pick a few major events and state them as a conclu-sion. For instance, "I went to the ball game on Saturday after-noon and the movies on Saturday night. I was really busy."

When you're asked to summarize information, you find the main ideas and weave them into a conclusion. Being able to sum-marize information is a school survival skill. You need it to take tests, write essays, have debates, and understand what you read.

Learn the Skill

You can summarize many types of information: a novel, a news report, a movie—even a museum exhibit. These steps show you how to sum up information.

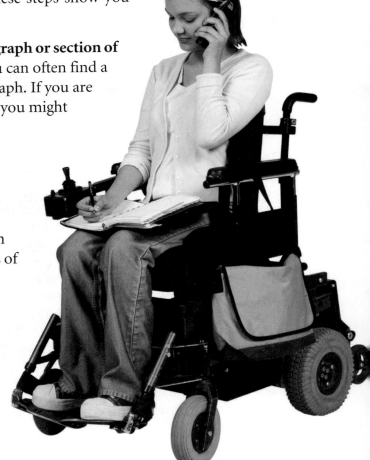

1 **Find and state the main idea of each paragraph or section of information you want to summarize.** You can often find a main idea in the topic sentence of a paragraph. If you are summarizing a large piece of information, you might want to jot down the main ideas.

2 **Identify what the main ideas have in common.** Look for the logic in how the ideas are presented. You might find events in chronological order. You might find causes and effects or comparisons. You can also look for main ideas that describe parts of a whole topic.

3 **Write a summary paragraph beginning with a topic sentence.** The topic sentence should draw together the main ideas you are summarizing. The main ideas on your list will become the supporting details of your summary.

Practice the Skill

Reread pages 156–157. Follow the steps on the previous page in order to summarize the text.

1 Read the heading and subheadings of this passage. List the main idea of each paragraph. For example, in the first paragraph, the first half of the topic sentence provides a strong main idea: "French culture first reached Quebec in the 1500s…." If no one sentence states the whole main idea, you should form a statement in your own words. Now write down the main idea for the other paragraphs in this passage.

2 The main ideas in this passage are mostly in chronological order. In what other ways are they related?

3 One possible topic sentence for your summary might be this: "The province of Quebec has struggled to preserve its French heritage in a country dominated by English culture." Use this topic sentence, or write your own, and then complete the summary paragraph by adding explanations and details. The details will come from the main ideas on your list.

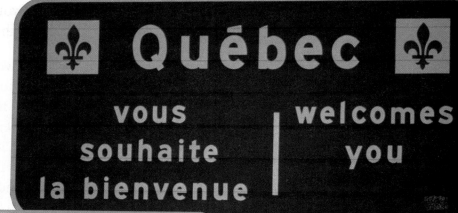

A welcome-to-Quebec sign in English and French.

Apply the Skill

Reread page 167. Follow the steps to summarize the information. Keep in mind that *change* is a major part of this passage.

Prepare to Read

Objectives

In this section you will
1. Discover what life is like for people in Canada's far north.
2. Find out about the remote region of the Yukon Territory.
3. Understand how the new territory of Nunavut was formed.

Taking Notes

As you read the section, look for details about the government of the Northern Territories. Copy the concept web below, and record your findings in it.

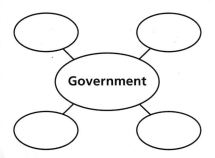

Government

Target Reading Skill

Use Context Clues Words and phrases can take on different meanings in different situations. For example, if you are watching a play, and someone says that the *cast* is very talented, you would know that *cast* means the group of actors. But *cast* can also mean "to throw a fishing line" or "something you put on a broken arm." The information surrounding a word—whether it is a few other words, or phrases and sentences—is the context of that word.

Key Terms

- **aurora borealis** (aw RAWR uh bawr ee AL us) *n.* the colorful bands of light that can be seen in the skies of the Northern Hemisphere
- **Inuktitut** (ih NOOK tih toot) *n.* the native language of the Inuit

Named for the Latin word for dawn, the **aurora borealis** (aw RAWR uh bawr ee AL us), or northern lights, is a colorful band of light that can be seen in the Northern Hemisphere. The farther north you travel, the better is your chance of seeing these colorful bands of light. Some of Canada's indigenous peoples believed the lights were spirits. One folktale described the lights as spirits playing games. Others said that if you whistled loudly, the spirits would whisk you away.

Scientists today think that the lights, shown here, are caused by the reaction that occurs when charged particles from the sun hit gases in Earth's atmosphere. The lights still attract many sky-gazers. These dazzling displays can be seen throughout northern Canada. The northern lights are a beautiful sight in the often harsh environment of these sparsely-populated territories.

The Far North

In addition to its provinces, Canada has three territories—the Northwest Territories, Yukon Territory, and Nunavut (NOO nuh voot). The territories make up more than one third of Canada's total land area and stretch far north into the Arctic Ocean. Despite the region's size, the people there comprise less than one percent of the nation's population. The main reason for the low population is the region's rugged terrain and harsh climate. The area is made up of tundra with little vegetation, icy waters, and subarctic forests.

Modern Inuits
This modern Inuit family travels on a snowmobile on Ellesmere Island. **Draw Conclusions** *How does technology influence Inuit life?*

People of the Far North Another characteristic unique to this region is the large number of indigenous people who live there. In the Northwest Territories, almost 50 percent of the population is made up of indigenous peoples such as the Dene, Métis, and Inuit. In Nunavut, about 85 percent of the population are Inuit. In contrast, only about 14 percent of the Yukon population is made up of native people. The rest of the population is of European or other ancestry.

Contact with Europeans has changed many of the ways in which indigenous peoples live. Technology has played a major role. For example, seal hunting is an important part of Inuit life. Today, Inuit hunters use snowmobiles instead of dogsleds to cross the frozen land.

A Different Form of Government Members of the House of Commons, a part of the Canadian Parliament, represent both territories and provinces in the federal government. Each territory has its own legislative, or law-making, body similar to those of the provinces.

But, the federal government exercises more authority over the territories. While territories do have control over many of the same local concerns as provinces, such as education, the federal government controls other areas, such as some natural resources. Territories also have less power to tax than the provinces do.

✓ **Reading Check** **What percentage of Nunavut's population is Inuit?**

Use Context Clues You know that *exercise* often refers to physical activity or putting something in action. Use part of that definition to help you understand *exercises authority*. What does *exercise* mean in this context? What is the meaning of the phrase *exercises authority*?

Northern Territories

Three territories—Nunavut, the Northwest Territories, and Yukon—make up this region. As territories, they have a different status from Canada's provinces. All three territories have legislatures, but there are no political parties. Decisions are made by agreement rather than by majority vote. Most of the territories' public land is controlled by the government in Ottawa. As you study the map and graphs, think about why and how Canada's territories are different from the nation's provinces.

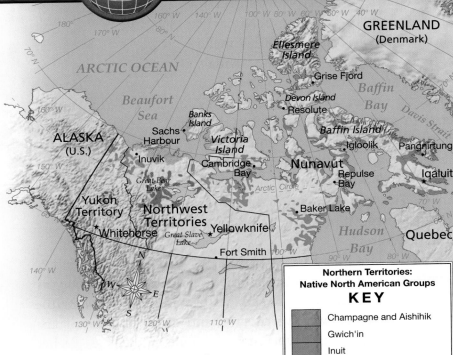

Northern Territories: Native North American Groups
KEY

- Champagne and Aishihik
- Gwich'in
- Inuit
- Inuvialuit
- Nacho Nyak Dun
- Sahtu Dene and Métis
- —— National border
- —— Provincial or territorial border
- ★ Provincial or territorial capital
- • Other town

0 miles 1,000
0 kilometers 1,000
Lambert Azimuthal Equal Area

Population and Area of Northern Canada

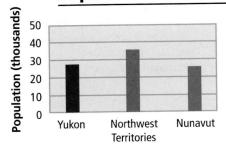

SOURCE: Statistics Canada

SOURCE: *Encyclopaedia Britannica*

Nunavut Legislature

Most provincial legislatures meet in a divided chamber. The party in power sits on one side, and the opposition sits on the other. The Nunavut legislature sits in a circle.

Map and Chart Skills

1. **Identify** What is the main ethnic group in Nunavut?
2. **Infer** How does the circular seating of the legislature serve the Nunavut decision-making process?
3. **Analyze** Would the organization of Nunavut's legislature work for the Canadian federal government in Ottawa? Explain why or why not.

 Use Web Code **lhe-4515** for **DK World Desk Reference Online.**

Forming New Territories

All of Canada's northern land used to be one giant territory—the Northwest Territories. Over time, this vast land was split up into three separate territories.

Yukon Territory The Yukon Territory was once a district of the Northwest Territories. In 1898, an act of Parliament made it a separate territory. Many people are familiar with the Yukon Territory because of the Klondike Gold Rush. After gold was discovered in a branch of the Klondike River in 1896, thousands of prospectors swarmed to the area. Within two years, the population of the town of Dawson swelled to about 30,000. Saloons, banks, theaters, and dance halls sprang up there.

It was amazing that so many people were able to get to the area, because one of the main routes was the treacherous Chilkoot Pass, known as "the meanest 32 miles in the world." The end of the pass narrowed to less than three feet wide and became very steep. But the Yukon's era of prosperity was short-lived. By the end of 1898, the rush began to slow, and the population of the settlement declined quickly. Today, fewer than 1,300 people live in Dawson.

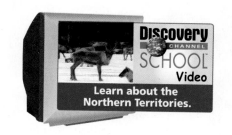

Learn about the Northern Territories.

Building a New Capital
A new building was constructed in Iqaluit to house Nunavut's legislature. **Draw Conclusions** *How might the construction of a new capital have helped Nunavut's economy?*

This stop sign is in Inuktitut and English.

Nunavut In 1993, the area now known as Nunavut was carved out of the eastern portion of the Northwest Territories. A constitutional act officially made Nunavut the third Canadian territory on April 1, 1999. A decades-long dream of the Inuit people to have their own self-governing territory became reality.

The Inuit, who make up most of Nunavut's population, proposed the formation of Nunavut in the 1970s. Nunavut means "our land" in **Inuktitut** (ih NOOK tih toot), the native language of the Inuit. When the matter came to a vote in 1982, residents overwhelmingly favored the creation of their own territory.

The construction of Nunavut's new capital, Iqaluit (ee KAH loo eet), provided many jobs for people. But Nunavut still faces several challenges. Leaders in the territory must work to keep its economy strong in spite of its remote location and harsh climate. The modernization of the area, which now has an Internet provider, a television broadcaster, and cellular phone service, may be a step in the right direction.

✓ **Reading Check** **Present-day Nunavut was once a part of which territory?**

Section 5 Assessment

Key Terms

Review the key terms at the beginning of this section. Use each key term in a sentence that explains its meaning.

Target Reading Skill

Find the word *bands* on page 180. Use your own knowledge and the surrounding words and phrases to explain what *bands* means in this context.

Comprehension and Critical Thinking

1. (a) List Which three territories make up the Northern Territories?

(b) Compare and Contrast How do the governments of provinces and territories differ? How are they the same?

2. (a) Recall What event made the Yukon Territory famous?

(b) Identify Effects How did that event cause the town of Dawson to grow?

3. (a) Recall What is the newest territory in Canada?

(b) Identify Point of View Why might Inuits have wanted to create a self-governing territory?

Writing Activity

Suppose that you are Inuit, and you have always been a part of a minority in a larger territory. Describe what it might be like living for the first time in a territory where you are part of the majority.

For: An activity on Nunavut
Visit: PHSchool.com
Web Code: lhd-4505

◆ Chapter Summary

Section 1: Ontario and Quebec

- Canada's central government is located in Ottawa, Ontario.
- Toronto is Canada's financial center and largest city.
- French Canadians are concerned about preserving their cultural heritage, and some think that Quebec should become an independent country.

Section 2: The Prairie Provinces

- Manitoba, Saskatchewan, and Alberta are called the Prairie Provinces.
- Many European immigrants settled the Canadian plains in the late 1800s.
- Disease and the destruction of the buffalo in the late 1800s led to the end of many indigenous peoples' way of life.

Section 3: British Columbia

- Following the discovery of gold in 1858, the population of British Columbia grew rapidly.
- Indigenous peoples were pushed onto small reserves and were not allowed to practice many of their customs.
- British Columbia has geographic, economic, and cultural ties to foreign countries, especially those of the Pacific Rim.

Section 4: The Atlantic Provinces

- Newfoundland and Labrador, Prince Edward Island, New Brunswick, and Nova Scotia make up the Atlantic Provinces.
- The location of the Atlantic Provinces has shaped the history, culture, and economy of the people there.
- The economy of the Atlantic Provinces is dependent on the fishing industry.

Section 5: The Northern Territories

- The Northern Territories— made up of the Northwest Territories, Yukon Territories, and Nunavut—are the least-populated regions in Canada.
- The Northern Territories have a different form of government from that of Canada's provinces.
- Nunavut is the homeland of the Inuit, and Canada's newest territory.

Totem pole

◆ Key Terms

Each of the statements below contains a key term from the chapter. If the statement is true, write *true*. If it is false, rewrite the statement to make it true.

1. A separatist is a person who speaks French as his or her first language.

2. A boomtown is a settlement that springs up to serve the needs of miners.

3. Colorful bands of light that can be seen in the Northern Hemisphere are the aurora borealis.

4. Descent is a natural resistance to disease.

5. Aquaculture has to do with navigation or shipping on the sea.

6. After the Quiet Revolution, Nunavut became a separate territory.

7. An exile is someone who is forced to leave his or her homeland.

8. A federation is a union of states, groups, provinces, or nations.

◆ Comprehension and Critical Thinking

9. (a) Explain What is the role of the British monarch in Canadian government?
(b) Compare and Contrast How does the Canadian government differ from that of the United States?

10. (a) Recall What were the results of the 1980 and 1995 referendums on Quebec's independence?
(b) Analyze Why do so many people in Quebec want to separate from Canada?

11. (a) List In what ways was the buffalo important to indigenous peoples on the Plains?
(b) Identify Effects How might the destruction of the buffalo have affected the native people who lived there?

12. (a) List In the late 1700s, which countries sent explorers to present-day British Columbia?
(b) Summarize What was the relationship between the early explorers and the indigenous people of the region?
(c) Compare and Contrast How and why did the miners' relationship with native peoples differ from that of the early explorers?

13. (a) Locate Where was the first French settlement in North America?

(b) Summarize How did the lives of Acadians change after the British gained control over the region in 1763?

14. (a) Explain Why are the Northern Territories not heavily populated?
(b) Predict How does climate affect culture in the Northern Territories?

◆ Skills Practice

Writing a Summary Review the steps you followed in the Skills for Life activity in this chapter. Then reread the part of Section 3 under the heading Economics and Culture. Find and state the main idea of each paragraph. Then, identify what the main ideas have in common. Finally, write a summary paragraph that begins with a topic sentence.

◆ Writing Activity: Language Arts

Suppose that you have been asked to develop a proposal for a film to be set in British Columbia. You may choose to make a documentary or a historical film. Outline the events or the plot of the film on a storyboard—a series of sketches that show the sequence of major scenes in the film.

MAP MASTER™
Skills Activity

Canada

Place Location For each place listed below, write the letter from the map that shows its location.

1. Quebec
2. Ottawa
3. Saskatchewan
4. Winnipeg
5. Vancouver
6. Prince Edward Island
7. Iqaluit

Go Online
PHSchool.com Use Web Code
lhp-4555 for an
interactive map.

Standardized Test Prep

Test-Taking Tips

Some questions on standardized tests ask you to analyze a reading selection. Read the passage below. Then, follow the tips to answer the sample question.

TIP Read for key words that may help you answer the question. In this case, the key word is *Nunavut*.

In 1982, citizens of Canada's Northwest Territories were about to vote on whether to allow the creation of a self-governing homeland. It would be known as Nunavut and would be carved out of the territories. Someone argued, "We're asking for a share in the resources. We don't want to appear as beggars dependent on government handouts, but we are now being denied the resources that we so willingly gave up to support this nation."

Who might have made this argument?

A a descendant of a French fur trader

B a descendant of an English farmer

C a descendant of an Inuit hunter

D a descendant of a German logger

TIP Try to answer the question before you look at the answer choices. Doing so may help you find the BEST answer.

Think It Through The key word *Nunavut* will help you answer the question. What does the passage have to do with Nunavut? The speaker says the government owes his people resources that had been taken away. Which group wants a separate homeland that would give them control over their own resources? You can eliminate B and D. That leaves A and C. Some French in Quebec do want their own homeland. But, their resources and land were not taken away. The answer is C.

Practice Questions

Use the tips above and other tips in this book to help you answer the following questions.

1. Who is Canada's head of state?
   A the monarch of Britain
   B the prime minister
   C the governor of Ontario
   D the president

Read the passage below, and then answer the question that follows.

In the late 1800s, life changed for a group of people who lived on Canada's plains. They could not hunt the way they always had, and their lands were taken away by new settlers. They also began to get sick in large numbers from new diseases.

2. Who does this passage describe?
   A French Canadians
   B Scandinavian immigrants
   C Native Americans
   D German immigrants

3. British Columbia has special economic and cultural ties to
   A Russia.
   B the rest of Canada.
   C the northeastern United States.
   D the Pacific Rim.

4. Who first settled Canada's Atlantic Provinces in large numbers?
   A the French
   B the British
   C the Vikings
   D Americans

Go Online
PHSchool.com
Use Web Code lha-4505
for **Chapter 5 self-test.**

Projects

Create your own projects to learn more about the United States and Canada. At the beginning of this book, you were introduced to the **Guiding Questions** for studying the chapters and special features. But you can also find answers to these questions by doing projects on your own or with a group.

1 **Geography** How has physical geography affected the cultures of the United States and Canada?

2 **History** How have historical events affected the cultures of the United States and Canada?

3 **Culture** How has the variety of people in the United States and Canada benefited and challenged the two nations?

4 **Government** How do the governments of the United States and Canada differ? How are they alike?

5 **Economics** How did the United States and Canada become two of the wealthiest nations in the world?

Project

RESEARCH YOUR LOCAL HISTORY

Make a Timeline
Read about the history of your community at the local public library. Write down dates and descriptions of between 10 and 20 important events. Then, make a timeline large enough to hang on the wall of your classroom. Draw a picture of each event and place it next to its description on the timeline. Add several major events of United States history.

Project

SET UP A WEATHER STATION

Create a Weather Log
Set up a weather station to measure and record your local weather as you read this book. Measure the temperature each day at the same time. Also record the amount of precipitation and the wind direction. Record all of your findings in a weather log.

Each day, compare your local weather with the weather in other parts of the country. You can get this information from television, radio, the newspaper, or the Internet. When you have finished your measurements and recordings, create graphs to display your local readings. Then, compare your findings with the climate map in the Activity Atlas.

Reference

Table of Contents

The World: Political

0 miles 2,000

0 kilometers 2,000

Robinson

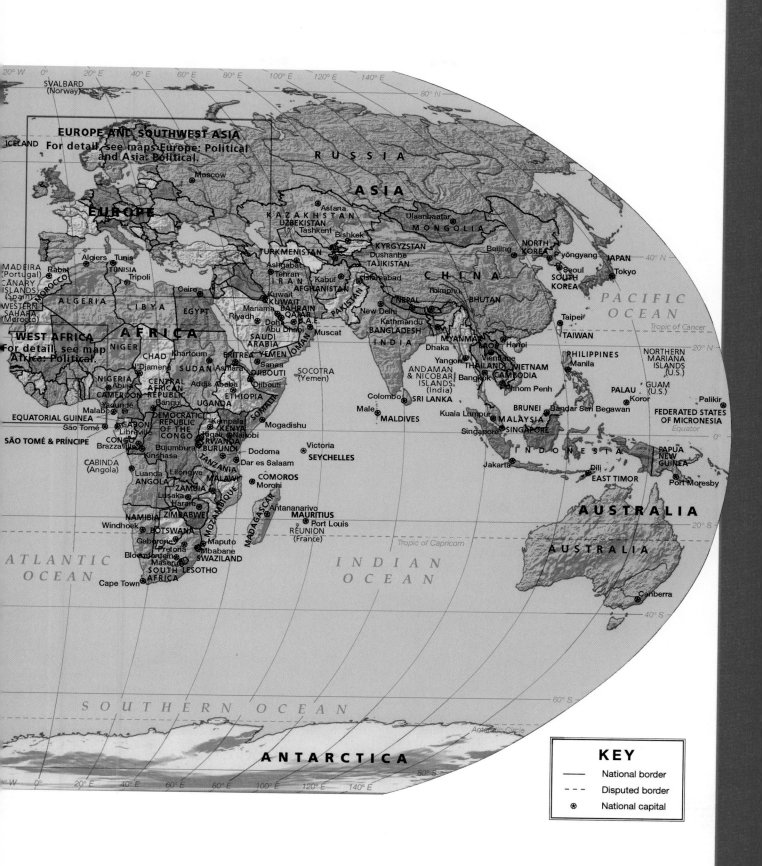

EUROPE AND SOUTHWEST ASIA
For detail, see maps Europe: Political
and Asia: Political.

SVALBARD
(Norway)

ICELAND

EUROPE

R U S S I A

A S I A

Moscow

80° N

KAZAKHSTAN
UZBEKISTAN
Tashkent

Astana

Ulaanbaatar

M O N G O L I A

Beijing

NORTH
KOREA

P'yŏngyang

JAPAN

40° N

Bishkek
KYRGYZSTAN
Dushanbe
TAJIKISTAN

Seoul
SOUTH
KOREA

Tokyo

PACIFIC
OCEAN

Algiers Tunis
TURKMENISTAN
Ashgabat
MADEIRA
(Portugal) Rabat
CANARY MOROCCO
ISLANDS
(Spain)
WESTERN
SAHARA
(Morocco)

TUNISIA
Tripoli

I R A N
Tehran

Kabul
AFGHANISTAN

Islamabad

C H I N A

Thimphu

BHUTAN

Taipei

Tropic of Cancer

ALGERIA

L I B Y A

EGYPT

Cairo

KUWAIT
Kuwait
Manama BAHRAIN
Riyadh Doha QATAR
Abu Dhabi U.A.E.

New Delhi
Kathmandu
NEPAL
BANGLADESH

TAIWAN

20° N

WEST AFRICA
For detail, see map
Africa: Political.

NIGER

A F R I C A

CHAD
Khartoum

NIGERIA
Abuja

N'Djamena
CAMEROON
CENTRAL
AFRICAN
REPUBLIC
Bangui
Yaoundé

SUDAN

SAUDI
ARABIA
YEMEN
ERITREA
Sanaa
Asmara DJIBOUTI
Addis Ababa Djibouti
ETHIOPIA

OMAN
Muscat

SOCOTRA
(Yemen)

I N D I A
Dhaka

MYANMAR
Yangon
LAOS
Hanoi
Vientiane
THAILAND VIETNAM
Bangkok CAMBODIA
Phnom Penh

PHILIPPINES
Manila

NORTHERN
MARIANA
ISLANDS
(U.S.)

ANDAMAN
& NICOBAR
ISLANDS
(India)

Colombo
SRI LANKA

PALAU

GUAM
(U.S.)

Koror

Palikir

EQUATORIAL GUINEA
Malabo
São Tomé
SÃO TOMÉ & PRÍNCIPE

GABON
Libreville

UGANDA
DEMOCRATIC
REPUBLIC
OF THE
CONGO Kampala
Kigali KENYA
RWANDA
BURUNDI Nairobi

SOMALIA

Male
MALDIVES

Mogadishu

Kuala Lumpur
BRUNEI
Bandar Seri Begawan
MALAYSIA
Singapore
SINGAPORE

FEDERATED STATES
OF MICRONESIA

Equator

0°

CONGO
Brazzaville
Kinshasa

CABINDA
(Angola)

Bujumbura
TANZANIA
Luanda Lilongwe
ANGOLA
ZAMBIA
Lusaka MALAWI
Harare

Dodoma
Dar es Salaam

Victoria
SEYCHELLES

COMOROS
Moroni

I N D O N E S I A

Jakarta

Dili
EAST TIMOR

PAPUA
NEW
GUINEA

Port Moresby

NAMIBIA
Windhoek

ZIMBABWE

BOTSWANA
Gaborone
Pretoria
Bloemfontein Maputo
Maseru SWAZILAND
Mbabane
SOUTH LESOTHO
AFRICA

MOZAMBIQUE

MADAGASCAR

Antananarivo
MAURITIUS
Port Louis
RÉUNION
(France)

AUSTRALIA

AUSTRALIA

ATLANTIC
OCEAN

Cape Town

Tropic of Capricorn

I N D I A N
O C E A N

20° S

Canberra

40° S

S O U T H E R N   O C E A N

60° S

Antarctic Circle

A N T A R C T I C A

80° E

20° W 0° 20° E 40° E 60° E 80° E 100° E 120° E 140° E

KEY	
———	National border
- - -	Disputed border
⊛	National capital

The World: Physical

0 miles 2,000
0 kilometers 2,000
Robinson

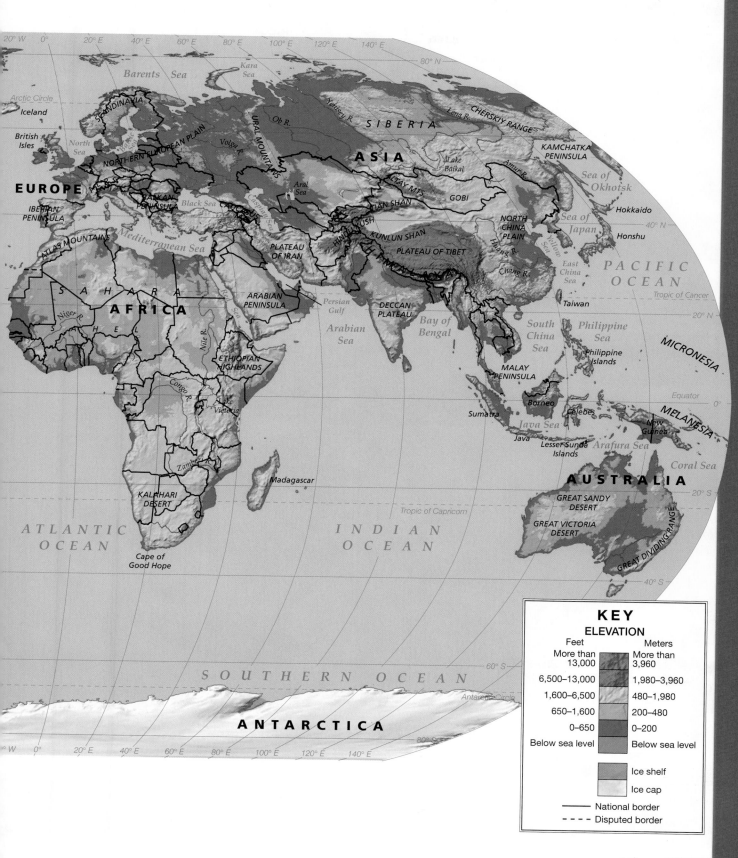

Barents Sea
Kara Sea
Arctic Circle
Iceland
British Isles
North Sea
SCANDINAVIA
NORTHERN EUROPEAN PLAIN
Volga R.
URAL MOUNTAINS
Ob R.
Yenisey R.
SIBERIA
Lena R.
CHERSKIY RANGE
ASIA
KAMCHATKA PENINSULA
Lake Baikal
Amur R.
Sea of Okhotsk
EUROPE
IBERIAN PENINSULA
BALKAN PENINSULA
Black Sea
CAUCASUS
Caspian Sea
Aral Sea
ALTAY MTS
TIAN SHAN
GOBI
NORTH CHINA PLAIN
Hokkaido
Sea of Japan
Honshu
ATLAS MOUNTAINS
Mediterranean Sea
PLATEAU OF IRAN
HINDU KUSH
KUNLUN SHAN
PLATEAU OF TIBET
Huang R.
Chang R.
East China Sea
Yellow Sea
PACIFIC OCEAN
Tropic of Cancer
40° N
SAHARA
AFRICA
ARABIAN PENINSULA
Red Sea
Persian Gulf
DECCAN PLATEAU
HIMALAYAS
Taiwan
20° N
SAHEL
Niger R.
Nile R.
Arabian Sea
Bay of Bengal
South China Sea
Philippine Sea
MICRONESIA
Philippine Islands
ETHIOPIAN HIGHLANDS
Congo R.
Lake Victoria
MALAY PENINSULA
Sumatra
Borneo
Celebes
Java Sea
MELANESIA
Equator
Java
Lesser Sunda Islands
New Guinea
Arafura Sea
Coral Sea
Zambezi R.
Madagascar
AUSTRALIA
20° S
KALAHARI DESERT
GREAT SANDY DESERT
GREAT VICTORIA DESERT
GREAT DIVIDING RANGE
ATLANTIC OCEAN
Cape of Good Hope
Tropic of Capricorn
INDIAN OCEAN
40° S
SOUTHERN OCEAN
60° S
Antarctic Circle
ANTARCTICA
80° S

20° W 0° 20° E 40° E 60° E 80° E 100° E 120° E 140° E 80° N

KEY
ELEVATION

Feet		Meters
More than 13,000		More than 3,960
6,500–13,000		1,980–3,960
1,600–6,500		480–1,980
650–1,600		200–480
0–650		0–200
Below sea level		Below sea level

Ice shelf

Ice cap

—— National border

- - - Disputed border

North and South America: Political

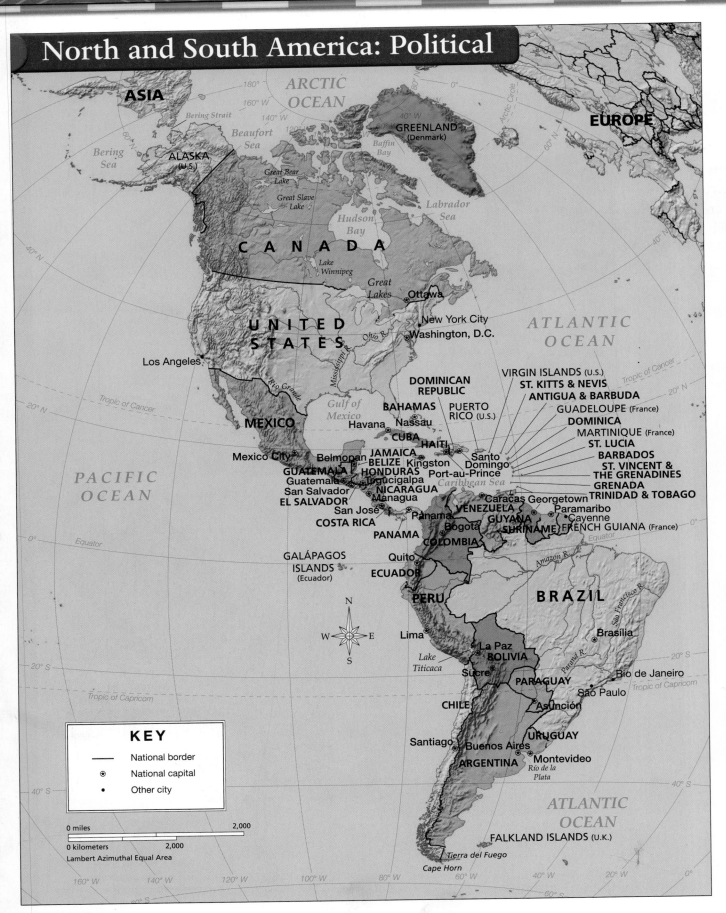

ASIA

ARCTIC OCEAN

180°
160° W
140° W
0°

Bering Strait

Beaufort Sea

Bering Sea

ALASKA (U.S.)

GREENLAND (Denmark)

EUROPE

Great Bear Lake

Great Slave Lake

Baffin Bay

Labrador Sea

40° N

C A N A D A

Lake Winnipeg

Hudson Bay

Great Lakes

Ottawa

New York City

ATLANTIC OCEAN

U N I T E D
S T A T E S

Ohio R.

Washington, D.C.

Los Angeles

Mississippi R.

Rio Grande

Tropic of Cancer

20° N

Gulf of Mexico

DOMINICAN REPUBLIC

VIRGIN ISLANDS (U.S.)
ST. KITTS & NEVIS
ANTIGUA & BARBUDA

Tropic of Cancer

20° N

MEXICO

BAHAMAS

Havana   Nassau

PUERTO RICO (U.S.)

GUADELOUPE (France)
DOMINICA
MARTINIQUE (France)
ST. LUCIA
BARBADOS
ST. VINCENT &
THE GRENADINES
GRENADA
TRINIDAD & TOBAGO

Mexico City

CUBA

HAITI

JAMAICA
Belmopan   BELIZE   Kingston
GUATEMALA   HONDURAS
Guatemala   Tegucigalpa
San Salvador   NICARAGUA
EL SALVADOR   Managua
San José
COSTA RICA   Panama

Caribbean Sea

Santo Domingo
Port-au-Prince

PACIFIC OCEAN

PANAMA

Caracas   Georgetown
VENEZUELA   Paramaribo
GUYANA   Cayenne
Bogotá   SURINAME   FRENCH GUIANA (France)
COLOMBIA

0°

Equator

GALÁPAGOS
ISLANDS
(Ecuador)

Quito

Amazon R.

Equator

0°

ECUADOR

PERU

São Francisco R.

B R A Z I L

N

W   E

S

Lima

Brasília

20° S

Lake Titicaca

La Paz
BOLIVIA

Sucre

PARAGUAY

Paraná R.

Rio de Janeiro

São Paulo

Tropic of Capricorn

20° S

20° S

CHILE

Asunción

URUGUAY

Santiago   Buenos Aires
ARGENTINA   Montevideo

Río de la Plata

ATLANTIC OCEAN

40° S

KEY

— National border
⊛ National capital
• Other city

FALKLAND ISLANDS (U.K.)

Tierra del Fuego

Cape Horn

0 miles   2,000
0 kilometers   2,000
Lambert Azimuthal Equal Area

160° W   140° W   120° W   100° W   80° W   60° W   40° W   20° W   0°

60° W

North and South America: Physical

ASIA

ARCTIC OCEAN

180°
160° W
140° W
Bering Strait
60° N

Beaufort Sea

Greenland

0°
40° W
60° W
80° N

EUROPE

Bering Sea

Mt. McKinley 20,320 ft (6,194 m)
Alaska Range

Aleutian Islands

Gulf of Alaska

Mackenzie R.

Great Bear Lake

Great Slave Lake

Baffin Bay

Davis Strait

Baffin Island

Labrador Sea

60°

40° N

Hudson Bay

CANADIAN SHIELD

ROCKY MOUNTAINS

GREAT PLAINS

Lake Winnipeg

Great Lakes

Missouri R.

Newfoundland

40° N

Colorado R.

Ohio R.

Appalachian Mts.

Mississippi R.

ATLANTIC OCEAN

Tropic of Cancer

20° N

Baja California

Gulf of California

Sierra Madre Occidental

Sierra Madre Oriental

Río Grande

Gulf of Mexico

Tropic of Cancer

20° N

PACIFIC OCEAN

Yucatán Peninsula

Cuba

Hispaniola

Greater Antilles

Lesser Antilles

Caribbean Sea

Isthmus of Panama

0°

Equator

Galápagos Islands

Orinoco R.

Guiana Highlands

AMAZON BASIN

Amazon R.

Equator

0°

N
W   E
S

ANDES

São Francisco R.

Brazilian Highlands

20° S

Lake Titicaca

20° S

KEY

ELEVATION

Feet		Meters
More than 13,000		More than 3,960
6,500–13,000		1,980–3,960
1,600–6,500		480–1,980
650–1,600		200–480
0–650		0–200

Ice cap

National border

ANDES

Gran Chaco

Paraguay R.

Paraná R.

Tropic of Capricorn

Aconcagua 22,834 ft (6,960 m)

Pampas

Río de la Plata

0 miles   2,000
0 kilometers   2,000
Lambert Azimuthal Equal Area

Patagonia

ATLANTIC OCEAN

40° S

Falkland Islands

Tierra del Fuego
Cape Horn

160° W   140° W   120° W   100° W   80° W   60° W   40° W   20° W   0°

60° S

United States: Political

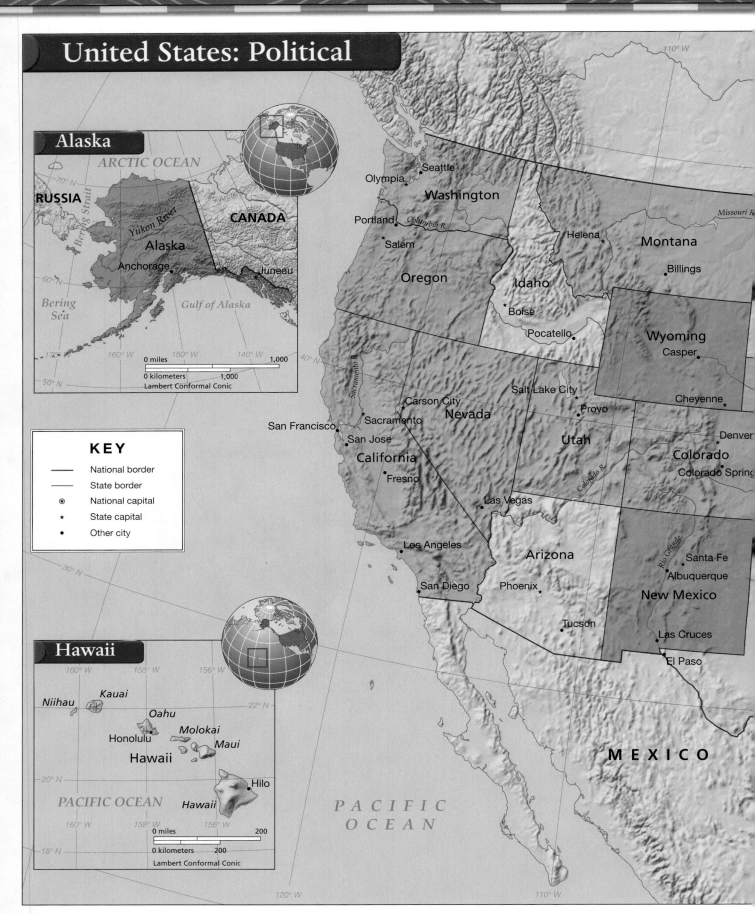

Alaska

ARCTIC OCEAN

RUSSIA

Bering Strait

Yukon River

Arctic Circle

CANADA

Alaska

Anchorage

Juneau

Bering Sea

Gulf of Alaska

0 miles 1,000
0 kilometers 1,000
Lambert Conformal Conic

KEY

——	National border
—	State border
⊗	National capital
★	State capital
•	Other city

Hawaii

Niihau

Kauai

Oahu

Molokai

Honolulu

Maui

Hawaii

Hilo

Hawaii

PACIFIC OCEAN

0 miles 200
0 kilometers 200
Lambert Conformal Conic

Seattle
Olympia
Washington
Portland
Columbia R.
Salem
Oregon
Helena
Montana
Billings
Idaho
Boise
Pocatello
Wyoming
Casper
Salt Lake City
Cheyenne
Carson City
Nevada
Provo
Sacramento
San Francisco
San Jose
Utah
Denver
California
Colorado
Fresno
Colorado Springs
Las Vegas
Colorado R.
Los Angeles
Arizona
Rio Grande
Santa Fe
Albuquerque
San Diego
Phoenix
New Mexico
Tucson
Las Cruces
El Paso

Sacramento R.

Missouri R.

MEXICO

PACIFIC OCEAN

CANADA

North Dakota
Bismarck
Fargo

Minnesota

South Dakota
Pierre
Sioux Falls

Lake Superior

St. Paul
Minneapolis
Mississippi R.

Wisconsin

Milwaukee
Madison

Michigan

Lake Michigan

Lake Huron

Grand Rapids
Lansing
Detroit

Lake Ontario

Buffalo

Lake Erie

Maine
Augusta

Vermont
Portland
Montpelier
New Hampshire
Concord

Albany
Boston
Massachusetts
Providence
Hartford
Rhode Island
Connecticut

New York

Nebraska
Omaha
Lincoln

Iowa
Des Moines
Cedar Rapids

Illinois
Springfield

Chicago
Fort Wayne

Indiana
Indianapolis

Ohio
Columbus

Cincinnati

Cleveland
Pittsburgh

Pennsylvania
Harrisburg

New York City

New Jersey
Trenton
Philadelphia
Delaware
Dover
Annapolis
Maryland
District of Columbia

Missouri R.

Kansas City
Topeka
Jefferson City

Kansas
Arkansas R.
Wichita

Missouri

St. Louis
Louisville

Ohio R.
Frankfort

Kentucky

Charleston

West
Virginia

Baltimore
Washington, D.C.

Richmond

Virginia

Norfolk

Oklahoma
Tulsa
Oklahoma City

Arkansas
Fort Smith
Little Rock

Memphis

Nashville
Knoxville

Tennessee
Tennessee R.

Raleigh

North Carolina
Charlotte

South Carolina
Columbia
Charleston

ATLANTIC
OCEAN

Red R.

Texas
Fort Worth
Dallas

Austin
San Antonio
Houston

Mississippi
Jackson

Shreveport
Louisiana
Baton Rouge
Gulfport
New Orleans

Mississippi R.

Alabama
Montgomery

Birmingham

Atlanta

Georgia
Columbus

Savannah

Mobile
Tallahassee

Jacksonville

Florida
Orlando
Tampa

Miami

Gulf of Mexico

N
W   E
S

0 miles   250
0 kilometers   250
Lambert Azimuthal Equal Area

100° W   90° W   80° W   70° W   50° N

90° W   80° W

Europe: Political

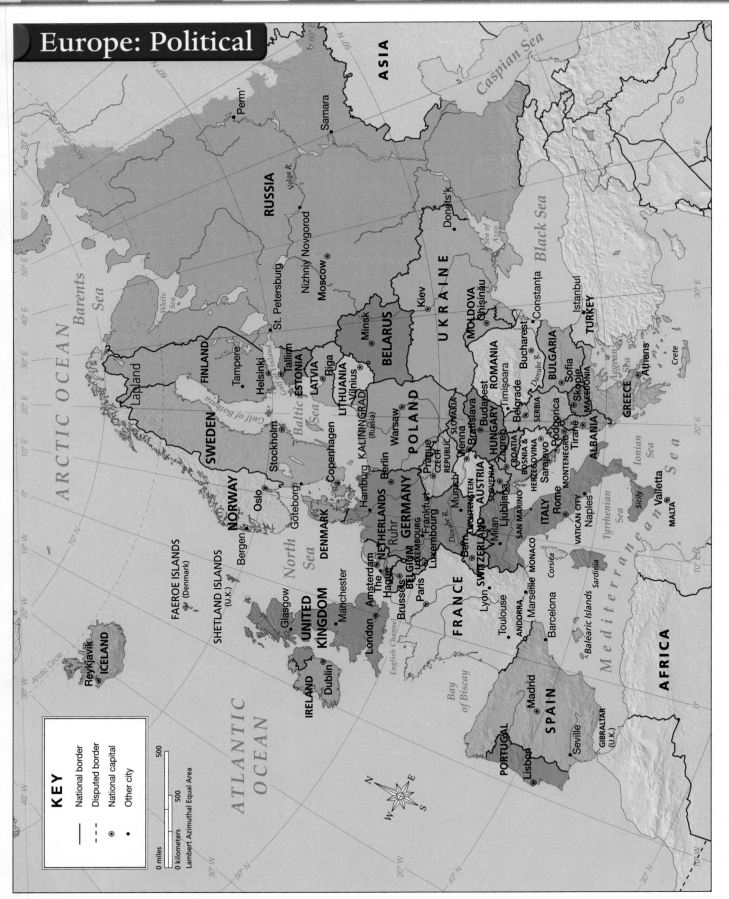

KEY

National border
Disputed border
⊛ National capital
• Other city

0 miles 500
0 kilometers 500
Lambert Azimuthal Equal Area

Europe: Physical

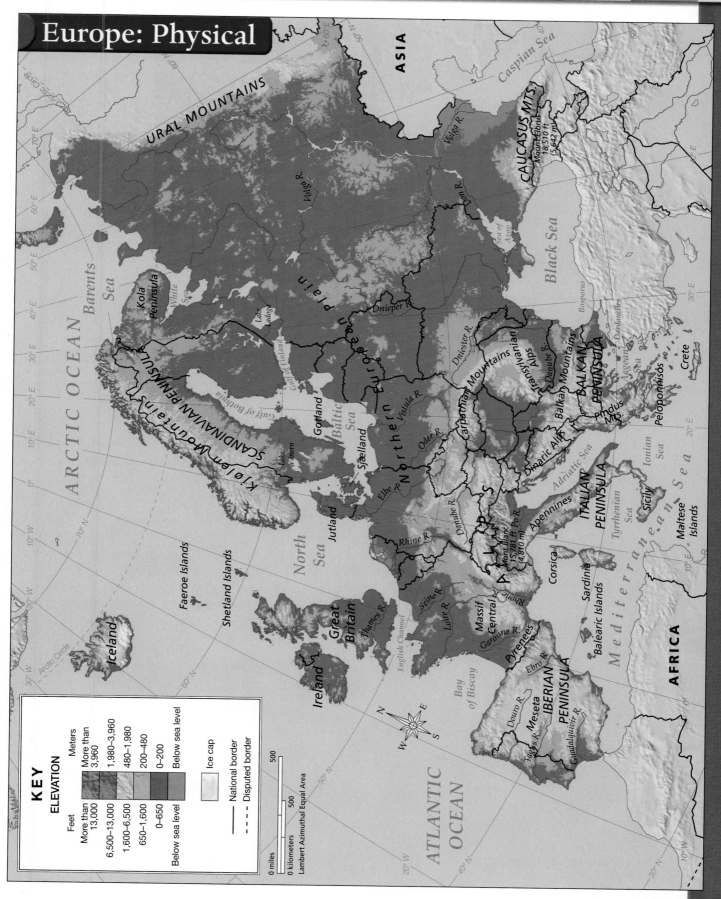

ASIA

URAL MOUNTAINS

CAUCASUS MTS.
Mount Elbrus
18,510 ft
(5,642 m)

Caspian Sea

Barents Sea

ARCTIC OCEAN

Kola Peninsula

White Sea

Volga R.

Volga R.

Don R.

Sea of Azov

Black Sea

Bosporus

Lake Ladoga

Dnieper R.

Northern European Plain

Dniester R.

Carpathian Mountains

Transylvanian Alps

Danube R.

Balkan Mountains

BALKAN PENINSULA

Dardanelles

Aegean Sea

Crete

Peloponnísos

Pindus Mts.

Dinaric Alps

Adriatic Sea

Ionian Sea

SCANDINAVIAN PENINSULA

Kjølen Mountains

Gulf of Bothnia

Gulf of Finland

Baltic Sea

Gotland

Sjælland

Lake Vänern

Oder R.

Vistula R.

Elbe R.

A L P S

Mont Blanc
15,781 ft
(4,810 m)

Apennines

ITALIAN PENINSULA

Sicily

Tyrrhenian Sea

Maltese Islands

Mediterranean Sea

Rhine R.

Danube R.

Faeroe Islands

Shetland Islands

Jutland

North Sea

Great Britain

Ireland

English Channel

Thames R.

Seine R.

Loire R.

Massif Central

Garonne R.

Pyrenees

Rhône R.

Po R.

Corsica

Sardinia

Balearic Islands

Iceland

ARCTIC OCEAN

Arctic Circle

Ebro R.

IBERIAN PENINSULA

Meseta

Douro R.

Tagus R.

Guadalquivir R.

Bay of Biscay

ATLANTIC OCEAN

AFRICA

KEY

ELEVATION

Feet	Meters
More than 13,000	More than 3,960
6,500–13,000	1,980–3,960
1,600–6,500	480–1,980
650–1,600	200–480
0–650	0–200
Below sea level	Below sea level

Ice cap

—— National border

- - - Disputed border

0 miles 500
0 kilometers 500

Lambert Azimuthal Equal Area

N E S W

Africa: Political

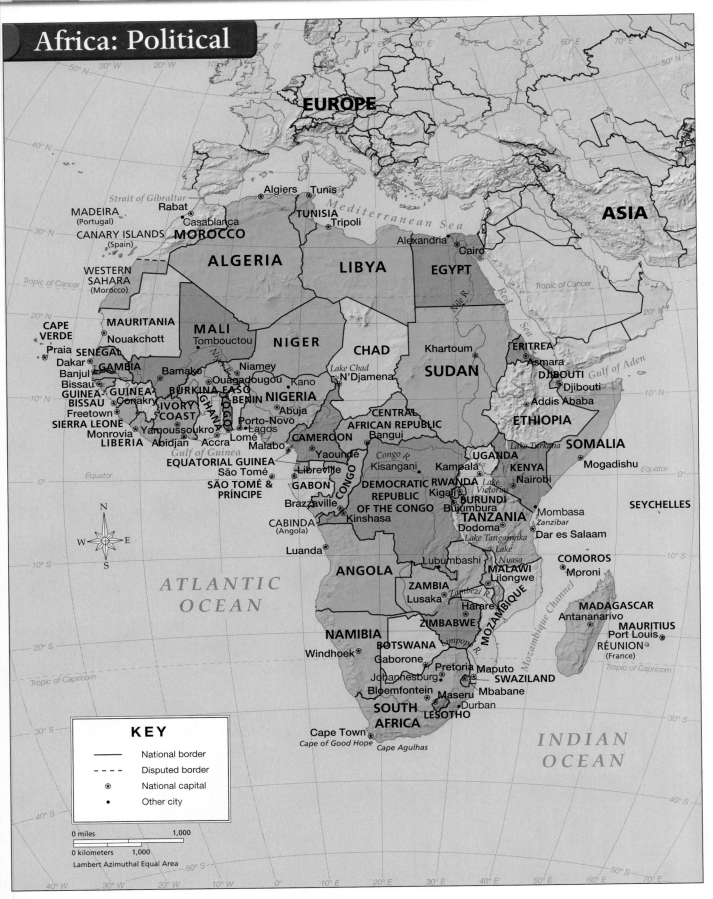

EUROPE

ASIA

Strait of Gibraltar

MADEIRA (Portugal)

CANARY ISLANDS (Spain)

Algiers Tunis

TUNISIA
Rabat
Casablanca
Tripoli

Mediterranean Sea

MOROCCO

Alexandria
Cairo

WESTERN SAHARA (Morocco)

ALGERIA

LIBYA

EGYPT

Nile R.

Tropic of Cancer

Tropic of Cancer

CAPE VERDE

MAURITANIA

Nouakchott

MALI

Tombouctou

NIGER

CHAD

Khartoum

ERITREA

Asmara

DJIBOUTI

Red Sea

Gulf of Aden

Praia
Dakar
SENEGAL
GAMBIA
Banjul
Bissau
GUINEA-
BISSAU
Freetown
SIERRA LEONE
Monrovia
LIBERIA

Bamako
Niamey
Ouagadougou Kano
BURKINA FASO
GUINEA
Conakry
IVORY
COAST
Yamoussoukro
Abidjan Accra

Lake Chad
N'Djamena

SUDAN

Djibouti

Addis Ababa

BENIN
NIGERIA
Abuja
Porto-Novo
Lomé
Malabo

CENTRAL
AFRICAN REPUBLIC
Bangui

ETHIOPIA

SOMALIA

Mogadishu

Equator

Gulf of Guinea

CAMEROON
Yaoundé

UGANDA

KENYA

Equator

EQUATORIAL GUINEA
São Tomé
SÃO TOMÉ & PRÍNCIPE

Libreville
GABON
Brazzaville
CABINDA (Angola)

Kisangani

Congo R.

CONGO

Kampala
Lake
Victoria

Nairobi

DEMOCRATIC
REPUBLIC
OF THE CONGO
Kinshasa

RWANDA
Kigali
BURUNDI
Bujumbura
TANZANIA
Dodoma

Mombasa
Zanzibar
Dar es Salaam

SEYCHELLES

N
W   E
S

Luanda

Lake Tanganyika

Lake
Nyasa

COMOROS
Moroni

ATLANTIC
OCEAN

Lubumbashi

ANGOLA

ZAMBIA
Lusaka

MALAWI
Lilongwe

Zambezi R.

MADAGASCAR
Antananarivo

MAURITIUS
Port Louis

Harare

MOZAMBIQUE

Mozambique Channel

RÉUNION (France)

NAMIBIA

Windhoek

BOTSWANA
Gaborone

ZIMBABWE

Limpopo R.

Tropic of Capricorn

Tropic of Capricorn

Pretoria
Johannesburg
Bloemfontein

Maputo
SWAZILAND
Mbabane
Maseru
Durban

SOUTH
AFRICA
LESOTHO

INDIAN
OCEAN

Cape Town
Cape of Good Hope Cape Agulhas

KEY

——	National border
- - -	Disputed border
⊛	National capital
•	Other city

0 miles   1,000

0 kilometers   1,000

Lambert Azimuthal Equal Area

Africa: Physical

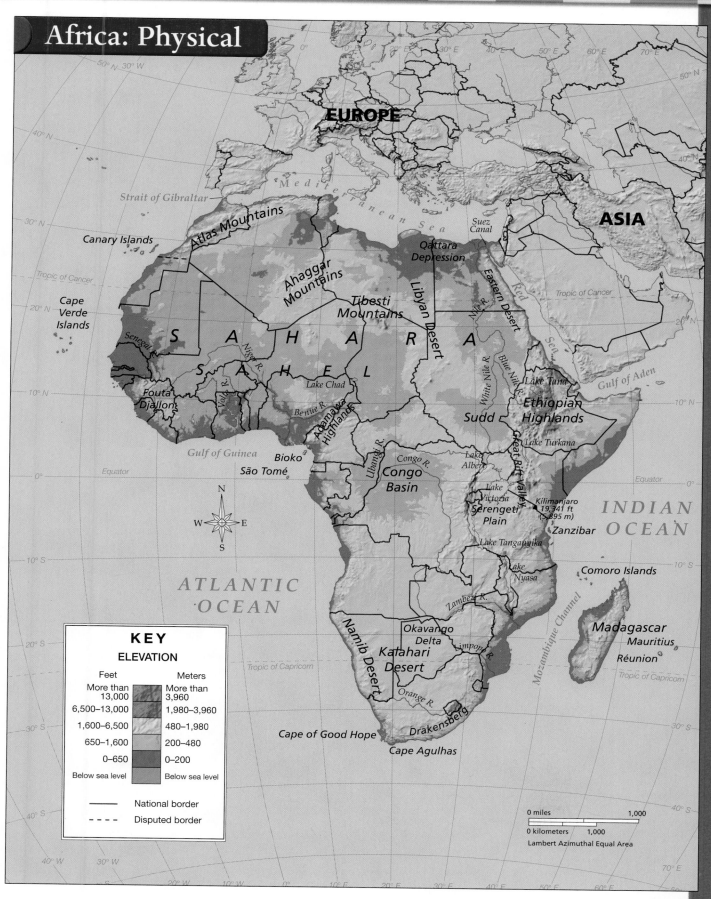

EUROPE

ASIA

Strait of Gibraltar

Atlas Mountains

Canary Islands

Cape Verde Islands

Mediterranean Sea

Suez Canal

Qattara Depression

Tropic of Cancer

Ahaggar Mountains

Tibesti Mountains

Libyan Desert

Eastern Desert

Red Sea

Tropic of Cancer

S A H A R A

SAHEL

Senegal R.

Niger R.

Lake Chad

Nile R.

White Nile R.

Blue Nile R.

Lake Tana

Gulf of Aden

Fouta Djallon

Volta R.

Benue R.

Adamawa Highlands

Ethiopian Highlands

Sudd

Lake Turkana

Gulf of Guinea

Bioko

São Tomé

Ubangi R.

Congo R.

Congo Basin

Lake Albert

Lake Victoria

Great Rift Valley

Equator

Equator

Serengeti Plain

Kilimanjaro 19,341 ft (5,895 m)

Zanzibar

INDIAN OCEAN

N
W   E
S

Lake Tanganyika

Comoro Islands

ATLANTIC OCEAN

Lake Nyasa

Zambezi R.

Mozambique Channel

Madagascar

Mauritius

Réunion

Namib Desert

Okavango Delta

Kalahari Desert

Limpopo R.

Tropic of Capricorn

Tropic of Capricorn

KEY
ELEVATION

Feet		Meters
More than 13,000		More than 3,960
6,500–13,000		1,980–3,960
1,600–6,500		480–1,980
650–1,600		200–480
0–650		0–200
Below sea level		Below sea level

——— National border

- - - - Disputed border

Cape of Good Hope

Orange R.

Drakensberg

Cape Agulhas

0 miles   1,000

0 kilometers   1,000

Lambert Azimuthal Equal Area

Asia: Political

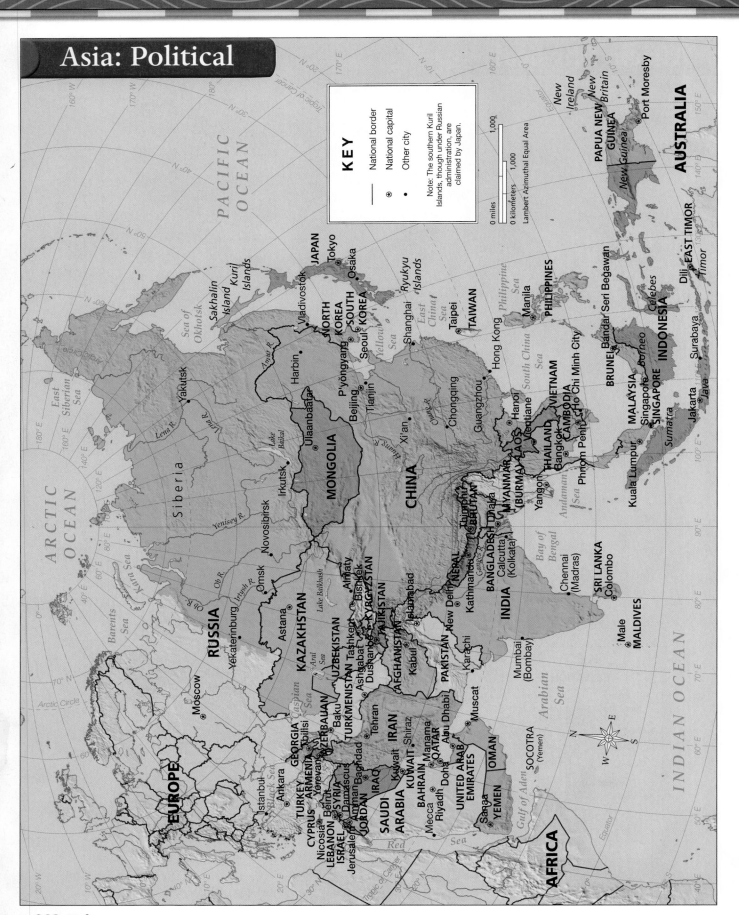

KEY

— National border

⊛ National capital

• Other city

Note: The southern Kuril Islands, though under Russian administration, are claimed by Japan.

0 miles   1,000

0 kilometers   1,000

Lambert Azimuthal Equal Area

PACIFIC OCEAN

ARCTIC OCEAN

East Siberian Sea

Kara Sea

Barents Sea

Sea of Okhotsk

Sakhalin Island

Kuril Islands

Yakutsk

Siberia

Lena R.

Tunguska R.

Yenisey R.

Ob R.

Irtysh R.

RUSSIA

Moscow ⊛

Yekaterinburg

Omsk

Novosibirsk

Irkutsk

Lake Baikal

Vladivostok

Harbin

Amur R.

JAPAN

Tokyo ⊛

Osaka

NORTH KOREA

P'yongyang ⊛

SOUTH KOREA

Seoul ⊛

Ryukyu Islands

MONGOLIA

Ulaanbaatar ⊛

Beijing ⊛

Tianjin

Shanghai

East China Sea

Yellow Sea

Taipei

TAIWAN

CHINA

Xi'an

Chang R.

Chongqing

Huang R.

Guangzhou

Hong Kong

South China Sea

Philippine Sea

Manila ⊛

PHILIPPINES

New Ireland

New Britain

Port Moresby

PAPUA NEW GUINEA

New Guinea

AUSTRALIA

ASTANA ⊛

KAZAKHSTAN

Aral Sea

Lake Balkhash

Almaty

Bishkek ⊛

KYRGYZSTAN

Tashkent ⊛

UZBEKISTAN

TAJIKISTAN

Dushanbe ⊛

Ashgabat ⊛

TURKMENISTAN

AFGHANISTAN

Kabul ⊛

Islamabad ⊛

PAKISTAN

Karachi

NEPAL

Kathmandu ⊛

Thimphu ⊛

BHUTAN

New Delhi ⊛

Ganges R.

BANGLADESH

Dhaka ⊛

Calcutta (Kolkata)

MYANMAR (BURMA)

Yangon

INDIA

Mumbai (Bombay)

Chennai (Madras)

Bay of Bengal

Andaman Sea

SRI LANKA

Colombo ⊛

Male ⊛

MALDIVES

INDIAN OCEAN

Arabian Sea

GEORGIA

Tbilisi ⊛

ARMENIA

Yerevan ⊛

AZERBAIJAN

Baku ⊛

Caspian Sea

Tehran ⊛

IRAN

Shiraz

TURKEY

Ankara ⊛

Istanbul

Black Sea

CYPRUS

Nicosia ⊛

LEBANON

Beirut ⊛

ISRAEL

SYRIA

Damascus ⊛

Jerusalem ⊛

Amman ⊛

JORDAN

Baghdad ⊛

IRAQ

Kuwait ⊛

KUWAIT

BAHRAIN

Manama ⊛

QATAR

Doha ⊛

Riyadh ⊛

SAUDI ARABIA

Mecca

UNITED ARAB EMIRATES

Abu Dhabi ⊛

Muscat ⊛

OMAN

YEMEN

Sana ⊛

Red Sea

Gulf of Aden

SOCOTRA (Yemen)

AFRICA

EUROPE

THAILAND

Bangkok ⊛

LAOS

Vientiane ⊛

CAMBODIA

Phnom Penh ⊛

VIETNAM

Hanoi ⊛

Ho Chi Minh City

MALAYSIA

Kuala Lumpur ⊛

SINGAPORE ⊛

BRUNEI

Bandar Seri Begawan ⊛

Borneo

INDONESIA

Sumatra

Jakarta ⊛

Surabaya

Java

Celebes

EAST TIMOR

Dili ⊛

Timor

Tropic of Cancer

Arctic Circle

Equator

Asia: Physical

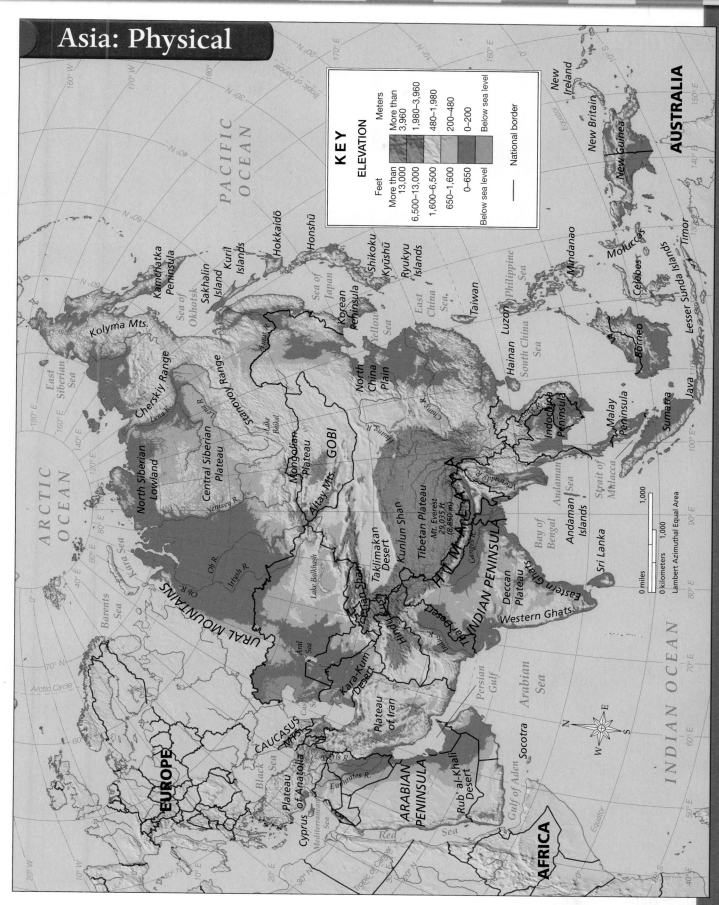

K E Y

ELEVATION

Feet	Meters
More than 13,000	More than 3,960
6,500–13,000	1,980–3,960
1,600–6,500	480–1,980
650–1,600	200–480
0–650	0–200
Below sea level	Below sea level

— National border

ARCTIC OCEAN

PACIFIC OCEAN

INDIAN OCEAN

EUROPE

AFRICA

AUSTRALIA

Kolyma Mts.
Kamchatka Peninsula
Cherskiy Range
Sea of Okhotsk
Sakhalin Island
Kuril Islands
Hokkaidō
Honshū
Amur R.
Stanovoy Range
Lena R.
Lake Baikal
North Siberian Lowland
East Siberian Sea
Barents Sea
Kara Sea
Central Siberian Plateau
Yenisey R.
Mongolian Plateau
Altay Mts.
GOBI
Sea of Japan
Korean Peninsula
Shikoku
Kyūshū
Ryukyu Islands
Yellow Sea
North China Plain
East China Sea
Taiwan
Philippine Sea
Luzon
Mindanao
New Ireland
New Britain
New Guinea
Moluccas
Celebes
Lesser Sunda Islands
Timor
Java
Sumatra
Borneo
Malay Peninsula
Indochina Peninsula
Mekong R.
Hainan
South China Sea
Strait of Malacca
Andaman Sea
Andaman Islands
Bay of Bengal
Sri Lanka
INDIAN PENINSULA
Deccan Plateau
Western Ghats
Eastern Ghats
Ganges R.
Brahmaputra R.
Irrawaddy R.
HIMALAYA
Mt. Everest 29,035 ft (8,850 m)
Tibetan Plateau
Kunlun Shan
Taklimakan Desert
Tian Shan
Hindu Kush
Pamirs
Lake Balkhash
Ob R.
Irtysh R.
URAL MOUNTAINS
Aral Sea
Kara-Kum Desert
Caspian Sea
CAUCASUS Mts.
Plateau of Anatolia
Cyprus
Black Sea
Mediterranean Sea
Tigris R.
Euphrates R.
Plateau of Iran
Persian Gulf
ARABIAN PENINSULA
Rub' al-Khali Desert
Arabian Sea
Gulf of Aden
Socotra
Red Sea
Indus R.

0 miles 1,000
0 kilometers 1,000
Lambert Azimuthal Equal Area

N E S W

Tropic of Cancer
Tropic of Cancer
Equator
Arctic Circle

Oceania

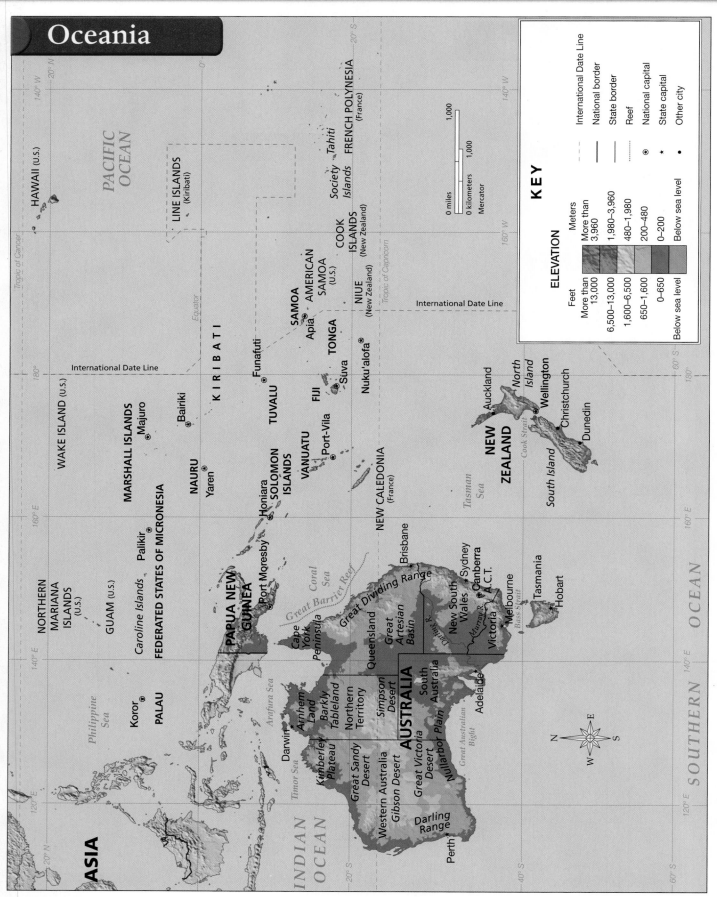

HAWAII (U.S.)

PACIFIC
OCEAN

ASIA

Tropic of Cancer

LINE ISLANDS
(Kiribati)

FRENCH POLYNESIA
(France)

Society   Tahiti
Islands

Equator

COOK
ISLANDS
(New Zealand)

AMERICAN
SAMOA
(U.S.)

NIUE
(New Zealand)

SAMOA
Apia

TONGA
Nuku'alofa

Tropic of Capricorn

International Date Line

WAKE ISLAND (U.S.)

International Date Line

K I R I B A T I

Funafuti

TUVALU

FIJI
Suva

NEW
ZEALAND

Auckland
North
Island

Wellington
Christchurch

Dunedin

Cook Strait

South Island

NORTHERN
MARIANA
ISLANDS
(U.S.)

GUAM (U.S.)

MARSHALL ISLANDS
Majuro

Bairiki

NAURU
Yaren

SOLOMON
ISLANDS
Honiara

VANUATU
Port-Vila

NEW CALEDONIA
(France)

Tasman
Sea

Philippine
Sea

Koror
PALAU

Caroline Islands   Palikir
FEDERATED STATES OF MICRONESIA

PAPUA NEW
GUINEA
Port Moresby

Great
Coral
Sea

Great Barrier Reef

Brisbane

Great Dividing Range

Queensland

Great
Artesian
Basin

New South
Wales

Sydney
Canberra
A.C.T.

Melbourne

Tasmania
Hobart

Bass Strait

Victoria

Murray R.
Darling R.

Arafura Sea

Timor Sea

Darwin

Arnhem
Land

Barkly
Tableland

Northern
Territory

Simpson
Desert

AUSTRALIA

South
Australia

Adelaide

Kimberley
Plateau

Great Sandy
Desert

Western Australia
Gibson Desert

Great Victoria
Desert

Nullarbor Plain

Great Australian
Bight

Darling
Range

Perth

INDIAN
OCEAN

SOUTHERN   OCEAN

K E Y

ELEVATION

Feet	Meters
More than 13,000	More than 3,960
6,500–13,000	1,980–3,960
1,600–6,500	480–1,980
650–1,600	200–480
0–650	0–200
Below sea level	Below sea level

- - - - International Date Line
———— National border
———— State border
·········· Reef
⊛ National capital
★ State capital
• Other city

0 miles   1,000
0 kilometers   1,000
Mercator

N E S W

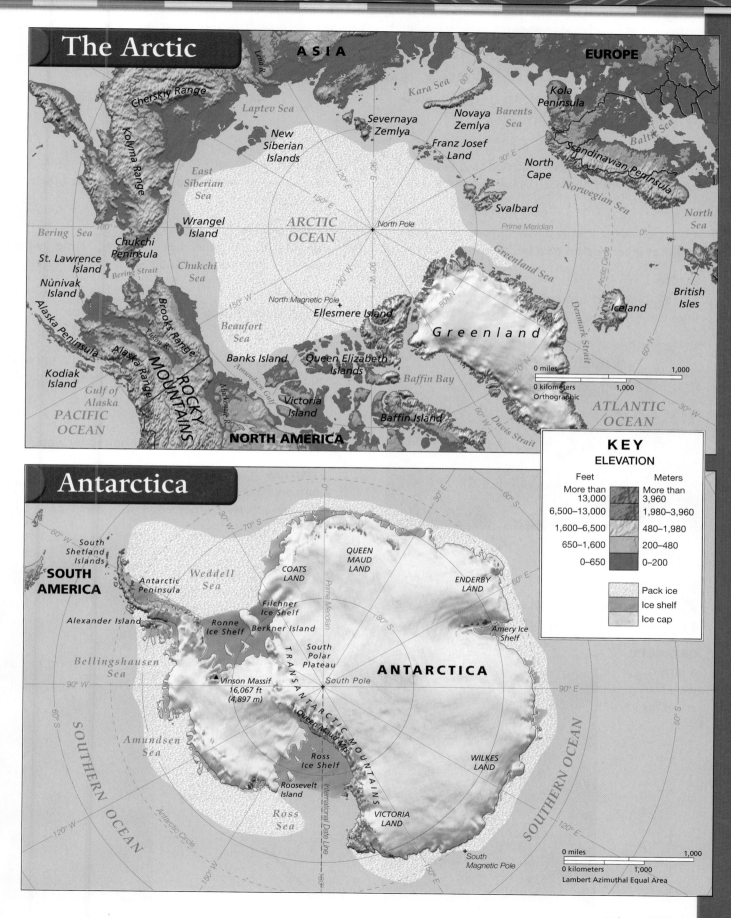

The Arctic

ASIA   EUROPE

Cherskiy Range
Kolyma Range
Laptev Sea
Lena R.
Kara Sea
60° E
Severnaya Zemlya
New Siberian Islands
Novaya Zemlya
Barents Sea
Franz Josef Land
Kola Peninsula
Baltic Sea
East Siberian Sea
30° E
North Cape
Scandinavian Peninsula
120° E
90° E
Svalbard
Bering Sea
Wrangel Island
150° E
ARCTIC OCEAN
North Pole
Norwegian Sea
Prime Meridian
0°
North Sea
Chukchi Peninsula
St. Lawrence Island
Bering Strait
Chukchi Sea
120° W
Greenland Sea
Arctic Circle
Iceland
British Isles
Nunivak Island
150° W
80° N
North Magnetic Pole
Ellesmere Island
Greenland
Denmark Strait
Alaska Peninsula
Brooks Range
Yukon R.
Beaufort Sea
70° N
Kodiak Island
Alaska Range
ROCKY MOUNTAINS
Amundsen Gulf
Banks Island
Queen Elizabeth Islands
Baffin Bay
0 miles   1,000
Gulf of Alaska
Mackenzie R.
Victoria Island
60° N
0 kilometers   1,000
Orthographic
ATLANTIC OCEAN
30° W
PACIFIC OCEAN
Baffin Island
Davis Strait
30° W
NORTH AMERICA

Antarctica

60° W
South Shetland Islands
30° W
70° S
QUEEN MAUD LAND
Prime Meridian
30° E
SOUTH AMERICA
Antarctic Peninsula
Weddell Sea
COATS LAND
ENDERBY LAND
60° E
Alexander Island
Filchner Ice Shelf
Ronne Ice Shelf
Berkner Island
South Polar Plateau
80° S
Amery Ice Shelf
Bellingshausen Sea
TRANSANTARCTIC MOUNTAINS
ANTARCTICA
90° W
90° W
Vinson Massif 16,067 ft (4,897 m)
South Pole
90° E
Amundsen Sea
Queen Maud Mts.
Ross Ice Shelf
WILKES LAND
60° S
Roosevelt Island
VICTORIA LAND
SOUTHERN OCEAN
120° W
Antarctic Circle
Ross Sea
International Date Line
South Magnetic Pole
SOUTHERN OCEAN
120° E
50° S
150° W
180°
150° E
0 miles   1,000
0 kilometers   1,000
Lambert Azimuthal Equal Area

KEY
ELEVATION

Feet		Meters
More than 13,000		More than 3,960
6,500–13,000		1,980–3,960
1,600–6,500		480–1,980
650–1,600		200–480
0–650		0–200

Pack ice
Ice shelf
Ice cap

Glossary of Geographic Terms

basin
an area that is lower than surrounding land areas; some basins are filled with water

bay
a body of water that is partly surrounded by land and that is connected to a larger body of water

butte
a small, high, flat-topped landform with cliff-like sides

▲ **butte**

canyon
a deep, narrow valley with steep sides; often with a stream flowing through it

cataract
a large waterfall or steep rapids

delta
a plain at the mouth of a river, often triangular in shape, formed where sediment is deposited by flowing water

flood plain
a broad plain on either side of a river, formed where sediment settles during floods

glacier
a huge, slow-moving mass of snow and ice

hill
an area that rises above surrounding land and has a rounded top; lower and usually less steep than a mountain

island
an area of land completely surrounded by water

isthmus
a narrow strip of land that connects two larger areas of land

mesa
a high, flat-topped land-form with cliff-like sides; larger than a butte

mountain
a landform that rises steeply at least 2,000 feet (610 meters) above sur-rounding land; usually wide at the bottom and rising to a narrow peak or ridge

▶ **glacier**

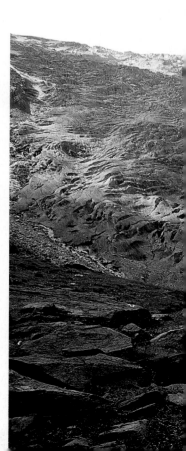

◀ **cataract**

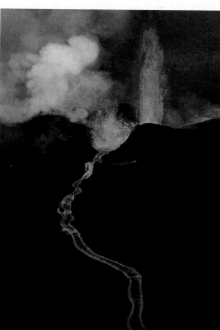
◀ **delta**

mountain pass
a gap between mountains

peninsula
an area of land almost completely surrounded by water but connected to the mainland

plain
a large area of flat or gently rolling land

plateau
a large, flat area that rises above the surrounding land; at least one side has a steep slope

river mouth
the point where a river enters a lake or sea

strait
a narrow stretch of water that connects two larger bodies of water

tributary
a river or stream that flows into a larger river

valley
a low stretch of land between mountains or hills; land that is drained by a river

volcano
an opening in Earth's surface through which molten rock, ashes, and gases escape from the interior

▶ **volcano**

Gazetteer

A

Acadia (51° N, 110° W) the first permanent French settlement in North America, p. 176

Atlanta (33°44′ N, 84°23′ W) the capital of the state of Georgia, p. 121

B

Boston (42°21′ N, 71°03′ W) the capital of the state of Massachusetts, p. 113

C

Calgary (51° N, 114° W) a city in southern Alberta, Canada, p. 165

Canadian Shield a region of rocky, rugged land that covers about half of Canada, p. 13

Cariboo Mountains (59° N, 116° W) a mountain range in eastern British Columbia, Canada, p. 169

Chicago (41°51′ N, 87°39′ W) a major city in the state of Illinois, on Lake Michigan, p. 130

Coast Ranges (55° N, 129° W) a mountain range stretching along the Pacific from southern California to Alaska, p. 13

Cuyahoga River (41° N, 82° W) a river in northeastern Ohio, p. 65

D

Dawson (64°04′ N, 139°25′ W) a city located in western Yukon Territory, Canada, p. 183

Death Valley (36° N, 116° W) the hottest, driest region of North America, located in southeastern California, p. 12

Detroit (42°20′ N, 83°03′ W) a city in the state of Michigan, p. 131

F

Fraser River (49° N, 123° W) a major river of western North America, mainly in British Columbia, p. 14

G

Great Lakes a group of five large lakes in central North America: Lakes Superior, Michigan, Huron, Erie, and Ontario, p. 13

I

Iqaluit (63°44′ N, 68°28′ W) the capital of Nunavut, Canada, p. 184

J

Jamestown (37°30′ N, 75°55′ W) the first permanent English settlement in North America, located in present-day Virginia, p. 40

L

L'Anse aux Meadows (51°36′ N, 55°32′ W) the earliest known North American Viking settlement, located on Newfoundland, p. 173

Los Angeles (34°03′ N, 118°14′ W) a major city on the southwest coast of California, p. 138

M

Mackenzie River (69° N, 134° W) a large river in the Northwest Territories of Canada, p. 14

Miami (25°46′ N, 80°11′ W) a city on the southeast coast of Florida, p. 122

Minneapolis–St. Paul (44°58′ N, 93°15′ W) two cities in Minnesota; also called the Twin Cities, p. 132

Mississippi River (29° N, 89° W) a large river in the central United States, flowing south from Minnesota to the Gulf of Mexico, p. 14

Missouri River (39° N, 90° W) a large river in the west central United States, flowing southeast from Montana into the Mississippi River, p. 14

Montreal (45°31′ N, 73°34′ W) the largest city in the province of Quebec, Canada, p. 156

N

New York City (40°43′ N, 73°01′ W) a large city and port at the mouth of the Hudson River in the state of New York, p. 115

Niagara Falls (43°05′ N, 79°04′ W) a waterfall on the Niagara River between Ontario, Canada, and New York State, p. 68

Northwest Territories (65° N, 120° W) a region of Northern Canada, p. 181

Nunavut (70° N, 95° W) a Canadian territory in the northern part of Canada, p. 181

O

Ontario (50° N, 88° W) the second-largest province in Canada, p. 153

Ottawa (45°25′ N, 75°42′ W) the capital city of Canada, located in Ontario, p. 153

P

Pacific Northwest the region in the northwestern United States that includes Oregon, Washington, and northern California, p. 135

Pennsylvania Colony a colony in America founded in 1682 by William Penn, p. 40

Philadelphia (39°57′ N, 75°09′ W) a city and port in Pennsylvania, on the Delaware River, p. 113

Portland (45°31′ N, 122°40′ W) the largest city in the state of Oregon, p. 136

Q

Quebec (52° N, 72° W) a province in eastern Canada, p. 157

R

Rocky Mountains (48° N, 116° W) the major mountain range in western North America, extending from central New Mexico to northeastern British Columbia, p. 11

S

St. Lawrence River (49° N, 67° W) a river in eastern North America; the second-longest river in Canada, p. 15

St. Lawrence Seaway (46° N, 73° W) a navigable seaway from the Atlantic Ocean to the western end of the Great Lakes, p. 68

St. Louis (38°37′ N, 90°11′ W) a major city in Missouri, on the Mississippi River, p. 131

San Jose (37°20′ N, 121°53′ W) a city in western California, p. 137

Seattle (47°36′ N, 122°19′ W) a city in the state of Washington on Puget Sound, p. 137

Sierra Nevada a mountain range in California in the western United States, p. 12

T

Toronto (43°39′ N, 79°23′ W) the largest and most populous city in Canada; the capital of the province of Ontario, p. 155

V

Vancouver (49°16′ N, 123°07′ W) a city in southwestern British Columbia, Canada, p. 166

Victoria (48°25′ N, 123°22′ W) the capital of British Columbia, Canada, p. 169

W

Washington, D.C. (38°53′ N, 77°02′ W) the capital city of the United States, located between Maryland and Virginia on the Potomac River, p. 123

Y

Yukon (64° N, 135° W) a territory in northwestern Canada, p. 181

Glossary

A

abolitionist (ab uh LISH un ist) *n.* a person who believed that enslaving people was wrong and who wanted to end the practice, p. 47

acid rain (AS id rayn) *n.* a rain containing acid that is harmful to plants and trees, often formed when pollutants from cars and factories combine with moisture in the air, p. 66

agribusiness (AG ruh biz niz) *n.* a large company that runs huge farms to produce, process, and distribute agricultural products, p. 26

alliance (uh LY uns) *n.* a formal agreement to do business together, sometimes formed between governments, p. 42

alluvial soil (uh LOO vee ul soyl) *n.* soil deposited by water; fertile topsoil left by rivers after a flood, p. 26

aquaculture (AHK wuh kul chur) *n.* the cultivation of fish and water plants, p. 177

aurora borealis (aw RAWR uh bawr ee AL us) *n.* colorful bands of light that can be seen in northern skies, p. 180

B

bilingual (by LIN gwul) *adj.* speaking two languages; having two official languages, p. 59

bison (BY sun) *n.* buffalo, p. 37

boomtown (boom town) *n.* a settlement that springs up quickly, often to serve the needs of miners, p. 169

boycott (BOY kaht) *n.* a refusal to buy or use goods and services, p. 41

C

civil rights (SIV ul ryts) *n.* the basic rights due to all citizens, p. 53

Civil War (SIV ul wawr) *n.* the war between the northern and southern states in the United States, which began in 1861 and ended in 1865, p. 47

Cold War (kohld wawr) *n.* a period of great tension between the United States and the Soviet Union, which lasted for more than 40 years after World War II, p. 53

communism (KAHM yoo niz um) *n.* a political system in which the central government controls all aspects of citizens' lives, p. 53

commute (kuh MYOOT) *v.* to travel regularly to and from a place, particularly to and from a job, p. 110

Continental Divide (kahn tuh NEN tul duh VYD) *n.* the boundary that separates rivers flowing toward opposite sides of a continent, located in the Rocky Mountains of North America, p. 14

corporate farm (KAWR puh rit fahrm) *n.* a large farm run by a corporation, often consisting of many smaller farms, p. 129

cultural diversity (KUL chur ul duh VUR suh tee) *n.* a wide variety of cultures, p. 76

cultural exchange (KUL chur ul eks CHAYNJ) *n.* a process in which different cultures share ideas and ways of doing things, p. 77

D

descendant (dee SEN dunt) *n.* a child, grandchild, great-grandchild (and so on) of an ancestor, p. 156

descent (dee SENT) *n.* ancestry, p. 161

dictator (DIK tay tur) *n.* a person who rules a country completely and independently, p. 54

discrimination (dih skrim ih NAY shun) *n.* the practice of treating certain groups of people unfairly, p. 53

dominion (duh MIN yun) *n.* a self-governing area subject to Great Britain; for example, Canada prior to 1939, p. 58

E

economy (ih KAHN uh mee) *n.* a system for producing, distributing, consuming, and owning goods, services, and wealth, p. 28

enslave (en SLAYV) *v.* to force someone to become a slave, p. 39

ethnic group (ETH nik groop) *n.* a group of people who share the same ancestors, culture, language, or religion, p. 78

exile (EK syl) *v.* to force to leave an area, p. 176

export (eks PAWRT) *v.* to send goods to another country for sale, p. 69

F

federation (fed ur AY shun) *n.* a union of states, groups, provinces, or nations, p. 153

forty-niner (FAWRT ee NY nur) *n.* one of the first miners of the California Gold Rush of 1849, p. 135

fossil fuel (FAHS ul FYOO ul) *n.* a fuel formed over millions of years from animal and plant remains, including coal, petroleum, and natural gas, p. 27

Francophone (FRANG koh fohn) *n.* a person who speaks French as his or her first language, p. 156

free trade (free trayd) *n.* trade with no tariffs, or taxes, on imported goods, p. 70

fugitive (FYOO jih tiv) *n.* a runaway; someone who runs from danger, p. 46

G

glacier (GLAY shur) *n.* a huge, slow-moving mass of snow and ice, p. 12

grasslands (GRAS landz) *n.* regions of flat or rolling land covered with grasses, p. 21

Great Lakes (grayt layks) *n.* the world's largest group of freshwater lakes, located between the United States and Canada and comprising Lakes Erie, Huron, Michigan, Ontario, and Superior, p. 13

H

haze (hayz) *n.* foglike air, often caused by pollution, p. 66

Holocaust (HAHL uh kawst) *n.* the killing of millions of Jews by the Nazis in World War II, p. 52

Homestead Act (HOHM sted akt) *n.* a law passed in 1862 giving 160 acres (65 hectares) of land on the Midwestern plains to any adult willing to live on and farm it for five years, p. 50

hydroelectricity (hy droh ee lek TRIH suh tee) *n.* electric power produced by moving water, p. 27

I

immigrant (IM uh grunt) *n.* a person who moves to a new country in order to settle there, p. 45

immunity (ih MYOO nuh tee) *n.* a natural resistance to disease, p. 163

import (im PAWRT) *v.* to bring goods into one country from another, p. 69

indentured servant (in DEN churd SUR vunt) *n.* a person who, in exchange for benefits received, must work for a period of years to gain freedom, p. 40

indigenous (in DIJ uh nus) *adj.* belonging to a certain place, p. 37

industrialization (in dus tree ul ih ZAY shun) *n.* the development of large industries, p. 121

Industrial Revolution (in DUS tree ul rev uh LOO shun) *n.* the change from making goods by hand to making them by machine, p. 45

Inuktitut (ih NOOK tih toot) *n.* the native language of the Inuit, p. 184

L

labor force (LAY bur fawrs) *n.* the workers in a country or region, p. 50

land bridge (land brij) *n.* a bridge formed by a narrow strip of land connecting one landmass to another, p. 37

landmass (LAND mas) *n.* a large area of land, p. 11

latitude (LAT uh tood) *n.* the distance north or south of the Equator, p. 19

literacy (LIT ur uh see) *n.* the ability to read and write, p. 80

lock (lahk) *n.* an enclosed section of a canal used to raise or lower a ship to another level, pp. 15, 69

Louisiana Purchase (loo ee zee AN uh PUR chus) *n.* the sale of land in 1803 by France to the United States; all the land between the Mississippi River and the eastern slope of the Rocky Mountains, p. 43

lowlands (LOH landz) *n.* lands that are lower than the surrounding land, p. 13

M

Manifest Destiny (MAN uh fest DES tuh nee) *n.* a belief that the United States had a right to own all the land from the Atlantic Ocean to the Pacific Ocean, p. 45

maritime (MA rih tym) *adj.* having to do with navigation or shipping on the sea, p. 177

mass transit (mas TRAN sit) *n.* a system of subways, buses, and commuter trains used to transport large numbers of people, p. 137

megalopolis (meg uh LAHP uh lis) *n.* a number of cities and suburbs that blend into one very large urban area, p. 111

melting pot (MELT ing paht) *n.* a country in which all cultures blend together to form a single culture, p. 89

migration (my GRAY shun) *n.* the movement of people from one country or region to another in order to make a new home, p. 37

missionary (MISH un ehr ee) *n.* a person who tries to convert others to his or her religion, p. 39

mixed-crop farm (mikst krahp fahrm) *n.* a farm that grows several different kinds of crops, p. 128

N

NAFTA (NAF tuh) *n.* North American Free Trade Agreement, signed in 1994 by Canada, the United States, and Mexico to establish mutual free trade, p. 70

navigate (NAV uh gayt) *v.* to plot or direct the course of a ship or aircraft, p. 15

nomadic (noh MAD ik) *adj.* frequently moving from one place to another in search of food or pasture-land, p. 91

P

Pacific Rim (puh SIF ik rim) *n.* the group of countries bordering on the Pacific Ocean, p. 171

permafrost (PUR muh frawst) *n.* permanently frozen layer of ground below the top layer of soil, p. 21

petrochemical (pet roh KEM ih kul) *n.* a substance, such as plastic, paint, or asphalt, that is made from petroleum, p. 120

plantation (plan TAY shun) *n.* a large, one-crop farm with many workers, common in the Southern United States before the Civil War, p. 40

population density (pahp yuh LAY shun DEN suh tee) *n.* the average number of people per square mile or square kilometer, p. 111

prairie (PREHR ee) *n.* a region of flat or rolling land covered with tall grasses, p. 21

prime minister (prym MIN is tur) *n.* the chief official in a government with a parliament, pp. 60, 153

province (PRAH vins) *n.* a political division of land in Canada, similar to a state in the United States, p. 21

Q

Quiet Revolution (KWY ut rev uh LOO shun) *n.* a peaceful change in the government of Quebec, Canada, in which the Parti Québécois won control of the legislature and made French the official language, p. 157

R

rain shadow (rayn SHAD oh) *n.* an area on the side of a mountain away from the wind, which receives little rainfall, p. 19

recession (rih SESH un) *n.* a downturn in business activity and economic prosperity, not as severe as a depression, p. 128

Reconstruction (ree kun STRUK shun) *n.* the United States plan for rebuilding the nation after the Civil War, including a period when the South was governed by the United States Army, p. 48

referendum (ref uh REN dum) *n.* a ballot or vote in which voters decide for or against a particular issue, p. 157

reservation (rez ur VAY shun) *n.* land set aside for a specific purpose, as by the United States government for Native Americans, p. 85

reserve (rih ZURV) *n.* land set aside for a specific purpose, as by the Canadian government for indigenous peoples, p. 90

responsible development (rih SPAHN suh bul dih VEL up munt) *n.* balancing the needs of the environment, community, and economy, p. 136

Revolutionary War (rev uh LOO shun ehr ee wawr) *n.* the war in which the American colonies won their independence from Britain, fought from 1775 to 1781, p. 41

Rocky Mountains (RAHK ee MOWN tunz) *n.* the major mountain range in western North America, p. 11

S

segregate (SEG ruh gayt) *v.* to set apart and force to use separate schools, housing, parks, and so on because of race or religion, p. 48

separatist (SEP ur uh tist) *n.* someone who wants the province of Quebec to break away from the rest of Canada, p. 157

slum (slum) *n.* a usually crowded area of a city, often with poverty and poor housing, p. 49

sod (sahd) *n.* the top layer of soil, containing grass plants and their roots, p. 160

standard of living (STAN durd uv LIV ing) *n.* the level that a person or nation lives, as measured by the availability of food, clothing, shelter, etc., p. 81

Sun Belt (sun belt) *n.* area of the United States stretching from the southern Atlantic Coast to the coast of California; known for its warm weather, p. 122

T

tariff (TAR if) *n.* a tax charged on imported goods, p. 70

tenement (TEN uh munt) *n.* an apartment house that is poorly built and crowded, p. 49

territory (TEHR uh tawr ee) *n.* a large division of Canada, p. 181

terrorist (TEHR ur ist) *n.* a person who uses violence and fear to achieve political goals, p. 54

textile (TEKS tyl) *n.* cloth, p. 45

totem pole (TOHT um pohl) *n.* a tall, carved wooden pole containing symbols, found among Native Americans of the Pacific Northwest, p. 167

treaty (TREE tee) *n.* an agreement between two or more nations, p. 85

tributary (TRIB yoo tehr ee) *n.* a river or stream that flows into a larger river, p. 14

tundra (TUN druh) *n.* a cold, dry region covered with snow for more than half the year; a vast, treeless plain where the subsoil is always frozen, p. 21

V

vegetation (vej uh TAY shun) *n.* plant life, p. 21

Index

The *m, g,* or *p* following some page numbers refers to maps *(m)*, charts, diagrams, tables, timelines, or graphs *(g)*, or pictures *(p)*.

Acknowledgments

Cover Design

Pronk&Associates

Staff Credits

The people who made up *World Studies* team—representing design services, editorial, editorial services, educational technology, marketing, market research, photo research and art development, production services, project office, publishing processes, and rights & permissions—are listed below. Bold type denotes core team members.

Greg Abrom, Ernie Albanese, Rob Aleman, Susan Andariese, **Rachel Avenia-Prol,** Leann Davis Alspaugh, Penny Baker, Barbara Bertell, **Peter Brooks,** Rui Camarinha, John Carle, **Lisa Del Gatto,** Paul Delsignore, Kathy Dempsey, Anne Drowns, Deborah Dukeshire, Marlies Dwyer, **Frederick Fellows,** Paula C. Foye, Lara Fox, Julia Gecha, **Mary Hanisco,** Salena Hastings, Lance Hatch, Kerri Hoar, **Beth Hyslip,** Katharine Ingram, Nancy Jones, John Kingston, Deborah Levheim, Constance J. McCarty, **Kathleen Mercandetti,** Art Mkrtchyan, Ken Myett, **Mark O'Malley,** Jen Paley, Ray Parenteau, **Gabriela Pérez Fiato,** Linda Punskovsky, Kirsten Richert, **Lynn Robbins,** Nancy Rogier, Bruce Rolff, Robin Samper, Mildred Schulte, Siri Schwartzman, **Malti Sharma,** Lisa Smith-Ruvalcaba, Roberta Warshaw, Sarah Yezzi

Additional Credits

Jonathan Ambar, Tom Benfatti, Lisa D. Ferrari, Paul Foster, Florrie Gadson, Phil Gagler, Ella Hanna, Jeffrey LaFountain, Karen Mancinelli, Michael McLaughlin, Lesley Pierson, Debi Taffet

The DK Designs team who contributed to *World Studies* were as follows: Hilary Bird, Samantha Borland, Marian Broderick, Richard Czapnik, Nigel Duffield, Heather Dunleavy, Cynthia Frazer, James A. Hall, Lucy Heaver, Rose Horridge, Paul Jackson, Heather Jones, Ian Midson, Marie Ortu, Marie Osborn, Leyla Ostovar, Ralph Pitchford, Ilana Sallick, Pamela Shiels, Andrew Szudek, Amber Tokeley.

Maps

Maps and globes were created by DK Cartography. The team consisted of Tony Chambers, Damien Demaj, Julia Lunn, Ed Merritt, David Roberts, Ann Stephenson, Gail Townsley, Iorwerth Watkins.

Illustrations

Kenneth Batelman: 153, 182; Geosystems: 68; Jill Ort: 83, 125; Jen Paley: 10, 18, 19, 25, 29, 36, 42, 49, 52–53, 55, 64, 76, 84, 86, 89, 90, 110, 112, 117, 118, 126, 127, 128, 133, 134, 137, 141, 152, 154, 158, 160, 162, 166, 168, 173, 175, 180, 182

Photographs

Cover Photos

tl, Miles Ertman/Masterfile; **tm,** Gunter Marx Photography/Corbis/MAGMA; **tr,** David Schmidt/Masterfile; **b,** Richard Cummins/Superstock.

Title Page

Richard Cummins/Superstock.

Table of Contents

iv–v, Andre Jenny/Visuals Unlimited; **vi,** Bonnie Kamin/PhotoEdit; **vii,** C. McIntyre/PhotoLink/Getty Images, Inc.; **xi,** Kevin Fleming/Corbis.

Learning with Technology

xiii, Discovery Channel School.

Reading and Writing Handbook

RW, Michael Newman/PhotoEdit; **RW1,** Walter Hodges/Getty Images, Inc.; **RW2,** Digital Vision/Getty Images, Inc.; **RW3,** Will Hart/PhotoEdit; **RW5,** Jose Luis Pelaez, Inc./Corbis.

Map Master Skills Handbook

M, James Hall/DK Images; **M1,** Mertin Harvey/Gallo Images/Corbis; **M2–3 m,** NASA; **M2–3,** (globes) Planetary Visions; **M5 br,** Barnabas Kindersley/DK Images; **M6 tr,** Mike Dunning/DK Images; **M10 b,** Bernard and Catherine Desjeux. /Corbis; **M11,** Hutchison Library; **M12 b,** Pa Photos; **M13 r,** Panos Pictures; **M14 l,** Macduff Everton/Corbis; **M14 t,** MSCF/NASA; **M15 b,** Ariadne Van Zandbergen/Lonely Planet Images; **M16 l,** Bill Stormont/Corbis; **M16 b,** Pablo Corral/Corbis; **M17 t,** Stone Les/Sygma/Corbis; **M17b,** W. Perry Conway/Corbis.

Guiding Questions

1t, Ohio Historical Society; **1b,** Bob Winsett/Index Stock Imagery, Inc.

Regional Overview

2, Staffan Widstrand/Corbis; **3,** R. Rainford/Robert Harding Picture Library; **4 t,** Jim Wark/Lonely Planet Images; **4 b,** Charles O'Rear/Corbis; **5,** Bohemian Nomad Picturemakers/Corbis; **6 t,** John Elk III/Lonely Planet Images; **6 bl,** DK Images; **6 br,** Inc. Luis/Castaneda/Getty Images; **7 t,** Richard T. Nowitz/Corbis; **7 m,** Yann Arthus-Bertrand; **7 b,** Peter Beck/Corbis.

Chapter One

8–9, Frank Perkins/Index Stock Imagery, Inc.; **10,** Scott Darsney/Alaska Stock; **11 t,** Andre Jenny/Visuals Unlimited; **11 b,** Discovery Channel School; **12,** Richard A. Cooke/Corbis; **13,** U.S. Geological Survey, Denver; **14–15 t,** Joseph Sohm; ChromoSohm Inc/Corbis; **14 b,** Joe McDonald/Corbis; **16,** Nancy Sheehan/PhotoEdit; **17,** J. Eastcott/Yva Momatiuk/Valan Photos; **18,** Donald Nausbaum/Getty Images, Inc.; **19,** Bob Winsett/Index Stock Imagery, Inc.; **20,** Alan R. Moller/Getty Images, Inc.; **21 t,** Gerry Ellis/Minden Pictures; **21 b,** Norbert Rising/National Geographic Society/Getty Images, Inc.; **23 t,** David A. Northcott/Corbis; **23 b,** Gordon Whitten/Corbis; **24,** Jean·du Boisberranger/Getty Images, Inc.; **25,** Royalty-Free/Corbis; **27 t,** Bruce Forster/Getty Images, Inc.; **27 b,** Randy Brandon/Alaska Stock; **28,** Melvin Grubb/Grubb Photo Service, Inc.; **29,** Jeff Greenberg/Visuals Unlimited; **30,** Vince Streano/Getty Images, Inc.; **31 t,** Joe McDonald/Corbis; **31 b,** David A. Northcott/Corbis.

Chapter Two

34–35, Robert Essel NYC/Corbis; **36 l,** Ohio Historical Society; **36 r,** Ohio Historical Society; **37 t,** Discovery Channel School; **37 b,** Tom Bean/Corbis; **38 t,** Marc Muench/Corbis; **38 m,** DK Images; **38 b,** Michael Freeman/Corbis; **40 t,** Sarony & Major/Library of Congress; **40 b,** Bettmann/Corbis; **41,** Kevin Fleming/Corbis; **42,** The Granger Collection; **45,** The Granger Collection, NY; **47,** Magma Photo News/Corbis; **47 inset,** Seth Goltzer/William Gladstone/West Point Museum Collections; **48,** Bettmann/Corbis; **48 inset,** C Squared Studios/Getty Images, Inc.; **49,** Bettmann/Corbis; **50–51 t,** Corbis; **50 b,** Bettmann/Corbis; **51 m,** Library of Congress; **51 b,** Underwood & Underwood/Corbis; **52 t,** Corbis; **52 b,** Bettmann/Corbis; **53 t,** Bettmann/Corbis; **53 b,** Mirrorpix/Getty Images, Inc.; **54,** Reuters NewMedia Inc./Corbis; **55,** Christie's Images/Corbis; **56,** Library of Congress; **57,** Hulton/Getty Images Inc.; **59 l,** Getty Images, Inc.; **59 r,** Bettmann/Corbis; **60,** Paul A. Souders/Corbis; **61,** Reuters NewMedia Inc./Corbis; **62 t,** Michael Newman/PhotoEdit; **62 b,** David Young-Wolff/PhotoEdit; **64,** Illustration by ML Kirk in Longfellow, Hiawatha 1910/Mary Evans Picture Library; **65 t,** Mark Gibson/Index Stock Imagery, Inc.; **65 b,** Bettmann/Corbis; **66,** Didier Dorval/Masterfile Corporation; **67 t,** Weyerhaeuser Company; **67 b,** Joel W. Rogers/Corbis; **68–69,** Nik Wheeler/Nik Wheeler Photography; **70,** AP Photo/Martin Mejia; **71 t,** Ohio Historical Society; **71 b,** Magma Photo News/Corbis.

Chapter Three

74–75, Kwame Zikomo/SuperStock Inc.; **76,** H A Strong/Mary Evans Picture Library; **77,** Library of Congress, Washington D.C., USA/Bridgeman Art Library; **78,** Mary Evans Picture Library; **79 l,** Connie Ricca/Danita Delimont; **79 r,** Nik Wheeler/Corbis; **80,** Rudi von Briel/Index Stock Imagery, Inc.; **81**